Building Hot Rods
30 Years of Advice from Fatman Fabrication's Brent VanDervort

Brent VanDervort

Published by:
Wolfgang Publications Inc.
P.O. Box 223
Stillwater, MN 55082
www.wolfpub.com

Legals

First published in 2015 by Wolfgang Publications Inc.,
P.O. Box 223, Stillwater MN 55082

© Brent VanDervort, 2015

All rights reserved. With the exception of quoting brief passages for the purposes of review no part of this publication may be reproduced without prior written permission from the publisher.

The information in this book is true and complete to the best of our knowledge. All recommendations are made without any guarantee on the part of the author or publisher, who also disclaim any liability incurred in connection with the use of this data or specific details.

We recognize that some words, model names and designations, for example, mentioned herein are the property of the trademark holder. We use them for identification purposes only. This is not an official publication.

ISBN 13: 978-1-929133-43-7

Printed and bound in U.S.A.

Building Hot Rods

Page 30

General Topics	*Page 6*
Air Conditioning	*Page 19*
Body	*Page 21*
Brakes	*Page 32*
Chassis	*Page 43*

Page 48

Design	*Page 53*
Drivetrain	*Page 71*

Page 72

Electrical	*Page 79*
Engine	*Page 83*
Steering	*Page 95*
Suspension	*Page 103*
Fabrication Skills	*Page 133*
Catalog	*Page 142*

From The Publisher

Years ago I made my living as an auto mechanic. After trading wrenches for a computer and camera, I wrote a series of Hot Rod books with Boyd Coddington. So, I figured I knew most of what there was to know about Hot Rods and chassis design. That was before I started to read all the articles that make up this book by the Fat Man. Not only does he convey to readers a huge amount of information, he does it in a way that's easy to read and understand.

Brent Vandervort has the brain and schooling of an engineer combined with the hands-on experiences that can only come from years of building hot rods. Though he cleaned up for the nearby photo, I go believe there's still a little grease under his fingernails - and gasoline in his veins. It's been my pleasure to combine these articles into book form so that at least two generations of Hot Rodders and car builders can continue to learn from the Fat Man.

Acknowledgements

I have been greatly blessed by God to have enjoyed a long association and career in the hot rodding motorsport. First and foremost is my dear wife Debbie, who has allowed me the time and freedom to pursue my interests. Mike Wright, Lew Parks, Nate George and many other hot rod buddies have passed on wisdom, knowledge and skills that have proven to be invaluable. Many friends have become customers, and customers became friends, stretching my own experiences in the hot rod building world. The opportunity to serve hot rodders and the National Street Rod Assn. as a State Inspector for 8 years greatly accelerated my learning curve and insight into where problems might begin. The Goodguys Rod and Custom Assn. has allowed me a forum since 1997 writing a monthly "Goodtips" tech column, where I have attempted to pass on all the accumulated knowledge in hopes of advancing the art of building and maintaining a hot rod. My fervent wish is that this compilation of some of those columns will serve you well in your own journey in hot rodding!

Foreword

It should come as no surprise that I am a longtime fan of Brent Vandervort of Fatman Fabrications. I have had the opportunity to author stories utilizing his product, have seen his product in use, and have ridden in many a hot rod that utilizes his company's product. But the telling truth rests in the very fact that I own and drive a '47 Chevy pickup with a Fatman chassis. As the saying goes, "The proof is in the pudding." And, if I may, my pickup is one "sweet" ride.

For well over a decade Brent has faithfully put together one great piece of advice after another on the pages of the Goodguys Gazette in a column titled, "Good Tips". It should also come as no surprise that he has often answered questions for the staff of Street Rodder as we try and answer the questions of rodders who write in to the magazine. On many an occasion I have called Brent to take from his vast "warehouse" of knowledge and experience on all things mechanical. Given his column has run for 13-plus years in the Gazette it would be safe to say many other rodders have found his advice helpful.

What you will read on the coming pages is a compilation of 13 years of knowledge shared willingly with rodders all over the globe. However, that only scratches the surface of the decades of mechanical and practical knowledge learned from years of theorizing, building, and driving. Nothing replaces real world experience. I always tried to keep my favorite "Good Tips" in a file and at the ready should I become stumbled by a reader's question. To now have them neatly arranged in a book makes going back and checking on these great ideas that have escaped my memory so much easier.

Brent's answers are based in his decades of research accompanied by proven engineering principles. The fact that he is so very willing to ask other experts in the world of street rodding for their input adds another level of credibility to his solutions to everyday problems all of us incur when building our hot rods.

Keep this book handy when building, refreshing, or performing maintenance on your ride and you will find yourself (and your hot rod) that much better for your efforts. "Now, let me see where is that column on installing U-joints?"

Brian Brennan
Editor/Editorial Director
Street Rodder

General Topics
Plan Your Project First!
The Best Hot Rods Don't Just Happen

The plain truth is that many good looking hot rods ride worse than the cars we drive to work, but it doesn't have to be that way. When a vehicle is lowered, axle travel is often reduced. Spring rates are usually increased and shocks made stiffer in order to control the potential of bottoming out. As the same amount of mass (weight) is decelerated over a shorter space, a higher "G" load is created. That higher "G'load is what you feel in the seat and up your back.

Most hot rod coil-overs are set up for 4 inches total travel. That is all you have to work with on a direct acting solid axle suspension. Most independent suspensions mount the shock on the lower control arm half way to the wheel, with that leverage doubling the actual wheel travel to a more forgiving 8 inches. I was recently in a conversation with a shock manufacturer who claimed that they could build a coil-over shock that would allow a car to sit with only 2 inches of total travel, yet never bottom out. My contention was that it is certainly possible, but not desirable. As the same amount of mass has to be controlled in half the distance, "G" loads will double. This adds to the structural load on the shock or coil-over mounting which can lead to bracket failure, as well as damage to the driver's body. Handling can also be compromised since a stiffer suspension will not do as good a job keeping the tire in contact with the road. No tread on the ground means no traction for stopping or turning.

If the axle travels so far that a bump stop is contacted, the spring rate goes to a value nearly infinite. That's why bump stops are a last resort to prevent component failure and should never be looked on as a way to support a vehicle in motion, even inside a fairground. Safety and comfort are both compromised when the suspension runs out of room.

The purpose of all the foregoing copy is to motivate hot rodders to spend more time Imagineering their rides before Engineering them. An all too common approach is to build a chassis, then later try to repair any problems that crop up. As we see more unusual cars and more radical stances, this becomes critical. Even proven hot rods like `40 Fords and '55 Chevys get built without enough prior planning.

We like to do some research first as to the rolling diameter of the tires to be used on a project. We then make discs out of cardboard or 1/8 inch paneling, which simulates the planned tire and wheel combination. Remove the original wheels and use jack stands, cinder blocks, or anything you have laying around to get the car sitting the way you want with the mockup discs in the wheel wells. You can easily see whether you'll like the proportions of wheel versus tire you selected. Try to do this in a large shop or even out in the driveway in order to get a full perspective of your mockup. "Small garage syndrome" is a curable disease.

Equally important is the ability to note the front and rear spindle heights relative to the frame. Armed with that info, you can confidently build the chassis. You may even find that altering the wheelbase will make for a more graceful finished product. Be absolutely sure to do whatever is needed to get sufficient suspension travel. That generally means at least 3 inches of compression and 2 inches of extension travel, measured at the wheel, as a bare minimum. More travel is better and will allow a slower deceleration of weight with lighter spring rates for improved ride and handling.

You'll often find it necessary to "C" or notch the frame to get this much travel. Don't just hope that a little less will be OK. Drop spindles and lowering blocks are often used to achieve a certain ride height without changing the suspension travel. Coil-overs are not used to lower a car, but rather as an easy way to get to the design ride height. Air ride springs can work very well to maintain proper suspension travel by changing air pressure to alter the spring rate as the load changes. This is especially handy with a sedan that is driven fully loaded on occasion. The axle ride height position can be preserved, maintaining sufficient travel. If you never defined that desired ride height by first doing a mockup, how can you know how to mount the axle and provide the necessary travel?

Make the goal of your next project to be the best it can be. Spending a little time planning before blindly starting to build can pay real dividends in having a hot rod that you never have to apologize for!

The pleasing stance and overall unity of design are a product of good planning and parts selection.

General Topics

Ten Things I Wouldn't Be Without

Everybody Needs a Wish List

I suppose everyone has a list of items they consider essential in a hot rod. Whether a modernized muscle car or a nostalgic rod, we all have our preferences based on style, speed, handling, comfort, and all the rest. It's another way of measuring a hot rod's performance based on the things we consider important. As the years go by our needs have a way of changing as well. Things you happily put up with at 25 may not be as important when life moves along. Since these items are naturally the results of opinion and personal experience, "your mileage may vary."

1) Radial tires. This applies largely to rodders who enjoy a nostalgic style on a restored vintage car as well as the hard core early roadster guys. The problem with restoring a car to a certain era is that you also get the technology of that era. Tires are only one example of an obsolete technology that looks good but drives poorly. Yes, the bias ply tires have the look, but I won't give up the immensely improved safety that radial tires provide. I just drive too far and too fast to risk it. I have been able to find some tall skinny radials in a light truck line but find that the heavy sidewalls are a little stiff for a light weight car like my '34 highboy. There have been worthy efforts to combine bias ply style with radial safety, but we don't seem to be all the way there yet.

2) Overdrive transmission. This one is something that was recognized in bygone years with optional overdrive transmissions, and then seemed to be forgotten for a while. An overdrive transmission will allow you to cruise at modern Interstate speeds without requiring your engine to be at elevated RPM levels on a continuous basis. Sure, your engine will rev high enough to run fast without an Overdrive, but will it do it for 400 miles? When the tire diameter, rear axle ratio and overdrive ratios are right, your engine will spend it's time right at the peak torque RPM at cruising speed. That will decrease noise and wear, get better mileage, be quieter and put less stress on your cooling system as well. Don't believe me? Take the family car out (it more than likely has an overdrive Trans) and run it about 20 miles at 75 MPH without using overdrive.

3) Modern engines. I love the look of vintage engines and the simplicity of a carbureted V-8. On a car where the engine is open to view, I would still put up with the oil leaks, moderate performance and poor fuel mileage. On a car where the hood is only open to check the oil, give me a modern engine. The GM LS series, Ford's Mod motors and the new Chrysler Hemis are terrific engines with the overdrive trans already attached. No more leaks due to better sealing, and great performance owing to excellent head design, fuel injection and roller cams. With some effort they can even be made to look pretty good.

4) Balanced brakes. Why put up with a mismatched system that requires extra caution when you drive it in traffic? Those problems can all be fixed by using the proper bore sizes on the master and wheel cylinders, along with proper valving. All drum or all disc systems require different combinations, as also a disc front/drum rear deal. The point is to continue to work on the system until another driver can get in it without having to be warned. Some prior-to-purchase conversations with rodders who have successful experience can be a big help in getting it right the first time.

5) Satellite radio. How cool is it to always have your favorite music at hand? No more searching thru endless commercials and talk radio. Just relaxing (or invigorating) music, the same at home or halfway across the country. Yes, you can get that with your Ipod as well, but XM does the programing for you. I like Bluegrass in the mountains, classic rock during the day, and it's gotta be dark to hear the blues.

6) Good air conditioning. I think this is way more than the obvious comfort issue. Wind in your hair is fun for a while but sustained highway runs can get pretty tiring with a lot of wind noise. And most hot rods have a healthy exhaust note that can get old after a couple hours. Being comfortable is a real boon in fighting fatigue and makes you a safer driver. You'll often get better mileage with the windows up, and it sure gets easier to hear those XM tunes.

7) Plenty of suspension travel. A hot rod that runs out of suspension travel has no suspension, but is rather a high powered go kart. Ride, handling and safety will suffer. Be realistic in your plan so that you can accept a more conservative ride height that allows good travel. If you want to be super low, be prepared to do whatever it takes to preserve travel. I had a chance to

Adding a simple tail-shaft mounted overdrive will transform the road manners of a hot rod while preserving the performance that made you build it in the first place.

ride in Gary Meadors yellow roadster that was built at Steve Moal's shop, and was amazed at how well it rode on rough San Francisco streets. Then I looked underneath at the longer than usual coil-overs and that the trunk floor had been raised to allow them room to operate. Start by mocking up your car at a stance that lights your fire and then design it all for at least 3 inches of compression travel and 2 inches of extension. You'll never regret making room for the suspension to work.

8) A good cooling system. An overheating hot rod will put a stop to your fun as soon as anything. Don't skimp on allowing sufficient space for a good radiator, fan and shroud. And think about how the hot air will get out. You almost cannot prevent the air from coming in, but restrict its exit at the risk of constant boil overs. Books have been and will continue to be written on cooling a hot rod, but problems often come down to not enough space to install the necessary parts to get the job done. If you have done all the "right" things and still have a problem, consider an engine oil cooler. That oil is all that cools the bottom of your engine. Buy a new 502 Chevy and it comes with oil cooler in the crate. Many of the new LS engines are factory equipped with an oil cooler. On the cars where I have added one, the operating temp went down 30-35 degrees, problem solved.

9) Shops with integrity. Very few rodders can handle every task on a complete build up. When you need help with paint, upholstery, wiring, parts, chassis etc etc, it is essential to carefully choose your contractors. When an earnest diligent shop combines with an informed and realistic owner the journey together can be a joy and a source of a long-term friendship. Or, lacking some of these qualities, an absolute nightmare. How can you tell the difference? Check out previous customers and make a couple visits to the shop. If a month later the same cars are in the shop without serious progress being made that is a danger sign. You also need to honestly appraise yourself as a customer and be sure that you have a solid plan and the finances to support that plan.

10) A clear title. Let's face it; the days of using junkyard "collector" titles on a newly built car are over. All the state DOT/DMV departments know what's going on. When these cars were worth a few thousand dollars, it was OK. But now we are talking serious time and money invested in a hot rod. How can you recover a car that got stolen or wrecked when it has a fraudulent title. Can you prove you owned it in the first place? The best plan is to approach the DOT Enforcement section in your State Police and find out what your own state requirements are. Build a little relationship with the man who can say whether or not you can title this car. Don't wait until it's done and painted; only to find out you have an expensive piece of garage art on your hands.

Just for fun, I've listed things I consider necessities. What's on your list? Regular readers of this column will recognize many of these topics as having been discussed in greater detail in these monthly columns. That is because I truly believe these to be essential points to building a hot rod which pleases you. Perhaps an honest appraisal of your personal top ten list will help you to define how your own next car should be built.

> **Don't skimp on allowing sufficient space for a good radiator, fan and shroud. And think about how the hot air will get out.**

General Topics
Shoebox Engineering

Structure vs Mass

Some cars such as the '49-'51 Ford and '55-'57 Chevy are known as "shoeboxes" but that's not what we're about to discuss. It has become clear that understanding some critical engineering concepts is made easier using a simple cardboard shoebox as a hands on example of just how torsional strength principles function.

You'll want to have a shoebox on hand to follow along. In fact you'll want to keep it next to your favorite TV chair to fiddle with during commercials. The insights you'll gain into just how a rectangular structure moves and reacts to stress will be quite instructive. The use of a simple model to simulate a structure has a very important history. The Wright Brothers discovered how to control an aircraft while absentmindedly twisting a cardboard inner tube box. Leroy Grumman discovered how to fold an airplane wing alongside the fuselage, saving space in an aircraft carrier to allow more planes to be carried, which was an immense help overwhelming the opposition during WWII in the Pacific. Modern engineers can use powerful drawing programs to simulate a structure, but this practical method remains useful.

Remove the lid from your box and twist the box itself. Your six-sided structure now has five sides and becomes quite unstable. The lid is also quite flimsy on its own. As shown in the photo, the upper edge of the box moves laterally as the box is twisted. Once the top is reattached the sixth side has been returned, which prevents the open upper edge from being warped out of square, returning the box to a stable shape. The lesson here is that shape means much in terms of torsional stability and that a small change can have a large effect. Do you think that doubling the wall thickness of the lower box would contribute as much strength as reattaching that flimsy lid? How can we apply this analogy to the design of a car?

When you look at the firewall forward structure of a unibody car such as a '62-'67 Nova or a '65-'73 Mustang, you'll recognize this box shape. The inner fenders, radiator panels and subrails form a shape much like that of our shoebox. Since these cars have no really substantial crossmembers forming the bottom of our box, we have a very weak structure where the rubber mounted engine has to try to act like the bottom of our box. The hood floats in a hole so it contributes very little. No wonder these cars suffer from chassis flex and fall out of alignment easily. You can also see how critical it is to maintain structural integrity with diagonal braces from the shock towers to the firewall and diagonally connecting the radiator core support to the inner fenders, along with a side-to-side brace for the shock towers. Those braces combine to act the same way as the lid on our shoebox example.

While a car with a structural, heavy wall frame can easily deal with sheet metal panel modification our unibody car requires much more careful design. When a unibody car is modified, simply removing these braces or replacing shaped panels with flat panels can seriously compromise strength. You know that beading and bent edges tremendously strengthen a flat panel. Tubular braces from the firewall to new frame rails are used with the well known Mustang II conversions on the Early Nova; Mustangs are often modified without attention to this issue. Plating the subrails certainly helps, but how is the integrity of the box being maintained?

Speaking of bracing, think of a roll cage as a skeleton of our box. The roll cage tubing on the corners frame the box shape with diagonal braces and thus serve the same purpose as the shoe box panels in terms of maintaining the rectangular shape of the box. Forward and rear legs added to a 6 or 8 point cage add even more stability to the box. Tremendous stability is added to the chassis when the cage is welded to it. We have in essence built the chassis into a truss shape, the favored way to bridge a river or span an open area of a building.

Think about why a truss is favored over a single heavy beam to carry over a gap. Just how deep and heavy would that beam have to be to accomplish the strength of a truss? If a truss was indeed used to cross the gap, how many members of that truss would have to be missing before the integrity of the truss is compromised? We've seen war movies where taking out just a few critical truss sections makes the whole structure collapse. When comparing mid 1930's frames from Ford and Mopar with X members to the Chevys lacking that design, one can see why the Chevy is recognized as being less strong. That is also why the larger GM cars such as Buick were built with an X member. Chassis Engineering Company X member designs have long been recognized as being the ideal way to open up an X member to clear an automatic transmission while maintaining structural integrity. Any removed member must be replaced with one that equals or exceeds the strength of the original item.

Now visualize the X member in a hot rod chassis as a truss. Will a single plane X member be able to be as strong as a dual plane design? A single plane design will flex much as the lid of our box, which is another form of a shallow box shape. X member designs which strongly brace the rails but are weakly joined in the center may flex more than is readily apparent. Remember that torsional loads move laterally through the frame members as well as feeding into the center of our X member. The beauty of an X member or at least K member design is that triangles are created which offer tremendous resistance to being forced out of shape. Strength is achieved thru shape rather than brute mass.

The integrity of the structure is maintained until one of the members or a weld joining them fails. With proper sizing of members and quality workmanship an enormously strong structure can be achieved with minimum weight. In fact, that is why race cars and airplanes are built with monocoque structures, that being literally the French name for what we call unibody structure with automobile manufacturing.

This technique of simulating a contemplated structural design with a simple mock up can be very valuable. You often gain insights as to how forces will try to alter your shape and compromise strength. The ingenious way that common structures we see every day are able to perform will be instructive in designing and modifying your hot rod into a stable structure that will convert torque into traction and allow your suspension to put the rubber to the road.

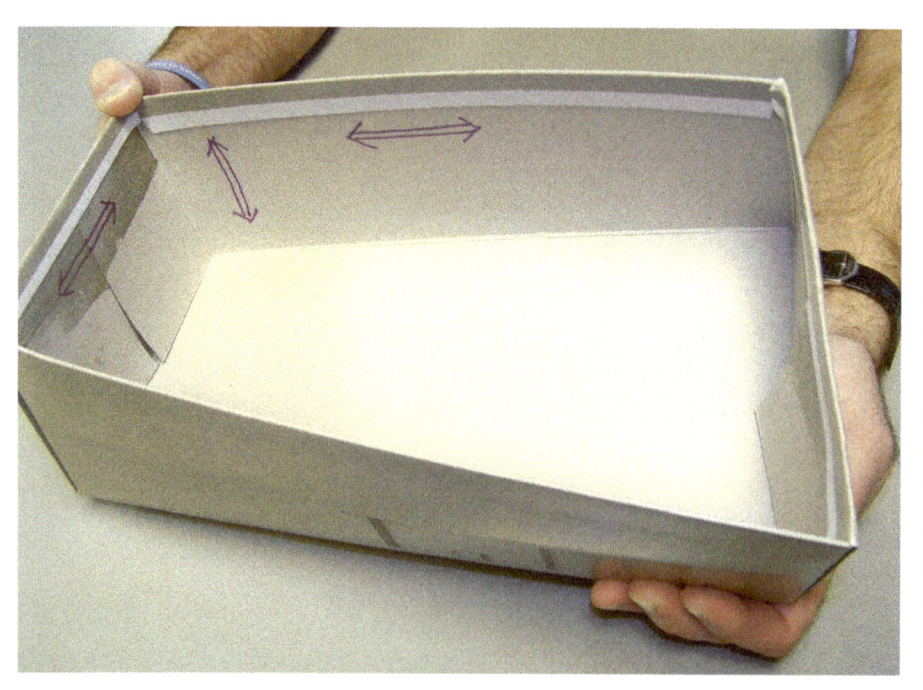

The arrows indicate which way the surfaces of the shoebox are twisted when under torsional stress. It's probably different than you might have supposed! These are the forces that must be controlled when designing a structure.

General Topics
Radical vs Practical
Get it Right the First Time

Good planning is essential to a successful street rod project. You must first decide WHAT you want; balanced by being honest with yourself about what is achievable, given your skills and pocketbook. The very worst plan is to switch styles halfway through.

You'll re-spend much valuable time going back over work you've already done, or paid for. Don't start with a smoothie concept, and then go a whole different route by adding nostalgia style wire wheels and whitewalls later.

This radical 40 Ford was designed from the beginning with Air Ride and the proper suspension and frame modifications that make it possible to park this low while preserving safe wheel travel.

A rod designed to be a driver won't really need a chassis detailed for show. Excessive chrome or extremely low ride height can create maintenance headaches on the road. Trick suspensions really get attention, but can lack durability and travel needed for survival in Pothole City. At the same time, leaf rear suspensions and factory type IFS won't get very far in the Pro's Pick.

I hear guys talk about their 900 horsepower blown big-blocks, but I don't see them on the Interstate. It's asking a lot to run 12-second times with an engine that has to idle for an hour with the A/C on while you're in traffic. Big engines are neat, but often compromise mileage, handling, serviceability and cooling. A good friend swapped his worn out small-block for a big-block and said it got twice the attention, but was half as good a car. A two-car garage may be the best answer to the age old quest for a dual purpose street-strip car.

Pro Street cars are probably the ultimate example of reality run amuck. They attract us with their wildness, being the epitome of the big motor/ big tire concept. As cool as they are, a fair share of them ride on trailers, which isn't really all bad. Road rash and thunderstorms don't coexist well with perfect paint and 20-inch tires. Maybe that guy was smart enough to make HIS choices and knows the strengths and limitations of what he built. After all, who are we to criticize?

It's especially important to be forthright with a pro shop. Go to a guy with a solid plan, and don't expect him to turn your beater into a winner in the Pro's Pick. This is referred to as making chicken salad out of chicken…..stuff! Neither can he get you a Top 25 jacket on a budget. If you start with a rare car in the worst condition and want it as a cover car, be prepared for some serious wallet wear.

It's all about choices. My own opinionated mind often sees "elephant cars" – I like to look at them, but I wouldn't want to own one. But that's cool, because a rod run populated by one guy's opinion of a proper hot rod would be boring indeed. We're blessed to live in a country/age/time where these choices can be made. Just try to define your dream before you try to make it happen!

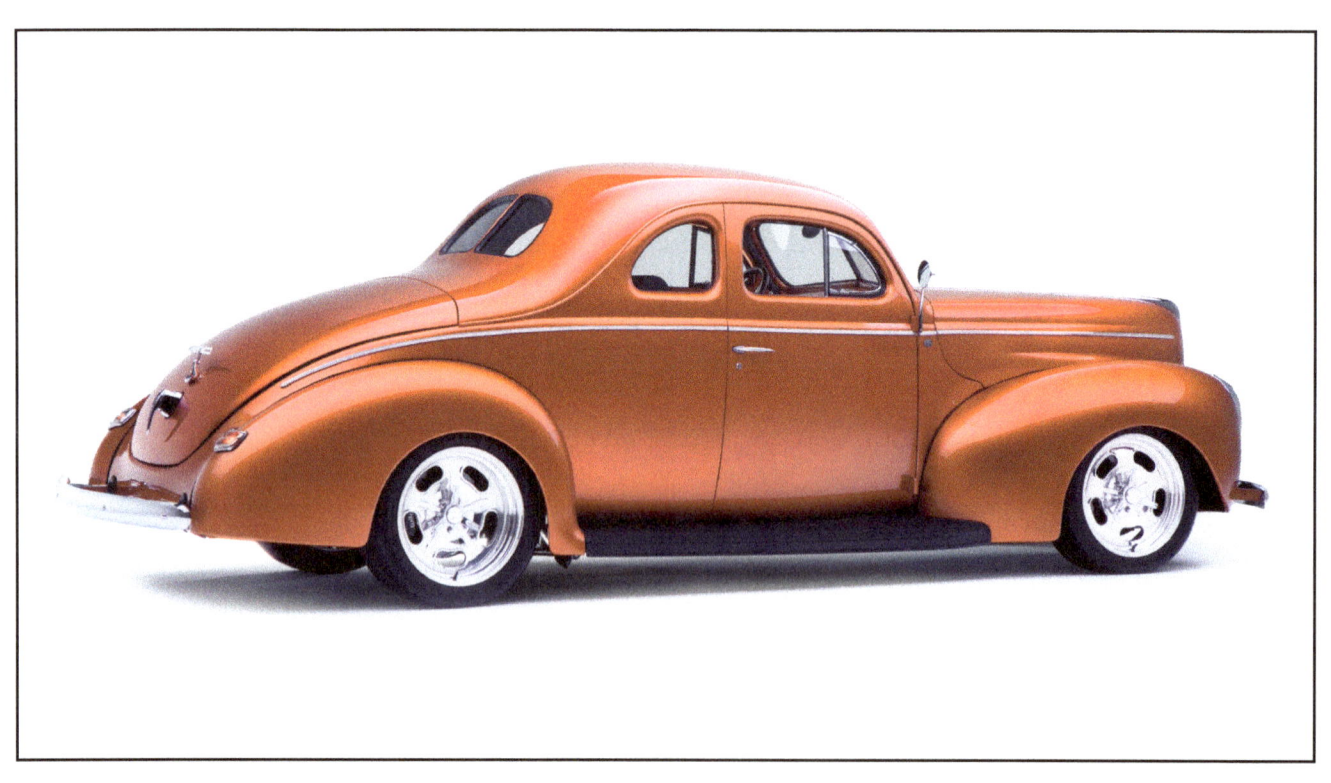

A well thought out hot rod such as the 2102 Street Rodder magazine tour car can make for reliable and comfortable rodding with remarkable performance.

General Topics

Organizing Your Project

Each Step Needs to be in Step with all the Others

Planning a project properly is one of the very best ways to keep costs and schedules under control. Having to redo work is both frustrating and expensive, and has led many rodders to abandon projects they could have finished. Once you've carefully reconciled what's doable, affordable, and sensible, it's time to begin.

Think of the total job as fabrication, then restoration. Don't rebuild the engine or brakes first, and then leave them around to rust while you're doing bodywork, or waiting for a painter to get done. It's tempting to knock out the chassis first, with finish paint, detailed engine and wheels in order to impress your buddies, and feel like you're really making progress. Later on, when the chassis paint is scratched, the engine won't clear the radiator, and the tires don't fit right, you'll be doing a very expensive backstroke.

Force yourself to do all the nitty, gritty fabrication tasks first. Sure, degrease or sandblast and prime the parts if they're just too nasty or rough to work with. A little floor rust or dinged fenders won't effect engine placement, so only do the rust repairs first if the car is flat out falling over the frame.

Set up the chassis next with the suspension you prefer, and mock up the stance that gives the look you're after. Be sure to allow plenty of suspension travel - you don't want to be "C"ing a painted frame rail later on! A good way to mock up the stance is using cardboard discs the same diameter as the tires you'd like to run. DO NOT SET THE CHASSIS LEVEL FRONT TO BACK! The suspension angles must relate to the ground not the frame rails. Why would you carefully set up all the suspension angles on a level frame, and then have a 3-degree forward rake when the rod is done?

The engine and trans mounts are next. You need to allow plenty of clearance for fans, firewall, and steering. Set the engine where it clears best. The semi-sacred 3-degree rule isn't that big a deal. You don't want the engine at 10 degrees, but if a 5-degree angle lets your small block Ford fit without major surgery, then do it. If engine angles were really all that critical, you couldn't go up any hills.

Too many rodders stop here, but you want to install everything except plumbing and wiring. Parts never get cheaper, or easier to install than now. Install the radiator, fan, shroud, and route the hoses, cooling and A/C. Hook up the steering and emergency brake system. All the pedals and linkage need to be installed sooner or later, doing it with a painted firewall only leads to trouble later! Run the brake lines and hoses, checking for clearance and travel. Figure the fuel lines and run the exhaust system. You still have time to be sure the rear axle won't rattle your pipes, and you won't have the local muffler jockey hammering that freshly painted chassis.

Don't stop until you could quick wire the engine, bleed the brakes and run around the block. Instead, pull up a milk crate, pop open something satisfying, and dream a little. Are those swap meet seats going to be comfortable? If you squint just right, surface rust can turn into perfect paint. You can check stance and tire clearance. Budding artists can chalk out scallops, flames, or even that trunk load of "Von Dutch" striping. If it's not turning you on, go back and change it now. Some folks are fans of leaving the car together in the rough, and driving it to a Goodguys event so you can see if everything works, and if it turns on your fellow rodders as much as yourself. Some of these test drives work out so well that the rod becomes a "prime" example of a well built hot rod.

With all the fab work done, you're ready to blow the car apart. Make a pile for the blaster, plater, and grinder. Proceed as fast as your time and budget allow. It makes sense to fix the sheet metal, finish the bondo (or lead), and put the car in primer next. This allows time for the primer to shrink, and any bad bodywork to bubble before spending any money on paint. You can rebuild the engine and brakes while the primer is curing. The pile of rough parts can be finished, painted, and set aside. The chassis can be painted and reassembled, and the local fender lizards and/or skeptical relatives can now be invited over for the unveiling. What you have is a great big model car to assemble, with every day in the shop showing real progress.

Start lining up your glass man and upholsterer-you'll need them soon. While you're at it, send in some pre-registrations for the next Goodguy event, and "Banzai" on the car until the big day.

Does this scene with the disassembled '57 Chevy look like your garage? Getting the project organized will make the work go faster with less frustration.

General Topics

Neutral Safety Switches

Safety First, Second and Third

This is one of those little details that is easily forgotten. We've seen enough Hot Rods run into each other and tool benches when an engine was started with the car in gear. Worse yet, I watched as a friend's T-Bucket (which "didn't need a neutral safety switch - I'm the only one who drives it") ran over his daughter's tricycle. Thank God, she wasn't on it, but he became a believer. You should too.

Using an automatic transmission makes it easy to add a neutral safety switch. The switch functions by interrupting the wire from the start post on the ignition switch going to the start post on your starter solenoid. Think of the ignition switch start function as the first switch in line to the starter solenoid, with the neutral safety switch also needing to be closed in order for the engine to turn over.

If you are using a column shift with a GM based aftermarket column, you can simply wire in the stock neutral safety switch at the base of the column. It can be relocated further up for foot room or a cleaner appearance. Many Street Rod shifters such as Lokar, and B & M include a neutral safety switch in the lever mechanism.

> **The switch functions by interrupting the wire from the start post on the ignition switch going to the start post on your starter solenoid.**

Most of the cheaper shifters do not. Factory floor shifts such as Vega, Camaro, and Mustang do not have the switch. On those cars, a linkage similar to shift linkage operates a conventional column type neutral safety switch. If you are unable to use the column and console switches, other options exist.

Ron Francis Wireworks invented the transmission-mounted switch for GM transmissions. As happens in our industry, other manufacturers picked up on the idea and produce similar items. Additional circuits for shift indicator lights are often included. Most N.S. switches also provide a function to operate back up lights. Not only can YOU see better, but many folks are accustomed to looking for back up lights in a parking lot, even during the day. Ford guys can get lucky here since many C-4 and C-6 trans have bosses for a trans-mounted factory N.S. switch.

Manual transmissions handle the neutral safety switch in a different way. A momentary (automatic return) push button switch will be activated by contact with the mechanical clutch linkage. The starter can only be energized when the clutch pedal is depressed, thus ensuring that a driver is in the car and can control it. Hydraulic clutch linkages are becoming more common, and can be controlled with a hydraulic brake light switch. The brake light switch would be used to supply a ground to a relay that would then allow the starter switch to send the energizing signal to the starter solenoid.

As a last resort, you can hide a normally open, push to close switch under the dash. These are used as a start button on most construction equipment, and are readily available at auto part houses. They won't guarantee the car is in park or neutral, but at least you'll have to stop, think and push a second switch. This idea gives you a little help in the anti-theft department too. I use one on my car with computer controlled Hilborn 8 stack injection to pre-oil the engine and get oil pressure before the fuel and spark are activated. The injection has such quick throttle response that the pre-oil procedure is good insurance against a dry bearing engine start. Smokey Yunick claimed that most engine wear occurs in the first 30 seconds that it's running, and that's a good enough authority for me.

Regardless of how you do it, be sure to include a neutral safety switch in your Hot Rod wiring. The safety of our sport, strangers, and loved ones depend on it.

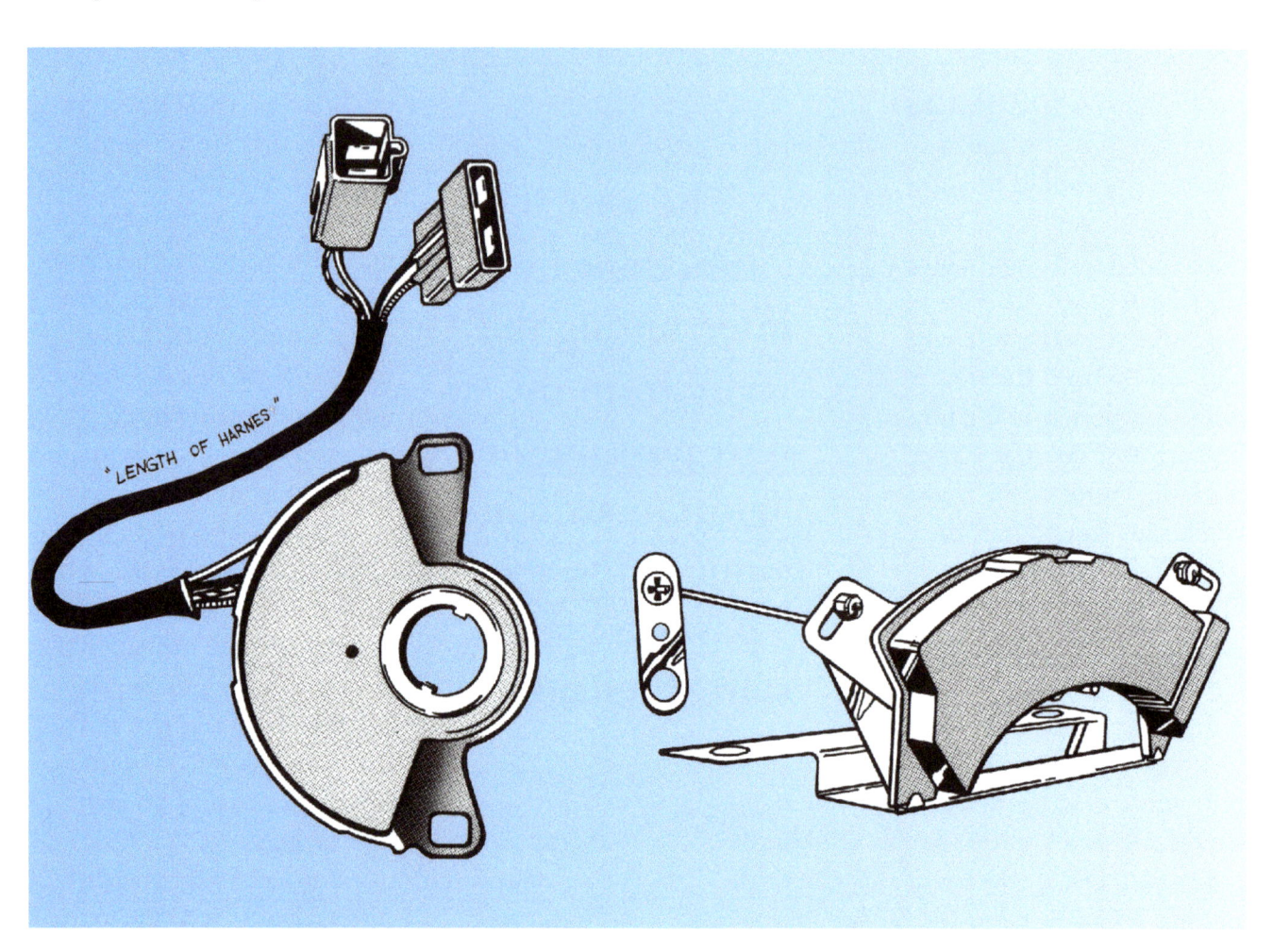

There's just no excuse for risking the safety of your car, yourself, and others when kits like these make installing a neutral safety switch so easy.

Air Conditioning

Sealing the Deal

Keep Cool Air In, Hot Air Out

I'm constantly amazed how a seemingly simple job turns out to have intricacies I never imagined! Choosing and installing weatherstrip is one of these deals where an overlooked detail can really affect the finished look of your hot rod project. Careful reading of the instructions is critical as always and will save much frustration if followed.

Rubber is molded under heat and pressure so it requires a mold release compound. This is the powdery stuff you see on the new parts. It is critically important that this be removed with a good wax and grease remover before any attempt to glue the rubber in place. It will inhibit adhesives just as well as stopping the rubber from sticking in the mold. Pre-fit the rubber to the mounting surface using masking tape to hold it in place. This step allows you to see where you might have problems before getting glue all over everything and everybody. Many cars have little metal clips to help retain the weatherstripping that can be very helpful, assuming you didn't throw them out. It's usually a good idea to let the rubber warm up in the sun to allow it to shape easily. Hard rubber parts like vent window channel cooperates much better with a little rubber lube. One of the best rubber lubes I have used is GoJo hand cleaner…..the smooth type without the pumice of course.

If you have to do any trimming, use a real sharp single edge razor blade. It's often necessary to cut and butt together rubber, especially when installing weatherstripping on a chopped car. The Cyanoacrylate-based adhesives such as "SuperGlue" work surprisingly well to make the butt seams nearly invisible. This seems to work better than ordinary rubber cement and does equally well on solid rubber or closed cell foam weatherstripping.

Most of us have had bad experiences with the rubber adhesive known as "yellow death" or "gorilla snot". This is a contact cement that is sloppy and ugly but we prefer a 3M product sold in body supply and regular auto parts stores. Part number 03602 is readily available in auto parts stores and is black to hide better, but it still has to be used right. Do not simply glob some cement on the rubber and cuss while it smears and slips all over, not sticking very well anyway. Since it is a contact cement, you must follow the directions by putting a thin coating on both surfaces to be joined then letting them dry. Then add just a very little bit to the body to reactivate the cement, doing so in short sections just before you press the weatherstrip in place. Doing it this way will avoid having the rubber stick to itself and having spider webs of stringy adhesive all over everything.

You will have to do some cleanup, so also get a can over 3M's adhesive cleaner #08984 or even "Goofproof" from the hardware store. These liquids do a terrific job of cleaning up excess cement. They will also dissolve contact cement if you need to reset the rubber for a better fit. I also use it to clean up window sealer, and just about anything else. It does a great job on removing excess anti-seize, silicon, and is helpful cleaning and detailing the entire car later. It won't damage cured paint either so it's great for cleaning painted firewalls and the like. Once you put a can on your bench you'll use it constantly.

Many excellent sources of rubber exist. The Ford guys can count on Bob Drake and Dennis Carpenter for really good parts. GM products are covered in enormous detail by Steele rubber. The more unique autos often have their own clubs and specialty companies listed in Hemmings, which can be of terrific help. The cheaper lightweight open cell foam stripping sold in discount stores and hardware stores usually don't hold up too well on a car. Some carry a closed cell black foam in strips that will hold up well though. You can find better quality universal rubber in body supply shops under the Auveco brand, as well as A.M. Sofseal and Metro Molded products. Where no specific listing for your car exists you can often find something that will work well by looking at the cross sections shown in the catalogs and websites. I found windshield rubber for my 1937 Citroen in the Steel catalogue listed as being for a 1937 Chrysler!

A common problem occurs when weatherstrip is added to the doors. Sometimes the rubber is too thick, holding the door open slightly and messing up your doors gaps. It may be possible to trim the rubber, or change to a smaller cross section type from the universal sources mentioned above. Model A's with their overlapping doors, benefit greatly from adding weatherstrip to seal out heat and noise. Many other cars benefit from an extra, small seal in the door edges in addition to the stock rubber. A.M. Sofseal has even gone to great effort in assembling specific kits for the fiberglass bodies common to our sport. Your local rod shop probably carries these.

A further trick for weatherstripping comes into play on light colored hot rods. A thick black rubber will often show, making the door gaps far too obvious. Try to find a smaller strip, which will do the job, yet not be so glaring. Most cars use a continuous welting to separate the hood from the cowl. This woven hemp based original stuff often doesn't look too good, and can be replaced with aftermarket universal closed cell foam rubber strips. These can be had in many thicknesses and can be stacked if necessary to get a good hood fit. They will compress slightly to keep everything snug. Another nice trick is to use just the fuzzy side of Velcro; either by itself or as a finish top on foam strips. It comes in many colors with self adhesive backing or plain, in sewing supply shops. The very effectiveness of this type seal can contribute to overheating by limiting airflow out of the hood of a marginally cooling hot rod. In that case you might try round rubber bumpers trimmed in height for proper hood fit .It won't look quite as nice as a continuous strip of hood welting, but will assist cooling by releasing the hot air that accumulates at the top and rear of your engine compartment.

Some time spent refining the weatherstripping will pay large dividends in a more quite ride and more efficient air conditioning, even on a car you've been driving for years. This little extra attention will make the next ride to your local Goodguys event much more pleasurable!

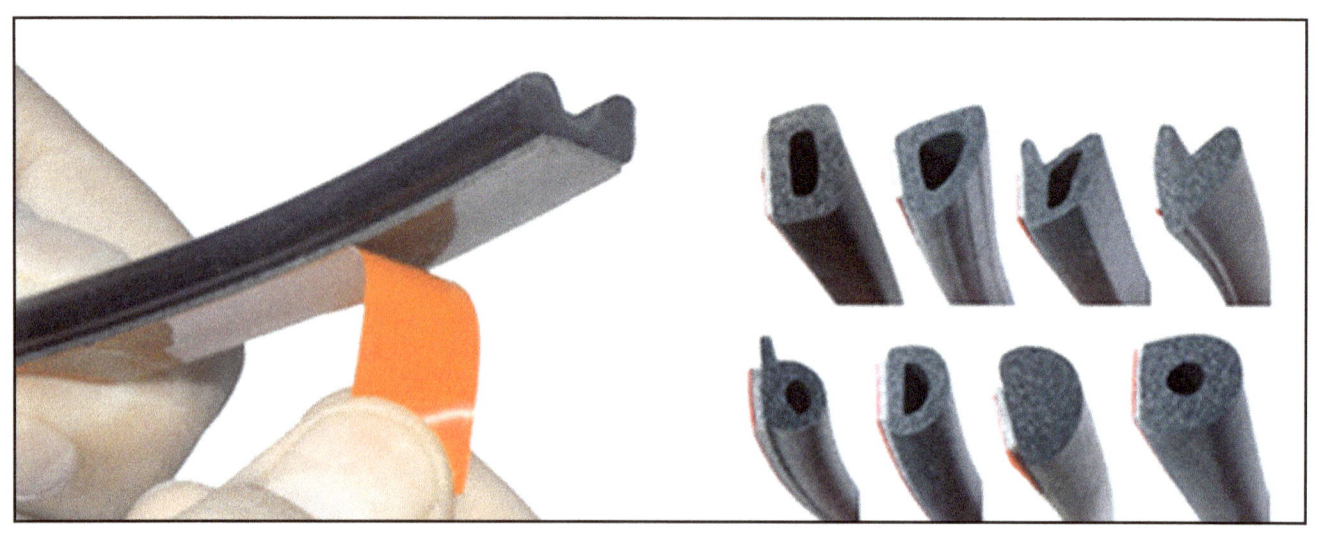

Weatherstrips are available in many different cross section shapes, one of which is sure to work for your unique application.

Body

Fitting Doors and Shimming Bodies

The Leg Bone's Connected to the Thigh Bone

"Fit" is the watchword of modern rodding. Never before have so many paid so much attention to the minute details that separate a nice rod from a super one. Stance and colors attract us at first, then workmanship takes over. It's surprising to find that many of the newer rodders do not realize that their bodies will not simply bolt in place on top of the frame, and fit without further effort. Some don't know that there are body mount kits that duplicate all the various thickness of mounting pads used by the original factories. If this is your first time chopping a car, you need to know that it is absolutely essential to have the doors fitting right BEFORE you start cutting. Otherwise, you'll go crazy trying to refit the doors to a misaligned body.

This month we'll talk about how to get those doors to line up on a vehicle with a full frame. Some of these approaches will work on a unibody car, the difference being that the unibody will be moved around by actually pulling and pushing on that structure with come-a-longs and jacks. We move the body around on a framed car by the use of shims at the mounting points, often assisted by the same type of pull/push devices as used with a unibody.

The primary concept is to realize that the main shape of the door cannot be changed, so the body must be matched to the door. Exceptions to that idea will be doors sagged due to worn hinges, and twisted by sagging. Once the perimeter shape of the door and the body match, the door can be twisted as necessary to fit correctly at the latch post. First, we need the body and door to fit with even gaps and properly fitted body lines.

The very first step is to have the body solidly bolted to the frame, and then remove the latch receivers and dovetails. You need the door to close naturally, without being forced into place by those parts. An ideal fit is even all the way around the door, with a 3/16" gap in bare metal, leaving room for primer and final paint. A wooden paint stick makes a good gauge. Make sure your painter doesn't build up the edges with Bondo and primer to where the door "grows" too large for the hole! Next, we'll change the shape of that hole to match the door. Think of the door opening as a parallelogram, and the following will make more sense.

Look first at the door edge on the hinge side. You need an even gap from top to bottom, and about the same at both sides of the door. If the gap is uneven, the hinges must be adjusted. Be sure the pins or hinge mount points aren't moving - they must be fixed first. Some hinges can be shimmed, but most must be bent. Move the door TOWARD the hinges by pulling the open door toward the hinge, or use a porta-power to push the pin, closing the gap. Move the door AWAY from the hinge by putting a wood block between the hinge halves and gently closing the door.

Now that the hinge post gap is right, look at how the body lines fit at the latch side of the door. If the door is low, the upper hinge must move away from the latch post. If the door is high, the upper hinge must move toward the latch post. In other words, the hinge post must be tipped forward or back to raise or lower the latch side of the door. This is accomplished by adjusting the shims between the frame, and the body mounts at either the firewall or the hinge doorpost. Adding shims at the post raises the door, adding at the firewall lowers the door. Suicide doors differ only in that the hinge post and latch-post positions are swapped.

If you can't get enough that way, you'll need to change the door opening shape by using a porta-power or a come-a-long to stretch the opening horizontally, or diagonally. In extreme cases you may even need to change shims at the latch side of the opening. I once had to shim up the left rear corner of a Model A Tudor body to push the right front corner forward enough!

Now that the gaps are right, you can twist the door to align the latch side of the door. An all metal door can be twisted against your knee, or by putting a wood block at a low point and pushing on a high point. The bow of the door can corrected by a properly rigged porta-power or come-a-long, or a combination of wood blocks and a helper to push.

Wood frame and fiberglass doors often flare out at the bottom. They really benefit from a support made with either a steel strap of braided cable, adjusted with a turnbuckle, running from the upper hinge side to the lower latch side. Find a way to keep the turnbuckle accessible for continuing adjustments. My 1934 Buick had these truss rods installed as original equipment, and they'll work as well for you today!

Reinstall the latch receiver and dovetail, and adjust them to keep the door in alignment, not forcing it into place. If the gaps have places that are still too tight, use a gas torch to melt back the edges. A wide gap can be filled with a weld bead, or 1/8" rod shaped and welded to fit. A little careful hand file work pays major dividends here. This final step is what the real Pros do to get fit quality far beyond what the factory ever achieved.

It does happen that the door and the fender or quarter panel character lines just won't connect. This can be a sign of poor quality replacement panels, or a less than skillful installation. In the real world, you occasionally have to split and re-weld the sheet metal to move a character line. A little judicious use of filler can help, but most body men will tell you that 1/8" buildup is the safe limit.

All this fitting can be tedious. If it's not working, relax, sit back and rethink the parallelogram concept, remembering we're changing the shape of the opening, and try it again - you'll be proud you did.

Did you know - An excellent poor mans porta-power can be made with 1" threaded rod, a matching nut, and some 1" pipe from the local hardware. A few different length pipes and couplers come in handy, and can easily be cut to length as needed. You'll be surprised how handy this tool will be.

We'll illustrate the door alignment process using a simplified drawing of a Model A sedan body. The body shape will change from car to car, but the principles remain the same.

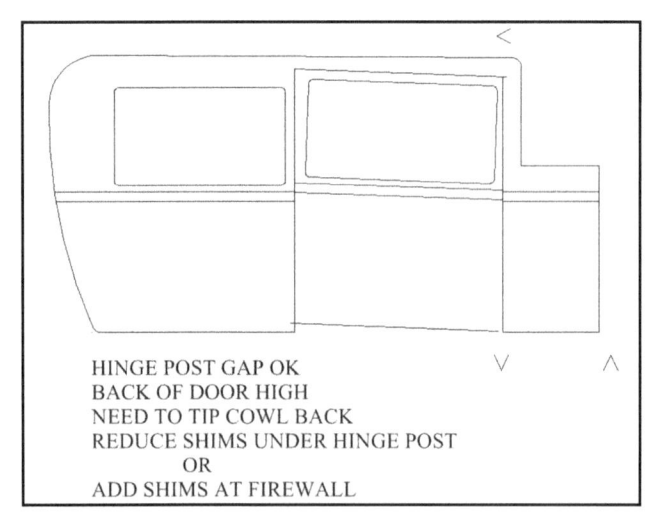

HINGE POST GAP OK
BACK OF DOOR HIGH
NEED TO TIP COWL BACK
REDUCE SHIMS UNDER HINGE POST
OR
ADD SHIMS AT FIREWALL

When your character line on the door is above the one on the body, follow this drawing to correct the fit.

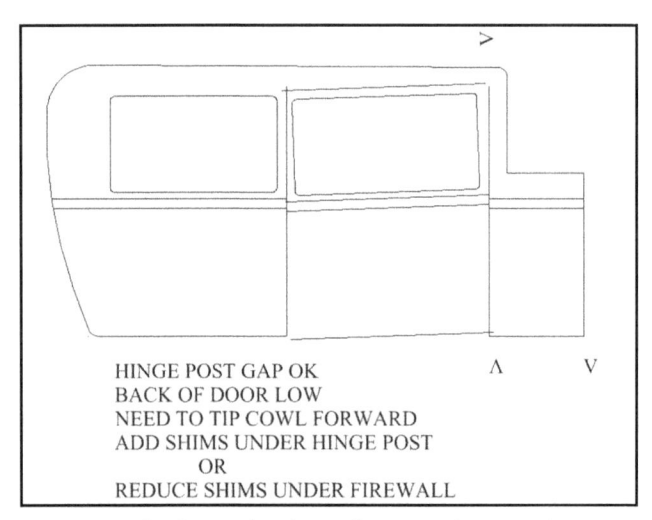

HINGE POST GAP OK
BACK OF DOOR LOW
NEED TO TIP COWL FORWARD
ADD SHIMS UNDER HINGE POST
OR
REDUCE SHIMS UNDER FIREWALL

You can also have the door character line too low, which is corrected with the changes shown on the drawing.

Body
Fitting the Fenders
Devilish-Details

Details can make or break a Hot Rod. It's tough enough to throw a project together, but the mark of excellence is careful assembly. The last column dealt with mounting the body so that the doors fit correctly. If you are building a fenderless and open engine traditional rod, you might be done with fine-tuning panel fit. On the other hand, a full fendered hot rod still needs more massaging.

It's generally best to begin by mounting the hood. Set the radiator in place using the necessary bushings, insulators, and springs. Be sure to have cowl and radiator lacings and rubber bumpers mounted since you'll need them in place to dial in fits. Different thickness hood lacings will affect the hood fit, and can be used to raise a hood that sits too low on the cowl or grill. It's not uncommon to use black closed-cell insulation, available in auto parts stores and better home improvement stores, to raise up the correct hood lacing, if the hood is too low. If the hood is too high, different hood lacing can be used, or layers of that closed cell insulation used to build up to the correct thickness.

If your car uses inner fender panels, mount them as well. All the bolts will be left finger tight for now, as with the entire process of mounting all the fenders and hood. If you try to first mount the fenders and then the hood, this process is much more difficult. The factory fit the hood and inner fender panels first, as seen in vintage photos showing bodies coming down the assembly line. The fenders are added later, and brought up to match the already fitted hood.

A problem can crop up with an IFS installation, when the original fender bracing has modified, or eliminated, as on the 1940 Ford. Be certain to have a way to mount the fender group so that it is properly supported to the frame, not hanging off the hood. Not to beat the popular '40 Fords to death, but this is a common problem on these cars, seen with a grill top and hood lower edge that don't meet well. Often, the only thing really holding up the nose is the hood latch. I have attached a drawing of a pretty simple stand used to solve this common problem, and the general idea will work on other cars as well.

Since the cowl of the body is our fixed starting point, begin by setting the hood in place. You'll want to fit the back of the hood to the cowl first. Shift the hood left and right at the front until the back fits the cowl with an even gap. Next you'll raise or lower the front of the hood as required to get the hood sides fitted evenly to the cowl sides. Raising the front of the hood will increase the gap at the bottom rear, and lowering the hood front will tighten that gap. The inner fender panels can also be adjusted to fit nicely to the bottom of the hood side panels.

Since the rear fenders can be adjusted only slightly to match the body, do that next. Leaving the bolts loose, move the fender to where the tail matches the body's tail pan nicely. Then the running boards can be mounted loosely. You'll probably find it necessary to readjust the rear fenders to get a happy medium between the tail pan fit and the running board position. 'Glass fenders are often easier since you can drill holes where the fenders fit best, rather than having to deal with predrilled holes. A nifty trick with fiberglass bodies is to use self-tapping sheet rock screws to hold fenders temporarily, replacing them with bolts later.

You can also use heat to improve the fit of fiberglass fenders. On something like a '32 Ford, you can cut a bunch of short pieces of 2 x 4, which are placed between a mounted tire and the inner side of the fender. The 2 x 4 spacers push the fender into a nice tight fit. Then a heat lamp is used to soften the fiberglass enough so that it will stay where it has been braced. Watch the heat closely so you don't get the glass too soft! This technique can be used all over the car. I've even known guys to push a 'glass car out into the hot Southern sun long enough to let the panels "relax" into a non-stressed position.

The front fenders are next. If you are lucky, they'll fit right up to the prefitted front end and hood. On later model cars, shims can be added under the fender's upper mounting lip (inside the hood) to raise the fender to a proper fit at the cowl. Otherwise, you may need to elongate some holes to get the fit you are after.

Repro parts can really give you difficulty. There is a difference in quality from brand to brand, so do some asking and checking around. It's another place where you get what you pay for. Good original tin will always be a great choice, but NOS parts can be a problem. All too often, NOS parts turn out to fit poorly. The reason is that the factories often used stamped parts that were off just a little as repair parts, trusting the body man to make in-shop changes on a collision repair. Occasionally the part fits so badly that a new one is ordered, and the out of spec part goes into storage until "we have more time to make it work". Later, some one finds that fender in a parts room, and sells it as NOS, which it is, but quite possibly with a checkered past. This is not to say all NOS is flawed by any stretch, just a word of warning passed on by old time parts men who were there when this scenario occurred. I prefer used tin, in good shape.

The fender braces are added last, holding the fenders in the necessary position. As always, leave all the bolts finger tight to make readjustments easier. Don't finish tightening all the bolts until you're satisfied with the total fit. Hopefully, all has gone nicely, but what do you do when adjustments don't give you the nice even gaps and fits you're after?

This is where you have to get clever. Sit back and think carefully about how the parts interrelate. Can you loosen one side at a time and move things into proper position? If you want to go past the limits of factory fit, you can expect to modify the mating parts. Whether steel or 'glass, the reality of working with 60 year old designs is that tolerances were much looser then. The average car from the 30s - 50s wasn't built to be a museum piece. If it went together without chipping paint, they had done their jobs well enough. That's why you'll see 1/4" factory gaps.

Just like fitting doors, once any available adjustments are made, consider trimming the edges, or adding to them for nice gaps. It's not uncommon to change the flanges of the fenders and running boards. They can be recontoured to match, and extended or shortened to get what you need. Fiberglass reinforced body fillers are very helpful on steel or 'glass fenders and running boards where a perfectly matched contour is required. We recently did a '36 Ford Roadster whose hood fit poorly. We first thought we'd have to lengthen the right hood side panel, but removing 5/16 inch from the length of the right hand running board moved the front fender back enough that the hood fit very nicely, with even gaps all around.

Like so many things in building a Hot Rod, the real key is patience. When you get frustrated, step back and think. Sometimes you need an hour, and sometimes you need a week, depending on the depth of your trouble and the length of your fuse. "Perfection" is wonderful, but getting it done is delightful!

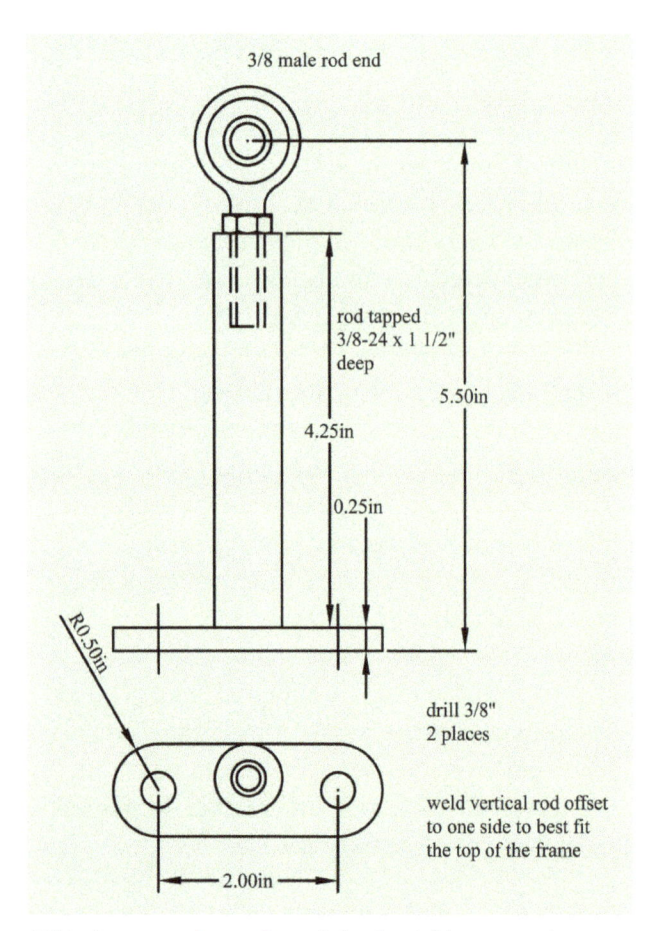

This brace replaces the original wishbone used on '39-'40 Fords and allows adjustment for a precise fit.

Body

Tips On Getting Slick Doors

Latches that Open and Close with Ease

Nostalgia is huge, and the resto-rod is on the comeback trail, but the smooth look will always be with us. Whether your project is a hi tech street rod, a '50s Kustom, or a Sport touring musclecar, hidden door handles are trick. Some neat effects can be achieved with smooth late model door handles, but the uninterrupted bodyline really works for these cars. Here are a few thoughts on ways to go about actuating those door latches.

The original type door latches that use a retracting wedge type mechanism are common on cars like '39 Fords and Chevys. They have a strong return spring that requires a lot of effort to move, along with a lot of friction between the striker plate and the pin. You'll need a real heavy-duty solenoid to pull these babies! An old favorite is the VW bug starter solenoids from the '60s, which are readily available and easy to mount. They can be connected to the latch with cable or rods. The problem is that all that pulling power is going to be hard on the mount and linkage. Failures and unreliable operations are quite common. We've tried weakening the return spring with a propane torch but it's a pretty hit and miss operation. Honestly, the best way to have reliable solenoid operated latches today is to use a rotary style latch.

Any car with a push button handle will have a rotary latch. These are super common from the late '40s on, so your job will be simplified on a car like that. We are all well aware of the aftermarket latches out there, which can be used to convert a slider latched door as above, as well as to replace a worn factory rotary latch. The beauty of these guys is that the only real friction is that of pulling the pawl lever, which releases the rotary latch (looks like a ratchet wheel). This lower friction requires a much lighter pull, and will be much easier on your mount and linkage. You will have a more reliable system that can use smaller solenoids and gear actuators with a smaller amperage load as well.

> It's really important to have a mechanical backup for any door latch or battery area. Plenty of folks have been stuck in cars ...

There are a wide variety of latches out there so shop carefully. There are big ones, small ones, locking ones, and cheap junk that wouldn't keep a suitcase closed, much less a suicide door! By the way, you did put safety pins on your SUICIDE doors, right? It seems like most everyone installs these with the pin on the jamb and the latch in the door. I'd like to campaign against that. If you put the pin in the door and the latch on the body, you will have less wiring in the door with potential for failure in the hinge area. What wiring you do have will be protected from weather and moving parts. More room is created to clear window tracks on cars with skinny doorposts like '39 Chevys. You won't need the notch in your door panel that breaks up that nifty and expensive interior. It also becomes very easy to have a backup release cable that runs under the car if any of the electrical components fail.

It's really important to have a mechanical back-up for any door latch or battery area. Plenty of folks have been stuck in cars with all electric actuation inside and out. You may get out in a gas station with a rock and a brave passerby, as long as your car isn't chopped to the point where the windows are skinnier than you are thick! Even then, 'ya gotta get in to get home to fix it! I have no idea how an EMT crew would get you out quickly in a wreck. Be sure to have a way out, without power.

Linkages from the actuator to the latch can be as simple as a piece of 1/8 inch rod bent to shape. Stainless steel welding rod is much stronger than plain steel rod so it will hold its shape better. You can easily get some from any welder. You can bend it slightly to dial in the length and it will hold better than slotted mount holes for the actuator. Another good way is to use braided 1/8 inch cable and crimp ends that can be had at any good hardware store. Use common 3/16 inch brake line tubing with a liberal coating of white grease inside as a more reliable cable guide than pulleys. You can easily route the cable where there's plenty of space. Just keep the cable entry and exit straight and the bend radius nice and gentle for smooth action. A simple loop with a secure crimp fitting on each end will set the length as needed.

The actuator will be operated by a relay, which gets power to go and a ground to activate. Be sure you use something heavier than a horn relay! Supplying the switching ground can be an exercise in creativity. Magnetic switches are a favorite on fiberglass cars, but will not work thru a steel body. They will work thru glass, or a small section of fiberglass worked into a section of a steel body. You can use remotes for either just the doors or simply to roll down the window to grab an inside handle. A weather sealed starter button for tractors can be hidden under a running board and pushed by your toe. We've also hidden miniature push buttons from Radio Shack under mirrors and headlights on '38 Chevys.

Back in the day of board step plates and cowboy boots with silver tips, we sometimes isolated a step plate bolt from the body with nylon washers, and ran the ground wire to it. Walk up, bridge the bolt to the step plate with your silver tip boots, and open sesame! A car with exposed stainless trim could easily work the same with a trim screw isolated and ground wired as above. Any conductive object like a coin or key becomes the bridge completing the ground circuit. The down side is that anyone who sees you do it can too, so a locking latch with remote actuator might be a good part of the plan.

A little thought goes a long way here, as on so many little projects on your hot rod. It's a nifty way to add a little personality to your car.

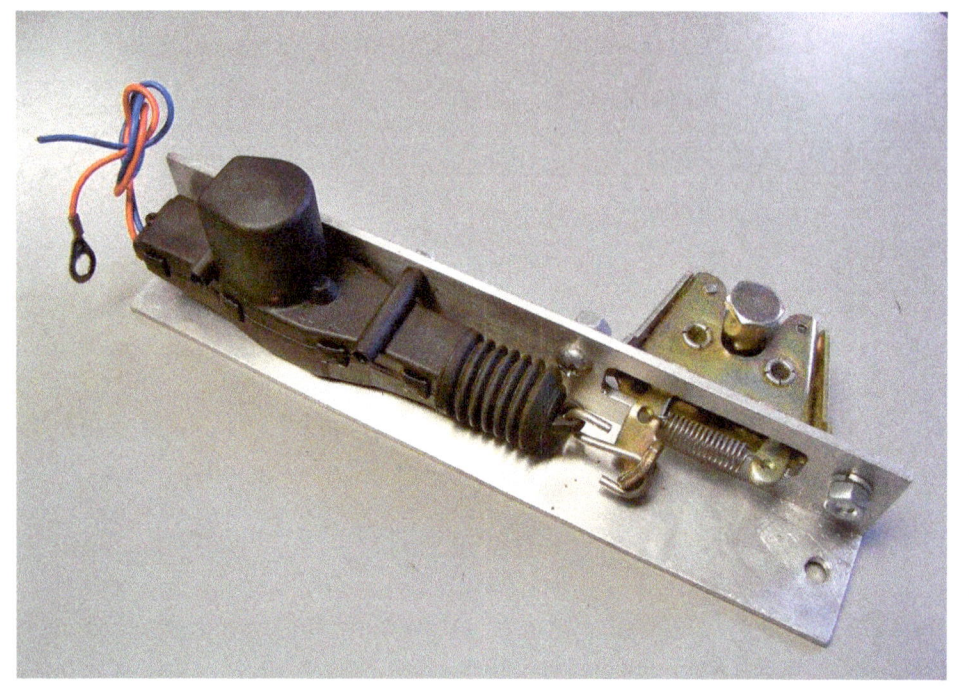

This solenoid kit works best with the light pull required to release the ratchet pawl on a small deck lid latch.

Body

Tricks With Tin

Clever Shortcuts

It seems like building a Hot Rod gets easier over the years. Specialty companies develop parts that make junk yard chasing unnecessary and sometimes actually more expensive when your time is considered. But sometimes, you need a part that just isn't available, so you have to make something else work.

With sheet metal work, it's possible to build or buy equipment to make virtually any panel. Our shop has all the English Wheels, Pullmax, shrinkers, etc. to make what we need. Even so, there are times it's more cost effective to rework an existing salvaged panel into what we need. What the panel manufacturers do is to trade your money for their time and expertise. For those lacking the tools, this is often a necessity. Here's some ideas to get you thinking!

There are plenty of rotted '40s to '50s pickups around which have a really useful shape over the rear window. This wide compound curve can make an excellent rear pan for a lot of fat fender cars. The tight radius upper corners can also be turned upside down to make corner patches. Now, this is more trouble than the excellent panels available, but it's another option when no exact fit parts are out there.

Filling the old cloth insert tops on thirties cars with factory panels has been going on for many years. Although a hammer welded seam is a sign of craftsmanship, an excellent cost effective alternative is slowly "stitching" it in with a wire welder. Be sure to overlap the hole about 1", and skip around with single spot welds until the seam is continuous. Do not try to run even short beads! New roof ribs made from 1 x 1 x .120 tube bent to the proper radius will help avoid warpage.

Ribbed tops look best in sedans. Our favorites are 61 - 64 Chevy, and 65 -67 Dart/Valiant wagons. Anglias with two hole grills look great with a 73 Corolla wagon top, which has lowered bands which match the grill. Coupes look best with a smooth insert; Mustangs and Pintos work nicely.

In all cases, the tops look best with the curved front near the windshield put to the rear of the project car in order to better match the contours. Try to use a pre-76 top, as the later cars use a much softer and weaker steel. If in doubt as to the required shape, a couple simple traced cardboard templates can be used to match the desired old and new top contours. Be leery of putting entire '60s tops on '40s cars since the early rounder shapes can look kinda weird with a boxy 67 Impala top.

Talking about templates reminds me of con-

> **There are plenty of rotted '40s to '50s pickups around which have a really useful shape over the rear window...**

verting a 33 Willys 4 door to a 2 door. After building the door framing, a simple template and a junk yard trip yielded a pair of Rambler tops that made beautifully fitted doorskins, with just the right compound curved shape.

    Firewall recesses can be beautifully made using a section from a large freon bottle. The local A/C guy tosses them away! For a full firewall recess in something like a Model A, try the local home improvement store. You can buy a replacement bucket for a light duty wheelbarrow in a home supply store for about 20 bucks. It has a real nice shape and can easily be trimmed to build an impressive looking coved firewall. (Tell the local fender lizards you banged it out over your knee!)

    A favorite and dirt cheap third light is found on Dodge Neons. It has a very pretty oval shape and is super simple to install. Hagan's gas doors work so well and cost so little that it just isn't worth hunting for a junkyard piece. Mazda Miatas have a trick door handle, but be sure to use the Mazda latch so you can lock it!

    When installing rotary latches, consider putting the pin in the door and the latch in the inside the post. This provides more glass clearance inside the door while eliminating weight. Your wiring is also simplified and it's much easier to hide a braided cable under the rocker to allow you to open the door when your battery goes dead. And your upholsterer won't have to put an ugly little notch in the door panel to clear the latch pin.

    Some of us prefer the more difficult junk yard method to 1-800 parts. Economics, an innovative spirit, and sometimes plain cussedness all play a part in this. The fun part is to see a shape and imagine it where "no man has gone before"!

New doorskins were fabricated using salvage yard roof panels when this 33 Willys was converted from a 4 door to this phantom design 2 door.

Body

Fixing The Sagging Door Blues

An Age Old Problem

You get a hot rod all done, and all the gaps are right on the money. But after a few miles and a season on the road, the bottom corner of the door, farthest from the hinge, is starting to come away from the body. The weight of glass, power windows, and upholstery has conspired with gravity to cause the dreaded sagging door syndrome. It doesn't look good and it leaks air. This is a common problem which occurs more often with fiberglass and wood-framed bodies than with all steel doors.

With a steel door, you can just put your knee against the door and pull judiciously on the top to pull some twist out. The welded corners and steel frame will hold the shape for a good long while. The Fisher Body guys who built wood framed bodies for GM back in the Thirties had the same problem and a clever solution for it. I found this out once when I had a '34 Buick with wood-framed doors. With the weight of the door and the unavoidable warping due to water getting into the wood framing, twisting was inevitable. I then discovered that each door had a turnbuckle built in that could be tightened as necessary to keep the door aligned. The edge of the door exposed a screw head that very quickly and easily solved the problem.

I once built a chopped and bobbed highboy '34 Ford Tudor in an old Sprint Car style with wire wheels, quick-change, injected fake Ardun…all that cool stuff. A look at the availability and the cost of a steel body (and the need to build the car in ninety days for LA Roadsters one summer) quickly turned me toward fiberglass. I acquired a phenomenally good fiberglass body from Wayne at Redneck. But I also inherited the dreaded drooping doors with the combination of the desert heat, a 6000 mile maiden voyage, and the upholstery. That's no reflection on the body quality of Redneck's, they all do it. A walk around any rod run will show you what I'm talking about if you look closely enough. I found that the Redneck body did it less than most. The fact is, these cars all need a turnbuckle added, just like the wood-framed cars had.

A trip to the local home improvement store will net you a couple of turnbuckles, jamb nuts for the turnbuckles, and some 1/8" x 1" aluminum strap. I have tried the smaller ones that are 10-24 thread, but they won't hold up. The larger 1/4-20 ones are a little more bulky, but they have the requisite strength. Being that all this stuff comes from across the water somewhere, be aware that the threads will be some bastard metric deal, so you'll want to open the package to find a jamb nut that fits the RH thread end while still at the store. This will save you a return trip later.

The pictures tell the story best but I'll try to describe the process. The idea is to find a spot to anchor the upper end of the aluminum strap near the top of the door, at the hinge side. Then find a

> **The Fisher Body guys who built wood-framed bodies for GM ... had a clever solution for it.**

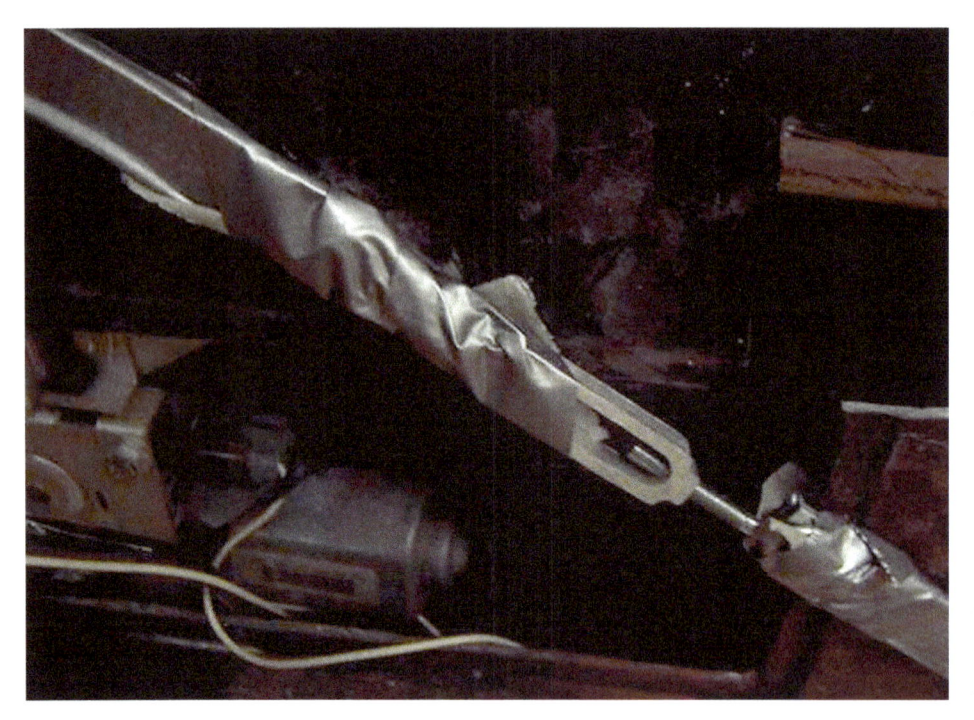

similar spot near the lower corner away from the hinge. You will need to locate, or cut an area that will accept the turnbuckle. There will often be a large access hole that serves nicely for this purpose. Then cut the strap as required. Use flathead screws to hold the strap to the door and the turnbuckles in the middle. Keep the bulk of this assembly at a minimum in order to keep from disturbing the fit of the door panel more than necessary. I like to use a couple layers of our old friend, duct tape to pad and anti-rattle the strap against the door inner panel. Be sure to add the jamb nut to the turnbuckle, and keep the RH threads on the up side to help prevent vibration from loosening the adjustment.

From there it's a simple matter of tightening the turnbuckle to pull the door back into the correct shape to fit the body. I like to let the door settle overnight before re-attaching the upholstery just in case final adjustments are necessary. It's also a good idea to bring the adjustment a little farther than right on, since the door panel adds a little weight and it will stretch in use.

In my case, I wanted to do all this before the body was painted, but like everyone in a hurry, I let it slide. This is a simple Saturday morning tune up to dial in a car that is finished, but it can and should be done on

A common hardware store turnbuckle can be the key to making your doors fit the body tightly.

Here you see the whole thing, the turnbuckle pull that brings the lower door corner into a tighter curve.

all fiberglass and wood framed cars while still in the build-up stages. It doesn't seem to be as necessary with an all-steel car, but it wouldn't be a bad idea there as well. I have seen it done on more than a few steel '32 Ford roadsters and 3 window coupes, especially when the top hinge has been eliminated during a chop.

Notice a good general fit, but the front lower corner has rolled out and is not snug in its body opening.

The turnbuckle adds an adjustable method to draw the door panel into a tighter curve that fits the body nicely.

Brakes

Brake Plumbing 101

Only DOT Approved Components

Once your chassis fabrication is done, it's time to plumb it for fluids. We'll discuss the brake plumbing first. You need to have all components mounted. That includes whatever valves your system requires. Be sure you've read additional articles, or a good catalog so that you clearly understand the purpose and differences between metering, proportioning, residual check, and combination valves.

Let's get some of hardest choices out of the way first. My personal opinion is that only legal, DOT approved components should be used. That excludes stainless hard lines, many S/S braided hoses, through the frame fittings, or any fittings with pipe thread in their design. The S/S hard lines come from aircraft use, with a totally different environment and inspection cycle than seen in highway use. The same goes for S/S hoses. In fact, most catalogs specifically state, "not for highway use." I'm not sure I'd want to defend my use of that component after an accident. There are S/S hoses with DOT approval, which have a nylon sleeve added to the ferrule to pass DOT's "whip" test. It is up to you to make certain those sleeves stay in place, but isn't that a better choice?

On the subject of pipe-thread fittings, DOT doesn't require double flare, inverted fittings just to be nasty. Pipe thread will not hold the necessary pressure, so don't build a weak link into your system. Finally, I hope we've finally seen the last copper brake lines, which work harden, break, and cause crashes.

Hard lines are normally made with tin plated steel lines, commonly sold in auto parts stores. The plating can be quickly polished with a 3-M pad, and clear lacquered with a spray bomb for a look almost as nice as stainless at a fraction of the cost. These lines must be double flared to length, which we'll cover later.

Stainless hard lines are used for a very trick appearance, but due to the brittle nature of stainless they do not flare well without special tooling. You can buy pre-made S/S lines from specialty companies, but most custom made, in-shop jobs make use of ferrule style aircraft quality fittings. Do not try to plumb the whole system with S/S braided hose, the expandable nature of that much hose causes a soft pedal.

As to proper line size, hydraulic theory explains that the transmission of pressure is dependent on cylinder size (piston face surface), not the conduit size. Your log splitter needs a lot of volume in a hurry, so it uses large lines, but flow rate isn't much of an issue in a brake system. GM used to run larger 1/4 inch lines in the rear, which I believe they thought would delay rear brake action, but today we use a metering valve to do a better job.

Rubber hoses are the old standby. We often use '85 Riviera front hoses (NAPA #36959) that are 17 inch long and accept 3/16 inch hard line. They fit as-is with metric GM calipers, and can be drilled out just a tiny bit to 7/16 inch for the earlier, larger calipers. A good rear hose for all 3/16 inch line comes from a 75 Jeep CJ-5 (NAPA # 36799). Stainless braided hoses are often actually cheaper, allegedly caused by the high liability premiums paid by the rubber hose manufacturers. Just be sure to get the DOT S/S hoses.

All hoses must be securely mounted at one end with a bracket and clip, not a tie wrap. The clips are Weatherhead # 5188, but we prefer a round 5/8 inch circlip from the hardware store for a nicer look. At each caliper end, you'll need 2 copper washers and a hollow banjo bolt. These are NAPA # 1243, #82703 for the metric, and # 82698 for 7/16 inch bolt. By the way, the Ford Motorsports rear disc kit using 96 Explorer calipers uses a 3/8 - 24 banjo bolt which is a special, available thru companies specializing in S/S braided plumbing. Be sure to route all hoses so that they never touch any other parts, moving or not. They will quickly wear through and endanger you. Calipers mount hoses through a gate to prevent rotation, thus loosening the banjo bolt. Hoses can be reoriented by carefully grinding a new gate in a different location. Since rear disc calipers float in their brackets, you can run two hoses in the rear as well for a cleaner axle housing. A neat trick on drum rear brakes is to swap the wheel cylinders side for side so the lines point forward, hiding on the forward side of the axle housing.

We prefer steel fittings to brass, in order to avoid rounding the hex. Inverted flare fittings seal internally, so Teflon tape is unnecessary. If the fitting leaks, re-flare the line and check the receiving seat. What follows is a list of handy fitting numbers from Weatherhead, which is the brand carried at most part stores. Spare 3/16 inch line nuts are # 105 x 3, 3/16 inch tee with mount tab # 7812. An oversize 1/4 inch nut to accept 3/16 inch line is made by drilling a 1/4 inch inverted flare plug. Corvette dual master cylinders which are commonly used on street rod power brake units need a # 7911 adaptor for 9/16 - 18 to 3/16 inch line for the rear brakes, which on GM cars are always serviced by the larger of the two fittings. The front brakes accept a 1/2-20 to 3/16 inch nut, which is not readily available, although it may come from your power brake supplier. This nut can be obtained in a salvage yard, as it is used on many GM cars. Take along a 1/2 and 9/16 fine thread bolt to check, since they match the thread in the Corvette cylinder. If you get both, you can put them on your lines and avoid adaptors altogether. Ford mixes their fitting sizes, but you can rely on the usual rule that the smaller reservoir will always service the drum brakes on a disc drum cylinder. (Remember small piston, small reservoir)

When routing the hard lines, avoid loops to shorten lines, and high spots that can trap air. Stay away from the bottom of frame rails and top of axle housings to avoid pinching the lines. Give a minimum of one-inch clearance from any exhaust as the heat will expand the fluid and cause dragging brakes. Use coat hangers to mock up bends, but as cheap as the line is, throw away your goofs and try again.

Bending tools are essential for the larger fuel and trans cooler lines, but the best 3/16 inch line bender is still two thumbs. When you need leverage for a tight final bend, slip a 3/8 inch box end wrench over the nut for a handle. You are using special line wrenches for the final tightening, right?

Clip the lines to the frame every 2-3 feet with the special clamps sold everywhere. Any of the nylon, aluminum, stainless, or rubber lined clips work well, but we really like the colored made-for-you sets with dual grooves for fuel lines running parallel where needed. We often use 1/8 inch pop rivets for easy setup and reinstallation. These provide a nice locating hole to tap for 10-32 screws if your project is more ambitious.

Don't forget to pump the pedal slowly to bleed the brakes. Vacuum bleeders make a one-man job much easier. Finally, regardless of the L or R cast on the calipers, the bleeder screws must be one top. You want to evacuate air, not fluid. You wouldn't believe how many guys fight a system, only to find their calipers are upside down!

Brake lines run with sharp corners and straight parallel lines look great and add to your chassis' professionally assembled appearance.

Brakes

She Won't Stop! Brakes

Solving Typical Brake Issues

Braking problems continue to be a major source of hot rod headaches. It's encouraging to see the efforts builders are making to produce a brake system equal to the best factory cars. Let's take a look at several of the most common concerns.

The most basic can be the most embarrassing. Calipers are cast with an L or R, signifying the position from the factory. Many hot rod brake kits switch the calipers side to side in order to clear steering linkage, causing confusion. Don't look at the casting mark; just install the calipers with the bleeder screw on top. You're trying to eliminate air, as evidenced by the appearance of clear brake fluid when you're done. When a rodder bleeds and bleeds with no luck, this is the first place to look for error.

Speaking of fluid, we all tried silicon fluid a few years ago in order to save paint and preserve rubber brake parts. Unfortunately, silicon fluid has a high surface tension, which tends to trap air bubbles. This leads to incomplete bleeding and spongy brakes. Experience has shown that good DOT 4 fluid gives a better pedal feel. Catalyzed paints have pretty much eliminated staining with short exposure to brake fluid. Just keep a rag handy and be a little neater when bleeding.

If you're getting clear fluid with bleeders on top, and it takes a second pump to get a good pedal, you have a volume problem. First and foremost, be sure the calipers don't get twisted by hitting the suspension, as this will actually pump fluid back out of the calipers.

Most hot rod pedal assemblies do very well with a 5 or 6-to-1 pedal ratio and around a one-inch bore master cylinder. You'll get around 1 inch of stroke, which produces enough volume to operate the wheel brakes we normally see. Original pedal assemblies can often have a 7-to-1 ratio. This increases leverage to decrease effort at the expense of increased foot pedal travel. That's why original pedals are often so high as to be awkward. When we adjust the linkage to lower the pedal, the master cylinder stroke is reduced and may not be enough to completely actuate the brakes. That second stroke produces the necessary added volume needed to stop. This same leverage versus stroke scenario is often created when a factory firewall mounted pedal is lengthened to keep the booster high enough to clear the valve covers. Aftermarket pedal assemblies are available which maintain proper leverage and design, so don't try it on your own unless you fully understand the physics involved.

The best solution to this volume problem is often a larger bore master cylinder. The larger bore compensates for the shorter stroke, providing the needed volume at the cost of increased pedal effort. Going from a 1 inch bore to a 1 1/8 inch increases volume and effort 26% (the surface area increases as the square of the diameter increases). To find a matching but larger cylinder, I look in the back of the catalog where the illustrations are. The EIS brand catalog is terrific, showing the different cylinder in the same casting "family" and detailing bore and fitting sizes. You can even find similar cylinders with outlets on different sides for ease of plumbing. The reverse part index will tell you what the new part application is.

Residual pressure valves (RPV) are used to ensure proper initial line pressure before the brakes are applied. Since drum brakes have actual return springs, they require a 10 psi RPV. Disc brakes use a 2 psi RPV, which keeps just enough pressure in the line to prevent the disc pads from pulling back too far. If the pads pull back too much, your first pump will be used up just getting the pads in position, with a second pump needed to apply pressure to the rotor. We always us a 2 psi valve with discs, whether in front or back. A dual disc/drum cylinder has a 10 psi RPV built in to the smaller reservoir to service rear drum brakes. You only need and external 10 psi RPV to drum brakes when using a Corvette 4 wheel disc cylinder as is common with hot rod power pedal assemblies.

A really weird volume problem can cause dragging brakes. We'll assume you've adjusted the pushrod for just enough free play at the pedal so the brakes aren't preloaded. If the pedal gets higher and harder while brakes are dragging, your probably have a case of bad brake fluid. Brake fluid is hygroscopic, which describes its affinity for water. When a can is opened it begins to absorb water. This happens much quicker in a master cylinder, especially with extended storage. The brakes heat the fluid, expanding the water tightening the brakes, accelerating the whole process. You might get home by temporarily opening a bleeder to relieve the pressure, but the only real solution is to blow out the system and change to fresh fluid. Buy the small cans and never save the opened ones.

When the "subframe era" arrived in the '70s, the thought was that by using all the suspension and drivetrain from, say, a '68-'74 Nova, your '40 Chevy will drive just like the Nova. What was missed was that the changes in total weight, weight distribution, and tire size completely change the vehicle dynamics. The engine is typically set back 4-5 inches, which makes the front springs too stiff and too tall. Since the Nova's brake proportioning valve was preset for that nose heavy car with equal tire sizes, it will be shutting down much of the pressure to the rear brakes, and be completely wrong for our hot rod. When the rear tires are taller than the front, the added tire diameter acts as a longer lever to reduce the power of the rear brakes. A 2 inch diameter difference amounts to an 8% reduction in rear braking. If the preset proportioning valve reduces the rear pressure another 16% (assuming the Nova had 58/42 weight distribution), this adds up to a 23% loss in rear brake power! That's why a preset valve will almost never work right. Our subject '40 Chevy with a small block (50/50 weight distribution), 11 inch front discs (MII upgrade), 10 inch rear drums (8 or 10 bolt axles), and 27/29 inch tires will stop great without any proportioning valve. You've increased the front brakes with the 11 inch setup, balancing the system while increasing the total brake power greatly. Isn't it a better idea to get balance by increasing the front rather than decreasing the rear? You'll only need an adjustable proportioning valve as you decrease front brakes (9 inch rotors), increase rear brakes (11 inch drums or rear discs), or run equal diameter tires.

A combination valve does have the desirable feature of a metering valve, which is used to hold off applying the front brakes until the rear pressure rises enough to take up the clearance between the shoes and drum. You can get a separate metering valve and install it as a tee for the front brakes. Take care to mount it in the center with equal length brake lines to avoid pulling under braking.

All of this is just high school Physics applied to real, "drive'em hard" hot rods!

This pedal assembly features a strong mount, proper leverage ratio and has a return spring which mounts over the pushrod.

Brakes

Parking Brakes - Gotta Have 'Em!

Not Very Exciting - Still Essential

There's nothing exotic or exciting about building an emergency brake system, but common sense and the laws of every state's DOT demand that you do so. Some folks call them parking brakes, which can be very important if all the good power- parking spots are taken, and you have to park in a sloped area. Setting the brake is certainly more dignified than using a brick, or tying off to a tree! One of the local comedians used to have a Vega E-brake handle screwed to a hunk of 4x4, and tried to con the inspectors into accepting it as a "mechanical parking brake". Hopefully you can be convinced to do a little better.

I prefer to think of the system as an emergency brake rather than a parking brake. With hot rods being essentially prototypes, there's always the possibility of brake system failure. Hoses can be stretched, master cylinder pushrods can bend or fall out...stuff happens. The point is, that you want a separate back up system to get you stopped. That's why a Line-Loc is not acceptable since it shares the primary hydraulic circuit.

It used to be pretty hard to build an effective and attractive system, which is probably why a lot of rods were built without this feature. We used to have to cobble up a bunch of old cables and hardware store clamps, but today the aftermarket rules. Lokar and Gennie Shifter were the innovators, and have their imitators, as always happens. You'll usually find their cable systems to actually be less expensive than trying to buy new OEM parts. Installation is a snap assuming you believe in reading and following instructions. Different levels of appearance and machining quality exist so it pays off to check out the available choices.

You can begin with a handle to actuate the system. Old favorites from the swap meet were Pinto and Vega handles, but they're getting pretty scarce. Most guys today will pick up an aftermarket handle that will be ready made to accept a hot rod cable set. You can get the normal floor mounted lay down style, antique appearing handles which mount to the trans like a Model A, and even foot actuated kick-panel mounted deals.

A nifty trick with limited floor space is to use a lay down handle mounted crossways in the car, just ahead of the seat base. This keeps it out of your foot space, and needs only a simple pulley to redirect the cable to the rear. You can use an original dash mounted handle with its original cable, or pick up one of the down cables that are now available made expressly to connect hot rod cables. I've seen them for '40 Fords and '47 Chevy pickups, but given how universal cable design seems to be, I wouldn't be surprised if they would fit a lot of other cars too.

Cables are pretty foolproof. You just have to fasten them securely and out of the way of exhaust and moving suspension components. The instructions tell you to mount the outer housing, insert the cable to mark the length and then take it all apart to cut to length with your Zizz wheel. If you try to cheat (like I have) by cutting the housing while the cable is still inside, you'll very likely remove some strands from the cable. That can cause the cable to bind in the housing or fail at just the wrong time. Do it the hard way - the right way like the instructions say. I like to leave the cable long until final adjustment is made after normal stretching occurs. Just wrap a little electrical tape or shrink tubing to prevent the cable unraveling. By the way, you'll avoid trouble by matching the rotation direction of your cutoff wheel to the cable's rotation spiral.

E-brakes on drum type rear brakes are pretty simple. Just make sure that the actuating pushrod is in place between the shoes. This is actually a flat, stamped steel piece that runs just below the wheel cylinder and pushes the shoes apart to hold the car whenever the cable is pulled. For some odd reason, this part is often missing on salvage yard rear ends. You'll have to go to a dealer for a new one as they are not stocked at most parts houses.

Rear discs are more complicated. Some have an actuating lever, which operates a screw that pushes the inner pad into the rotor. Watch out for frame clearance with these levers. Where most calipers are self-adjusting, these require you to use the parking brake every time you park the car in order to keep the pads close to the rotor. This is the downfall of the infamous Versailles disc brake rear. If all the parts are in good shape and the park brake is always used, you're usually OK. I've seen good mechanics fight these deals for a year before giving up and converting back to drums. Personally, I'll be glad when they're extinct - Ford abandoned the design after 3 years!

Many other OEM rear discs such as Corvette and later Fords use a small drum machined into the disc rotor. These usually work pretty well. We've been using a lot of the Ford Motorsports rear disc kit, which is based on '96 Explorer parts. It's adaptable to most 8 and 9 inch rears and is fairly priced. There are quite a few rear disc kits in the aftermarket which actually use an OEM front caliper. These will not have any provision for a park brake, so be careful what you buy, although one can be added. Some of the aftermarket disc kits also lack this feature.

A separate small caliper is often used to provide a parking brake, but considering their small size and lack of mechanical advantage in their simple wedge design, they may hold a car but I wonder if they could stop a car in case of hydraulic system failure.

The Model T had a normal service brake which acted only on the driveline with emergency brakes on the rear wheels, opposite to how we do it today. It was a common thing for T drivers to ignore the service brake and use the lever operated rear brakes instead. Our heavier and faster hot rods might be in real trouble relying on such a small backup system. This may be another case where the trick show-car stuff isn't so hot on the interstate. Show-ponies and workhorses aren't good or bad, you just have to match them to the job at hand.

If you do want to use rear calipers, which lack a strong emergency brake, consider installing the unique deal made by ECI. Their special caliper mounts the pinion flange on Ford rears and uses a spiral ball actuator, which provides 1800 foot-pounds of static retarding force with 35 pounds of effort at the handle. These works so well that ECI has used them to develop a line of brakes for use on industrial processing equipment.

You'll hopefully never need the hand brake for anything other than parking. If you ever have a failure of your hydraulic service brakes, having them available for emergency use may save lives. Get them working!

Both OEM and aftermarket rear brake kits generally incorporate a small emergency drum brake system hidden inside the rotor hat and actuated by a lever that connects to normal E brake cables.

Brakes

Strange Brake Problems

Always go back to the Basics

Problems with brake function can be difficult to solve, especially when you have used all the "right" top quality parts that have a proven track record of working together in everybody else's systems. You will find, almost without fail, that there is a solution so simple you'll slap your forehead when you find it. Always go back to the basics.

Before we can diagnose any functional problems, we have to get the brake system full of fluid, a process known as bleeding the brakes. We are actually getting rid of trapped air, evidenced by a flow of clear fluid at the bleeder screws. It is not uncommon for calipers to be installed on the wrong side, and inverted. As we've mentioned, this allows fluid to come out the bleeder at the bottom, but does not release the trapped air. Just be sure to install the caliper with the bleeder screw on top. Most aftermarket calipers have dual fittings for the input line and the bleeder, so be sure to still keep the bleeder on top. This is often the root cause when a novice rodder says they have bled much fluid through without ever getting a good pedal.

Another common cause of never getting a good pedal is a problem with the master cylinder putting out less volume of fluid than is required to actuate the wheel cylinders. Again, the symptom of this mismatch is bleeding through too much fluid without getting a good pedal feel. Every master cylinder in common hot rod use will need a one-inch stroke at the pushrod. Be sure to actually measure that pushrod travel if you have this problem, especially if you have played around with the pedal leverage ratio. That ratio of foot-pad to pushrod travel is generally in the 5 to 1 range, which works great with master cylinders with a bore size from 15/16 to 1 1/8 inch.

You can gain volume output with larger bore master cylinders, but you increase pedal effort since the pressure output is reduced. This is why power boosted systems become essential on heavier cars, especially when larger calipers and four wheel disc systems require more volume than the master cylinder can produce. I saw this once on a T coupe with a home fabricated pedal assembly that only had ¾" stroke at the master cylinder. Replacing the original one-inch bore master cylinder with a 1 ¼ inch bore unit got us brakes on the first try. We got the volume by trading stroke for bore size…just like it works in an engine cylinder.

Brake system pressures are generally in the 1500-2000 psi range. Actual delivered pressure at the wheel can be checked with a brake pressure gauge, which is of enormous value when diagnosing brake function. Even though pressure is being delivered, a too-small caliper piston-bore will lack clamping force. This is a common problem when using the '78-'87 GM Metric calipers, which have a very small piston diameter, even smaller than a standard MII caliper. Although larger-bore special Metric calipers are on the market, we avoid their use on cars weighing over 3200 pounds, preferring the disc kits using the larger bore '70-'81 Camaro caliper.

If you have power brakes, be sure to use as much hard line as possible to feed the booster, with genuine vacuum hose at the ends. Fuel hose will collapse under high vacuum and block airflow, driving you nuts since the problem never occurs when you are sitting still at idle speed.

A common place for fluid leaks is the hose connection to the caliper. The GM calipers so widely used are machined to accept a hollow bolt and loop end hose, usually referred to as a banjo fitting. These need a copper seal on BOTH sides of the hose end to seal properly.

Hoses do have a top and bottom side, the difference being a step on the side on top, under the bolt head. The hoses will also have a shoulder where the hose is crimped to the end fitting. That can also bottom out into the "gate" machined in the caliper, and again prevent the washers from sealing. Turning the hose over, a little grinding on the caliper, or an extra washer as a spacer will solve the problem once you find it. The copper washers do an excellent job of sealing, so if it leaks, the installer is usually the cause.

Brakes that drag can be caused by an improperly adjusted pushrod with no free play, or a batch of contaminated fluid. Brake fluid actually attracts moisture, which over time converts to an acid that rusts your brake parts. It also causes a major reduction in the boiling point of the fluid. When normal driving puts heat into the fluid, the expanding fluid can cause trouble. If your brakes are getter higher and harder as you drive, try flushing the system with alcohol and rebleeding with all new fluid.

It is also possible that the brakes will overheat due to drag produced when fluid cannot flow back out of the wheel cylinder. It's quite common to find a line over a rear end that has been smashed flat in contact with a tailpipe. Rubber hoses can swell over time causing an internal restriction. Any little trash in the fluid gets trapped and acts as a check valve. It's better not to trust old brake lines and hoses. That original line that looks shiny and nice on the outside can hide a pinhole or internal corrosion.

Backing plate wear from normal motion of the brake shoes must be repaired so that the brakes both expand and retract smoothly.

Master cylinders with lines reversed will also give you fits. It's worth repeating that drum brakes need a 10 psi residual pressure valve (RPV) to operate properly with their retraction springs, while disc brakes with no retraction device require a 2 psi RPV. A dual master cylinder with two different size reservoirs will almost always run the smaller bore drum brake wheel cylinders off the smaller reservoir. That smaller reservoir for the drum brakes will have an internal 10PSI residual pressure valve, and will not need an external one. Hot Rod power brake units generally use a Vette 4 wheel disc type master cylinder with a cap that looks like an oval race track, and equal size reservoirs. The line outlet nearest to the booster is for the rear brakes. That type master has no internal residual pressure valves at all and will need external pressure valves to match disc or drum brakes.

Combination valves with preset rear brake proportioning often shut off far too much rear line pressure. If your rear brakes aren't working, bypass the combination valve to see if that is the problem. An adjustable proportioning valve is a far better idea. Cars which are not nose heavy and those with larger rear tires often need no proportioning valve at all.

You can lose your brakes if the caliper interferes with the suspension at full lock in a turn. If there is enough contact, the caliper gets cocked in its bracket, causing the pads to retract. Your first pedal pump merely takes up that clearance, and you can't stop (Thank goodness you added that return spring, huh!). You will need to limit steering travel or change the caliper to one with a different shape to fix this.

Dual diaphragm brake boosters are defined by the two different diameters seen on the master cylinder side of the booster. The very popular Corvette style master cylinder has been nicely plumbed with the residual pressure valves near the master cylinder and the port nearest the mounting flange connected to the rear brakes for correct sequence of brake actuation.

Brakes

Simple Brake Math

You can't Ignore the Laws of Physics

Analyzing brake system performance can sometimes be complicated, but an understanding of the simple math involved will prove to be a big help in understanding how the system does, or does not, function. It's really all about the surface area of the face of the piston(s) involved whether you are looking at the master cylinder or wheel cylinder/caliper. The laws of hydraulics don't care if you have disc or drum brakes.

Forget about line and hose diameters for our hot rods. The conduit line inside diameter does influence possible flow rates but the volume of fluid movement associated with our brakes is so small that flow rates are not meaningful. Flow means a lot for a hydraulic log splitter but not in a brake system. Normally 3/16 inch ID lines are used.

A basic principal of Hydraulics is that an equal force is exerted at all points in the system, expressed as pounds per square inch or psi. Even though a proportioning valve operates as a needle valve limiting delivery of line pressure to rear brakes, if you hold the pedal down long enough the rear pressure will equalize to the same as delivered up front. So our job designing and assembling a system has to do with how MUCH line pressure can be produced and HOW we use that available line pressure.

This is where the diameter of the piston face comes into play. If we know the diameter we can easily calculate the face surface area. Multiply those square inches by the line pressure in pounds per square inch and you get the applied force in pounds. Taking the one-inch bore size face of .785 square inch, times say, 1200 psi (which is pretty normal for a car brake system) and you get 942 pounds of clamping force. That's a good reason for not getting your fingers in the way when bleeding a brake system! If you want to take the math to the next level you could then multiply that clamping force by the brake pad surface area, times the leverage supplied by the rotor diameter and you would have a pretty good estimate of the available braking force.

Experience has shown that a one-inch bore master cylinder mounted with a 5:1 pedal ratio works well for lighter cars. You can produce more line pressure with a smaller bore master or a greater pedal ratio but what you gain in pressure you lose in the volume produced. The volume can get so low that you no longer have enough fluid flow to operate the brakes. You'll find that most master cylinders have a full stroke of about one-inch of depth and that a properly adjusted and bled system will use about ½ of that to have a pedal stroke reserve for safety. Looking at the chart attached shows that going from a one-inch bore master cylinder to a 7/8 inch bore will produce 31% more line pressure but also require a matching 31% increase in stroke. That would mean that our example has us down to only a .19 inch cylinder stroke reserve. With a 5:1 pedal ratio we need only a .95 inch pedal reserve….not good!

This example makes clear why power brakes had to be developed. Engineers simply could not produce the line pressure they needed with an acceptable pedal stroke until the input effort at the pedal could be increased by mechanical means beyond mere driver leg power. If enough pedal power boost is added (again a function of booster diaphragm diameter times atmospheric pressure) master cylinder size can be greater thus producing greater line pressure and/or a shorter pedal stroke.

It seems that most pedal assemblies and booster are designed for a one-inch bore master cylinder. I have found that a 15/16 inch bore master is an excellent compromise for a little more line pressure without too much increase in stroke or effort. Referring to our chart shows a 14% increase in that critical line pressure, or the same line pressure with 14% less effort, but only .7 inch increase in stroke based on our 5:1 Pedal ratio. That's generally a pretty good trade off. The master cylinder I use is from the '74-'78 Mustang II, the power type easily accepts the pushrod supplied with most pedal assemblies.

Piston face surface area is every bit as important on the wheel cylinder end. Once you have produced a reasonable line pressure, the wheel end piston will translate that psi into pounds of force to push the shoes against the rotor or drum. In fact, as an illustration of how this principal is used, Ford increased the bore size of their wheel cylinders from 1 ¼" for '39-'41 to 1 3/8 inch for the heavier '46-'48 cars. I think many suppliers use the larger for all applications today but its worth having the larger bore for better braking power. You can also get into the better parts catalogs (this info is almost NEVER on line) to play this bore size game with different modern rear axles like the 8 and 9 inch Fords. You can certainly use a proportioning valve to REDUCE rear brake force, but using a larger bore wheel cylinder would be a way to INCREASE rear brakes. I find that larger cylinder by going into my brake parts catalogs. My EIS brand catalog will list the current wheel cylinder by application and then the casting family. I can then look under that casting family and easily find a large bore wheel cylinder that is a simple bolt in replacement. Generally it will be for an application where a larger heavier car with bigger drums is using the same rear end as a smaller car, the larger bore wheel cylinders being used to provide more brake force.

A similar situation occurs with disc brake calipers. Again, the total piston face area determines how much clamping force can be developed. The classic GM '70-'77 Camaro caliper used on many brake conversions has a 2-15/16 inch bore for a piston area of 6.25 square inches. The Metric caliper, known for its smaller 5 ½ inch mounting pin spread and originally used on '78-'87 Monte Carlo and Malibu has a much smaller 2 ½ inch bore for only 4.45 square inches of area. That is a reduction of about 39% in clamping force! Be careful of using these Metric calipers on cars over 3200 pounds. This is enough of a problem that special larger bore Metric calipers have been developed with a 2 5/8 inch piston and 5.43 square inches of piston area. Now we are only 22% smaller than the big GM calipers, so this is a real improvement you should consider. You'll also find that aftermarket disc brake companies such as Wilwood know this too, and supply similar calipers with different piston sized for each application. They generally have the application dialed in well, but if you lack stopping power a larger bore caliper is worth considering.

There's a lot more to brake system design, but understanding the relationships between cylinder bore size, line pressure and braking power is essential to assembling and diagnosing a problem in your brake system.

BORE SIZE	FACE AREA	FACTOR
3/4"	.44 sq. in	1.78
7/8	.60	1.31
15/16	.69	1.14
1	.785	1.00
1 1/16	.88	.89
1 1/8	.994	.79
1 1/4	1.227	.64

Cylinder bore size directly affects the cylinder face area and therefore can alter both the master cylinder pressure output and wheel cylinder braking force.

Chassis

Setting the Wheelbase

Should be Simple but Ain't

Where's the axle centerline? A question we hear on the phone almost every day. For a common car like a '40 Ford, that question is easy to answer. If your project is something really different in terms of stance or rarity, some pre-planning work is critical. With stance so important today, proper tire to fender centering is critical to "the look". Published wheelbase figures are seldom accurate, often needing fine tuning, especially because a lowered car on a rake will appear to change the perceived center of the wheel in the fender opening. A real good beginning is to look at the car BEFORE you tear it down.

Stand back and see if the front and rear tires look centered in the fenders. It's helpful to cut cardboard or plywood discs that represent the diameter of the tires you plan to use. You can even draw in wheel diameters to see if you like the "big and little" of it. The original wheels can be removed and the lowered onto jackstands or blocks until you get to a stance that lights your fire. The discs can be easily placed in the fenders and moved as necessary. The wheelbase positions can then be transferred to the frame using a plumb bob. Don't settle for less than a perfect stance!

This is also the perfect time to determine where you want the height of the front and rear axles, relative to the frame bottom. Having that knowledge allows you to properly position the suspension with plenty of travel for a good ride and handling. Too many rodders blindly install a suspension and then wail away later trying to raise or lower the car to get it looking and working right. It's easier and cheaper to have a plan to follow.

> **Some specific cars that benefit from stretching the front axle placement forward ½ inch are '32 Fords and '34-'35 Chevy Standards.**

Drop is an almost meaningless word in hot rod suspension. It's going to depend on where you start (tire diameter, spring fatigue, engine weight, etc.), and how you dress the car out in terms of those variables. Figure out where you want the wheels, build the suspension in that position, and then change springs so that design ride height is achieved with all the weight in place. You cannot do that without HAVING a design to begin with!

If you are doing a totally custom tube chassis, you need to plan the wheel placement very carefully. You are working smart by working backwards from the final design we just planned, and building to that standard. This careful pre-planning is the sign of a pro, who needs to know spindle placement to build his frame. It is amazing how many rodders cut a car in half to install a subframe without first finding the proper ride height and wheelbase. After it's done, they spend a lot of time and money installing springs, spindles, and narrowed control arms. Be smarter than that!

Some specific cars that benefit from stretching the front axle placement forward ½ inch are '32 Fords and '34-'35 Chevy Standards. The '36 Chevy Standard looks better with the front axle moved back one-inch. An old trick Dan Carpenter and Mike Chesser taught us with the '53-'56 F100 is to move the front axle forward one-inch to avoid the stock "run into a stump" look.

Rear fenders vary also. Willys changed the wheelbase on their '37-'41 Coupes and Sedans by moving the wheel cutout on the same basic fender stamping. The '35-'37 Fords often need an offset lowering block with multiple holes to look right. This is so common that Chassis Engineering offers just such a lowering block set to go along with their excellent rear spring kits.

We've found that many '37-'39 Chevy fenders don't match left and right. It's common to split the difference on these cars. Also, the '37-'48 Chevy axles move back and forth quite a lot as the spring arch is flattened to create different ride heights. That may require a lowering block with multiple holes like on the '35-'37 Ford. All of this backs up the advice to totally assemble the car, and fine tune the details, before disassembly for paint. You'll still have some stuff that magically (or tragically) refuses to line up without a fight, but the experience of final assembly and that first test drive will happen sooner - and easier!

This F100 suffers from a slightly awkward appearance with the front wheel one inch off center in the fender opening rather than extended as discussed.

Chassis

Start With a Firm Foundation

Do be level side to side, but NOT front to back

Any big project needs a plan. Whether building a house or a hot rod, you start with a conceptual drawing or model of what you want to accomplish, and then modify and dial in the finished design. We'll assume you have mocked up your hot rod project, or at least done some measuring on a car you like. That gives you an idea of proper wheel placement as well as front and rear axle height in relation to the frame. With that info, it's time to begin on the foundation, or in the case of a hot rod, the frame.

The frame has to be leveled, plumb, and square so that everything built on it will come out correct. If you have ever tried to remodel a house with crooked walls and floors, you know how important this is. The body can be on the frame without causing too much trouble, and can actually be helpful in determining things such as firewall to engine clearance. Having fenders handy to recheck wheel locations can prevent costly errors as well.

You will need the normal hand tools and welding equipment common to most hot rodders' garages. A simple carpenter's level, plumb bob, tape measures, squares, and angle finder will be essential. Digital versions of the level and angle finder, along with laser pointers, have come way down in price. They make an excellent gift suggestion for that upcoming anniversary or birthday too! What man can resist having more tools? Visit the art supply store for a box of silver metallic pencils. They are just great for marking and will pick up more light for those whose vision may be getting a little dicey.

You do not need a surface plate, frame jig, or a perfectly level floor. You need to work off the top of the frame anyway, so its distance from the floor is not critical. Anything from jackstands, cinderblocks, or temporary legs can be fitted to the frame to get it level. Shims of scrap steel work very well to exactly dial in the stand height. Tack them in place so they don't vibrate out as you work, causing you to lose your place. You can get stands with screw tops, or make them with inexpensive floor jacks from the home supply, cut down as needed. Frame jigs and tables are great timesavers for production work but are not absolutely necessary in the home shop. If your frame measures level from side to side at the front, rear, and several locations in between, it cannot be twisted. You do want to be level from side to side, but probably NOT front to back!

Most any hot rod will sit on a forward rake. We've measured hundreds of cars and find 2-3 degrees to be a good average. Your frame should be set on that 2-3 degrees so that it closely simulates the finished stance. This is very important as it affects the placement of the front crossmember, engine and trans, rear suspension and pinion angle to mention a few. Think of the stands as a way to push the ground down for underneath access rather than raising the car. If you set the car level and the engine at the normal 3 degree rear rake, it will be only 1 degree with the car at a 2 degree finished stance. All your careful work will be for naught. If your engine needs a couple extra degrees of rake to clear the oil pan or the floor, the incorrect set up angle exaggerates that angle and makes it look goofier than it really is. Sure, I know you can figure the angles into the level frame, but it's easy to get confused and go the wrong way. (Especially if you are working on the frame upside down). If you go the wrong way, you DOUBLE your error. Setting up the frame level front to back seems like an intuitive first step, but it's wrong!

You will also want to check the frame for square. This is best done with diagonal, corner to corner measurements. Pick matching holes on an existing frame, or work from the ends of a scratch built frame. That requires the rail blanks to be very precisely the same length, or you'll never get it square. If you are installing new suspension it is also necessary to locate the axle centerlines. Use the plumb bob to mark the location directly on the floor with a permanent marker like a Sharpie. The radiator core support is critical for remounting the nose sheet metal, so carefully measure, mark, and record that position as well.

It's very important that the frame not move from it's now carefully located set up position. You can tack weld the stands in position or add temporary legs. We like to pile on a lot of weight such as spare engine blocks. They won't leak like punctured sandbags. You will be sawing, hammering, and pounding on this deal and you do not want to get lost.

The axle positions you have determined can be set up next. Since you know their heights in relation to the frame rail, you can mock them up in position without worrying about the springs for now. An unloaded suspension will fool you into thinking it will not sit right when you are done. Build the car at the mock-up height, and select, swap, or adjust springs to get to that design height. You must wait until ALL the weight is on the car to do this. Having two fat guys stand on the frame is not good scientific practice. You are just guessing and wasting your time trying to set up springs with an unknown load! Coilovers and Air-ride have the distinct advantage of very simple ride height adjustment. Solid struts are easily used in the build up phase to preserve the design stance. The expensive suspension parts are also protected from weld spatter and overspray as well.

Welding can really pull a frame out of shape. Be sure to jump around and let things cool before continuing in an area just welded. It's even a good idea to just tack everything securely, and save the final welding for later. That gives you a chance to make easier design changes as the work progresses. Later, you can weld a little, go work on something else for a while, and then weld some more. It's a good practice to do the welds in a symmetrical pattern. As you perform matching welds on the left and right sides, shrinking stresses are generally equalized. I would suggest welding boxing plates in less than 4 inch stretches, with matching passes left and right as well as top and bottom. Never start on the top and run the bead 20 inches, no matter how well it's flowing. You will get warpage beyond belief. We've seen Model A frames so warped that they look like Olympic ski jumps. You'll find that your best critical welding will be done in the morning when you are rested.

It's time to build, so turn off the tube (at least the one in the house) and get out in the garage. Now is the time to bring that project to life. What a great opportunity we have to put opinions into action!

Rear suspension for a '50 Olds - A hot rod with a fundamentally well designed chassis, one with good geometry and plenty of wheel travel, will always create excellent ride and handling.

Chassis

Frame Swaps - A Good Idea?

Not as Easy as you Think

I hear it all the time, "My Uncle gave me his '83 Buick LeSabre. Will it fit under my Model A, '48 Chevy, '50 Merc?" Everybody who has ever read a tech column will recognize the question. It's tempting to think that there is a magic combination of donor and transplant cars that will match perfectly. It would be even better if the two cars you just happen to have in the driveway made up that perfect marriage. But in the real world it just doesn't work that way.

There are several things you need to know: The wheel-base must match, and the track width must allow sufficient tire-to-fender clearance. If you have to widen the fenders or buy special wheels to get out of trouble, that great-deal you found on the suspension was no bargain. The frame horns and bumper mount need to be the right shape and location, and the floor pan needs to fit the frame kick-up. It's far too easy to get out the torch without first checking these items. You don't want to hit a dead end resulting in a still-born project rusting away out back. Do the homework first by comparing the wheel location and the general frame shape. Look at where the radiator will have to sit. Too often the newer car's suspension and steering box gets in the way of the radiator mounting parts. Have you determined the finished ride height or will you hope that changing springs and spindles will get you out of the woods later on?

> It's tempting to think that there is a magic combination of donor and transplant cars that will match perfectly.

We are hearing a lot about S-10 frame swaps. With plenty of rusted out S-10s around, the price is right. The '47-'54 Chevy PU frame is flat on top while the S-10 has an 8 inch deep belly that will rquire some pretty big adapters to fit the early PU Body. Then the front rack is 6 inches too narrow and 3 inch wheel adapters are not a good idea. Makes us wonder if the whole thing is a good idea.

The '49-'51 Mercs will sometimes receive a '73 Pontiac LeMans 4-door chassis. This swap has been done and publicized by the late, great Dick Dean, one of my best and most experienced customizers. The follow up articles that were written went on to explain how the rear axle links have to be altered to dial in the wheelbase, and the truck floor and rear frame horns have to be modified to fit together. For a guy with Dick's ability, these are relatively minor challenges. For a guy with a lot of enthusiasm and maybe not quite as much equipment and experience, it may be overwhelming.

If your project car has a rotted out floor, or you're willing to cut out a perfectly good floor, your project may actually be simpler. You can build rockers and floor pans to match the donor frame's body mounts and shapes. Some talented rodders have even been able to include the donor car fire-wall and dash. The quality of a car done that way by a custom builder like Canada's Ron Box or George Bickel makes it clear how good these guys really are. They almost make it look easier than it is which can tempt less talented folks to get in over their heads.

In my personal experience dealing with thousands of rodders all over the country, it seems that most are more capable of making chassis modifications than attempting radical body fabrication. The beauty of our hobby is that you can exercise your abilities and learn new skills as you build that new rod. However, it's all too easy to get in over your head, get frustrated, and never finish what might have been a really nice car. Dare I say it? Some that get finished even look a little awkward. Out-of-position tires and tires with interference problems can be symptoms of the "too small garage" syndrome. Don't forget to roll your project outside once in a while and take an objective look at where you're headed.

I'm sure many of you may disagree with me. I thought seriously of putting an "OPINION ALERT" sign at the top of this chapter. Some readers will even say my opinions are influenced by the fact that I make my living manufacturing parts to modify stock chassis. My honest opinion is that, for most rodders, it's easier to first use the frame that already fits their hot rod's body and then to adapt different suspension and steering to that frame. So if you still want to do a frame swap, by all means go ahead but perhaps you will consider some of the issues raised earlier, and your project will turn out to be all you've wished it to be.

A '41 Chevy shop job - many rodders have discovered that the best way to build a chassis is to adapt the suspension you want to the frame that fits your hot rod, rather than trying to adapt dissimilar cars and chassis to one another.

Chassis

How Much Tire Will Fit

The Combo is Crucial

Hot rods are all about stance and fenders full of tires. A basically stock drivetrain and chassis can be lowered and fitted with the right rubber combo for an amazing transformation from ordinary to exceptional. The trick is to begin with the right type wheel that matches your intended build style. If you are going with a nostalgia theme, 20 inch billets probably won't look just right, anymore than would wire wheels on a smooth contemporary theme. As with anything in hot rodding, someone will break those "rules" and carry it off OK, but mixing build styles generally produces a confused looking car.

Once the style wheel has been determined, it's time to do some research on the tires. You may be fortunate enough to have seen a car like yours that really has the combo right. The owner will always be happy to fill you in on the wheel size and spacing, as well as the tire size that works so well. Or maybe you can borrow a set of mounted tires and wheels from a buddy to give you a starting point for what will fit correctly. But first it is important to know exactly how tires and wheels are measured.

Tires have a stated size, using numbers and letters that denote the diameter and ratio of sidewall height to section width. Section width is the dimension across the fat part of the sidewall, not the tread width. You need to know that tread width and section width are two entirely different things, and two tires with the same numerical size from two different manufacturers will be totally different physical sizes. The best way to sort all this out is to get a look at each manufacturer's size charts either at the dealer or on line. The chart will show you the height, tread width, section width, and recommended rim size. By now you should have been able to mock up your car with borrowed tires or even cardboard discs to find the diameter that provides the right stance. Tires that look good in a tire store showroom and are the latest for factory cars are often far too short to look good on a vintage car.

There is a strange conflict of information that often gets hot rodders into trouble with their wheel selection. Sometime in the deep dark past, it was decided that wheels would be identified by the diameter and width of the seat for the tire's bead. So, a 16X7 inch wheel accepts a 16 inch tire with a width that properly fits a 7 inch bead width. The contradiction comes in when wheel offset is determined.

Wheels offset is measured from the outside of the rim, not the bead seat inside. So, our 7 inch rim example will actually measure around 8 inch overall width. The backspace is measured from the wheel mounting surface to the outside of the lip, not the inside bead dimension. You would think that a centered 7 inch rim would have a 3 ½ inch backspace, but it is actually 4 inch (half of the 8 inch overall width). This simple conflict of measurement basis is the cause of many rubbing tires. If you are not aware of this, you can easily end up with your tires ½ inch further outboard than you had planned. On a low cars with fat tires, trouble is often the result.

Front tires will be more difficult than the rear. We have to deal with keeping the tire out of the fender when turning, especially when the tire rides up in the fender when entering a driveway. The best way seems to be to mount an actual wheel and tire on the car, turn the wheels to full lock, and see how much room you have. Then you can make an educated judgment based on the backspace and diameter of that mock up combo. A rule of thumb is to have the track width at least 12 inch narrower than the inside of the fenders. That has proven to be reliable on most cars with a 4 inch backspace 7 inch rim with 4 inches front space. Narrower fenders will require less front space, and wider wheels will need a narrower track width.

Another rule of thumb I have learned is to go down one wheel size and two tire sizes from what fits comfortably in the back. That would be a 14x6 inch wheel with a 215/70 up front and a 235/70 x 15 in back, for old guys like me that still like 14 and 15 inch wheels and tires. The same logic holds for 16s and 17s. You aren't changing the outside dimensions that much going from 15s to 17s - you are trading wheel diameter for sidewall height to get tighter handling at the expense of harsher ride, with the esthetics being a matter of personal taste.

The rear fitment is easier than the front since we don't have to be concerned with steering the car. Get hold of a simple plumb bob to transfer the dimension of the rear wheel house and axle, and we'll begin. Hold the plumb bob the inside of the outer fender lip to find the outer limit, and mark that point on the floor. Then mark the axle flange where the wheel actually sits in that flange. Finally, find the point on the inner wheel house that would be first contacted by the tire, and mark that point to the floor. Experience has shown that you need about one-inch of clearance from the fat part of the tire (its section width) to the outside fender lip, and 1-1/2

Proper planning of frame and axle width will provide the clearance needed for your chosen wheels and tires to fit the hot rod as they should.

inch to the inside, giving you a little extra space to get the wheel off the axle studs.

Several manufacturers and hot rod supply houses now have a really cool wheel simulator. You can bolt these onto your wheel hub, front or rear, and then expand the tool to simulate different ties sizes and wheel offsets. You can even check clearance with the front wheels turned for steering. The tool isn't cheap, but if you build a lot of cars or can share the tool with friends or a car club, they are well worth the expense.

Now we will do a sample calculation for a '40 Ford coupe, knowing that this procedure is no different for a '69 Chevelle. Follow the same procedure for any car to determine what will fit without cutting, or how much you need to cut to add space for larger tires.

We'll figure stock '40 Ford wheel wells and frame with a 7x15x4 inch backspace (8 inch overall for a 4 inch front and back space), and a 235/70 x 15 inch tire mounted, for an 8 inch section width.

> A basically stock drivetrain and chassis can be lowered and fitted with the right rubber for an amazing transformation...

Inside fender lip	67 inches
Outside clearance (1 inch x 2)	minus 2 inches
Outside tire	65 inches
Front space (4 inches x 2)	minus 8 inches
	Hub to Hub axle width 57 inches (which means an 8 inch Maverick axle is perfect)
Backspace (4 inches x2)	minus 8 inches
Inside tires	49 inches
Inside Clearance (1-½ inches x 2)	minus 3 inches
Final max. frame width	46 inches

Since a '40 Ford will measure at 44 inches frame width with 45 inches inside the inner wheel house, we're looking good. We do have an extra half inch per side on the inside to play with so we can get brave and push the limit by ordering a 15x8 inch rim with a 4-1/2 inch backspace and front space (9 inches total) and fill that fender all the way.

You can easily run the same arithmetic to see how a 10 inch rim with a 4-1/2 inch backspace and 6-1/2 inch front space with a 12 inch section-width tire will have a mounted backspace of 5 inches and front space of 7 inches. That figures to an axle width of 51 inches and maximum inner wheel house of 38 inches. Since our subject car has 45 inch stock inner wheel wells, we need to do a 3 to 4 inch narrowing job per side, and get an axle cut to 51 inches hub to hub.

You won't find any factory axles that width, so it's time to call one of the fine manufacturers that advertise in the Goodguys Gazette. They can dial you right in and produce a very straight and square housing, with the axles and brakes of your choice. A pilot shaft is used to put all the inner and outer bearings in alignment for a perfect running assembly. If an original housing is used, you will often see an offset in the axle tubes where the tube is welded back together. Since original housings are often bent in use over many years and miles, the housing may be slightly out of alignment. This shows up when the alignment fixture puts the bearing right, and the tubes are out a little. It all works just fine, but lacks a little in the cosmetic department. The better axle shops use new housings or straighten them first for a better looking finished part. In fact, most used housings are out a little, and the bearings can handle some misalignment without difficulty. Proof of this is the NASCAR guys having run as much as 2 degrees camber intentionally bent into the housing for more cornering power. (until the inspectors made them stop).

At the risk of getting a less careful builder in trouble, there is an easy way to narrow your own

Ford 8 or 9 inch rear axle. Ford 28 spline axles with the 2.875 inch small bearing, are used on both assemblies, meaning that a shorter axle from either type can be used in either housing. You might have a 9 inch housing that's too wide, say from a '67-'79 F100 pickup, and a '70-'77 Maverick 8 inch that's the right width. Both have 3 inch axle tubes and the gears both accept the 28 spline axles. Cut off the ends of the 8 inch housing and get a machinist to turn down the welds at the ends in order to release the outer bearing cups, leaving the small pilot diameter that registers to the inside of the axle tube. Disassemble your truck housing and use a pair of jack stands and a digital level to check that the bearing cup ends are square to the housing where the gearset attaches. If it's out much, the housing will need to be straightened first. If it's square, you can compare the old and new axles to see how much the axle tubes will need to be shortened. Leave them a little long for the moment.

Before inserting the salvaged 8 inch housing ends, insert the new short axles all the way into the gear, and pull them back .125 inch for a little end play. Then remove the extra bit of housing that will put the housing ends in proper position. Tap the new housing ends into the axle tubes, being careful to keep the backing plate bolts right side up and properly rotated. Use the digital level to check the ends for square, rotating the housing 90 degrees to check both ways. Tack weld, recheck for squareness, and trial fit the axles one last time. If all is in order, weld the ends in place, moving from side to side and welding 90 degrees at a time. Give it time to cool between welds to keep the warpage down. The donor-axle brakes will bolt right in place, and you are in business.

This technique can also be used to narrow just one side of the housing. Most Ford housings will have the right axle about 2.5 inch longer than the left side. You can use two short side axles, and narrow the housing to match for times when you just need a little shorter assembly. This also centers the housing for a clean appearance on cars like Model A's where the axle assembly is in plain view. The design of these fine units requires that when the driveshaft is centered, the housing is not. Since the driveshaft is just as happy with horizontal or vertical misalignment, the u-joints easily handle an offset driveshaft resulting from a centered housing. The driveshaft rotates, and doesn't know up from sideways.

The absolute correct way is to use a set up bar as detailed above. That's why the pros do it, and why they can offer you such fine work. A clever and careful amateur can get it right too, if he has a straight housing to begin with, a good level, and a little patience. A club with a good machinist could even build their own loaner line up bar fixture for a few bucks and have the satisfaction of doing it themselves.

Having been through all the calculations above, I hope it's clear how a swap meet bargain can end up in disaster. You may be able to have special wheels made to get a wrong width axle to work, but I'd bet the "savings" will be used up. Better to mock-up and calculate to get what you need and want the first time. Buy the wheels and tires based on your stock rear axle and wheel house if you are going conservative. Still buy them first if you are going wild and then have the housing made to suit. It's no more expensive to have the housing cut one length or another so you might as well get what you need the first time. It's just one more thing that sets the noticed cars apart from the not so noticed ones. It's a subject we discuss often, since it is so often a cause of misunderstanding amongst rodders. Simple planning and thinking skills are still your most important tools in building a trick piece for the next Goodguys season!

> **Since the driveshaft is just as happy with horizontal or vertical misalignment, the U-joints easily handle an offset driveshaft resulting from a centered housing.**

Design

Reverse Engineering

Know what the Final Result will be

You wouldn't start off going to a Rod Run without knowing your final destination and then planning an efficient route. If you blindly head off in the general direction and then continually adjust your route as you get closer to the goal you may indeed get there, but will have lost a lot of time and gained extra expenses. You will be a little frustrated as well and enjoy the journey less than you could have. Building a Hot Rod is no different.

If you are building a fairly common car you have great resources to see what you like and what you don't. Looking at photos and talking to owners of cars you admire is great. It's even better to spend a day with your new project and a couple buddies with a good eye for a Hot Rod. This process can be more difficult if you are building an unusual car, or a common car in an unusual style. You need to stand back and walk around the car. A big shop is great and outdoors is even better. A two-car garage won't provide the perspective you need. How can you know where to set the front and rear axles as to wheelbase or drop? Don't fall victim to "small garage syndrome" with a poorly proportioned Hot Rod.

The placement of the wheels and tires on the car are critical to getting the look you want. The diameter of the mounted wheels and tires as well as any front to rear stagger are just as important. The really top builders often build a car around a chosen set of wheels and tires and then make what ever modifications are necessary to make them function on that car. Even if you aren't yet so sure what rolling stock will look right on your project, you can simulate their effect easily even with the car's original suspension still in place. Make some plywood or cardboard discs which approximate the diameter and sidewall to rim proportions of the tires you plan on running and tack them to some heavy chunks of wood so they will stand up. Since they are skinny, the mock up discs can be easily set up with the old suspension still mounted. Set the complete body down on jack stands, cinderblocks, or scrap 4 x 4's. Put your mockup wheels in the fenders and adjust the ride height and rake until everybody says it's cool.

Step way back to make sure you have the same perspective as walking up from a hundred yards away at a show. A couple side view snapshots, enlarged and copied, can be cut up and scaled to consider any body modifications. Maybe a 2 inch chop will actually look more proportionate than the radical 4-1/2 inches you've been thinking of. It's sure easier to cut and paste paper than tin!

This is a great time to look carefully at the track widths front and rear. Do you have a combination of suspension width and wheels that will fill the fenders with tires, yet without creating interference? An actual set of borrowed tires mounted on rims are of great benefit here. Do the arithmetic and get it right rather than hoping you can buy some goofy offset wheel later to fix a mistake.

Now you can get real serious. Use a plumb bob to mark the wheel centerlines that give you proper tire-to-fender placement. It's often quite different than the advertised wheel base. You'll also want to locate the wheel center heights as compared to the frame. Only by doing so can you be sure to get the chassis right with the axle centerlines where they belong. Measure and record the front and rear frame height, and set your chassis at that rake angle in the shop. Suspension angles relate to true ground level, not the frame itself. This step is often missed, with dire effects to geometry, alignment, and drive ability.

Your front suspension spindle center height is based on information from the kit supplier, or from measuring the normal driving height of the donor car. Don't make the mistake of just throwing in the suspension, hoping to adjust the ride height and alignment with special springs, spindles, or control arms. In fact, it's best to remove the coil springs, and add either washers or a short piece of tube to immobilize the shock at its proper ride height length. This allows you to set up the chassis without regard to the final weight loading. Later on, you'll use springs that will maintain that proper ride height. (This is the true benefit of coil-overs.)

Most suspensions are ideally designed so that the lower control arm hinge axis is parallel to the ground. Be sure to check this, and adjust accordingly. You can be within 2 -3 degrees of level and will still have enough adjustment for final alignment.

We often use scrap steel to actually tack the rear axle housing, or a length of 3 inch tubing, at its proper position. This works especially well with four-bars since you can assemble the four-bar and tack the frame brackets so that the bars are level to the ground. This avoids roll steer due to an axle that cocks out of square in the chassis as it travels vertically. Leaf springs are a little tougher. I'd suggest removing a couple leaves to approximate the final loaded spring arch, adding enough leaves later to match that with a fully loaded car. Try to keep the front half of the spring level since it acts just like the lower link of a 4-bar. Dearched springs are often better than a lowering block for that reason.

With the suspension in place it's easy to verify things like proper shock travel and ground clearance. The engine and trans can be fitted and any sheet metal clearance provided. Setting the engine first, then modifying steering linkage to clear an oil pan is a big mistake that this preplanning will avoid.

Knowing what the final result will be makes it easy to confidently and efficiently build your chassis. Expensive mistakes and bad driving/riding Hot Rods can be avoided. You've got to see the finished Hot Rod in your mind before you start. A few good photos of the mock up will keep you inspired. This reverse engineering works for every job from mounting an alternator to installing power windows. Don't build the bracket until you've located the components for proper fit and function. This is how the pros do it, as well as the best home builders. Try thinking backwards - it works.

A '34 DeSoto Mock-up - Time spent mocking up wheel to fender position and ride stance are especially important when hot rodding an unusual car.

Design

An Exercise in Practical Design

Imagineering

Many rodders find that one of their favorite projects is the opportunity to imagine, design and fabricate a special bracket needed for a certain function. The particular bracket may not be available, or you may want to design your own to save money, time, or just exercise some creativity. The key is to first "see" the needed part in your mind. One of my most clever friends refers to this process as "Imagineering", a title which I think goes back to the folks who built the Disney parks.

You have to be able to envision the part and how it needs to attach to the existing structure while mounting the object you need to add. If that bracket can serve multiple purposes you have stumbled onto a pro fabricator's best practice. Maybe it can hold one part while also functioning as an engine mount or something along that line. I find that my high school drafting courses were wonderful in teaching me how to think in 3D. To draw a part, as well as design and build it, you need to see how it relates to all the other pieces with which it interfaces. If you have never taken any drafting, it might be a worthwhile use of your time to take a night class or even self teach from a good book on the subject.

A typical project might be adding a hydraulic power steering pump to a Ford Coyote four-cam engine. The more "normal" Ford Mod series engines came with a power steering pump but the advent of the EPAS (Electrically assisted Power Rack) caused the Coyote 4 cam engine to lack that provision. You can buy entirely new aftermarket drives from guys like Vintage Air, which are wonderfully made and also upgrade to a smaller yet more efficient A/C compressor. Or, you may want to make your own bracket to mount the common and inexpensive GM Saginaw integral reservoir PS pump we all know from the 1960-2000 era.

Without going into exact details for a real installation, let's make up some dimensions for a practice drill. First, you need to mount a pulley that matches the serpentine drive on the engine to the new PS pump. An aftermarket supplier or a really cooperative salvage yard can help you find the pulley you need. Then hold the pump with that pulley up against the engine to get basic dimensions such as set back so the belt lines up. Think about how the pump will need clearance around the steering connection, access to hoses for the steering box, exhaust manifolds, etc., etc. Fortunately, the mount can be rigid, as belt adjustment will be made with the original tensioner. Make certain that you have figured out how to route the belt and that it will turn your PS pump the right direction. They will not work running backwards like an alternator can. If the belt runs on it's outside, the pulley will be smooth, and the pulley will be grooved for running on the inside. It's probably a good idea to get a measurement of the belt length you will need and to be sure you can get one. A good trick there is to cut an old belt and measure how much longer the new one has to be in a straight part of the routing. A good parts man can take it from there to find your new belt length.

So let's make up some dimensions for the sake of illustration. Perhaps you have found some unused mount bosses on the engine that are exactly 2 inches behind the center of the belt position you found would work. The PS pump you want to use has mount holes that are one-inch behind the bolt center. We want to make our mount plate with ¼ inch thick steel, so we need to space the plate ¾ inch forward of the mount bosses on the engine. That takes care of the fore and aft position of the pump.

We got lucky and our PS pump has two mounting bosses that are stacked directly above one another, each 1-1/2 inch vertically from the pump shaft center, and 2 inches outboard of the pump shaft center. Next let's say we found that the PS pump position works best when the upper engine mount boss is 4-1/2 inches inboard and one-inch below the pump upper mount boss. Also, the engine lower mount boss we want to use is 3-1/2 inches inboard and 1/2 inches above the pump lower mount. That will let us design the front view of our theoretical bracket.

There is a basic rule for distance from a hole to the edge of a part. It is often stated as having the center of the hole 1-½ times the hole diameter from the edge of the part. I think it's simpler just to say that the material between the edge of the hole and the edge of the part should not be less than the diameter of that hole. It's just two ways of saying the same thing. Experience says that parts thinner than 1/8 inch need to be very lightly stressed, and parts as thick as 3/8 inch are generally used only on highly stressed parts. We have found that 3/16 inch is plenty for parts that don't see a lot of vibration, but we'll design for ¼ inch steel in our example since the PS pump will see a good deal of vibration from the belt drive and pump pulses.

The drawing below may be helpful in deciphering these dimensions we just imagined. Available space for this article prevents us from finished the design job with a gusset or rear bracket that would stabilize the pump on a real installation. We are avoiding sharp corners that can become stress risers that give birth to cracks. Curved edges can be used to clear obstacles and lightening holes can be added for extra style as you wish. The idea here is to understand what dimensions you might need and how to use them for any fabrication challenge.

It can be very helpful to whip up a trial bracket out of plywood to help you see what is happening. Plywood is easier to cut and then throw away if you missed a good design on your first attempt. You can either start over or use glue to attach more plywood for your next attempt. You can go so far as to finish the entire mockup job with glued up wood until you have settled on your final version. In fact, if you wanted to make the final part as a casting, this wooden model can be smoothed with Bondo until you have a pattern the foundry can use to make the forms. The wooden parts can be used as a pattern, or your drawings/sketches can allow the building of your steel parts.

Again, this is a very loose illustration of how a part gets designed. In essence you are locating the necessary holes and then using basic rules of hole to edge distance to let the part tell you how it should look. Our purpose here is to show the thought process that succeeds in the real world.

This sample bracket begins by drawing the critical mount holes in their proper positions and then creating a bracket that accommodates those holes in a graceful design.

Design

Avoiding Small Garage Syndrome

Stand back to get a Good Look

A well thought out Hot Rod instantly grabs your attention with a clear statement of its purpose. Whether built as a show car or a driver, nostalgic or high tech, pro street or resto-rod, a unified design concept creates a certain impression; a clear statement of its purpose. The challenge is to make that statement clearly. It is possible to build design features that look great close up in the shop but maybe don't work so well when viewed in the real world at a distance.

I just attended a very major indoor event where some unbelievable fabrication and detailing work was displayed. The funny part was that of my personal favorite cars, two kept bringing me back. One had many subtle tricks that took a while to see and just kept drawing me in for another look. The more I looked at the other car, it seemed that much of the gorgeous craftsmanship that first grabbed my attention seemed to be a little overdone, as if it had been built to make more show points. In other words, it began to lose interest in my own view as I looked at again.

Stance is certainly the first thing that catches your eye, with wheel and tire selection a critical part of the look. A chopped and slicked hot rod just doesn't look right with wire wheels. Your '32 Ford sedan resto-rod is going to look a little strange with 20 inch rims and 45 series tires better suited to a late model Camaro. Wheel selection can be such a major factor in setting the tone of a car that top builders often design the entire car around them. You can choose to run the tires and wheels that will fit within your cars dimensions, or you can select the rolling stock first and then commit to making whatever modifications are necessary to make the car fit the wheels. How do you know when you have the wheel and tire sizes nailed?

Much of this thought process began the moment you visualized the finished car. This process was covered in the Reverse Engineering article, but it bears repeating. The best way to end up where you want to be is to know what that goal is. In other words, mock up the body and wheels with the finished stance you want. If you don't have the wheels and tires, make cardboard cutouts that represent a size you think might work right. Then take pictures and measurements to guide you in the build process. Measure the position of the floor to several key points on the chassis, and how the wheel centers relate in terms of both ride height and position in the fenders. Now you will know how high the axles need to be in the chassis, and whether you will need dropped spindles, rear axle "C" in the frame, etc. Refer to the chassis in terms of axle height, not drop. Drop depends on many factors such as tire size, and is a relative number. Axle height is absolute, and can even be mocked up with temporary solid struts that hold the design axle position. Building a chassis without this planning can be an expensive exercise in frustration.

Color is right next to stance in creating that all-important first impression. Paint ain't cheap, so spend lots of time on this decision. The ladies generally have a much better color sense than the guys. Try taking pictures in the mock up stages, and experiment with colors schemes over 8x10 copies of those pictures. Or, if you are an old guy, be really high tech and have the local 14 year old computer whiz help you do the samples with Photoshop.

Body modifications are really prone to Small

Garage Syndrome. You may find that a milder chop really looks better than the 5 inch chop your buddies all fantasize over. The rake on a level chopped '67-'72 Chevy pickup looks backwards, unless it gets rolled outside to see that the front needs to be cut an extra inch to make the side glass look right. We once built a '40 Ford, three window coupe, with longer Tudor doors, and spent most of a day getting the side window shape and lofting of the top to look as if Ford had built the car. You just cannot see the car's lines while leaning against the wall in a two-car shop. A basically stock bodied hot rod with a trick engine needs the hood up, but I personally don't like to see cars displayed with the hood open when the body mods are the main draw to the car design.

A '70 Mustang fastback has a very tasteful one-inch tall ducktail rear spoiler…would it look better if it was 3 inches tall? Maybe so, in your shop. Does the cowl induction hood really need to be the tallest you can find or make? Would a '69 Camaro chin spoiler look better if it was 2 inches deeper? How much fender flare can you add until the car looks like it belongs in a cartoon? Some cars miss the mark just a little while others are right on. These are all matters of opinion for sure. We never get tired of seeing the true classic shapes of a beautiful woman, a Les Paul guitar, a Colt 1911, and your favorite cars. Could it be that lasting appeal involves some tasteful restraint?

All these questions lead us to the need to get the car outside, and spend some time looking at it. You have to be able to get back a fair distance and see the car from all angles. I call the lack of this perspective "Small Garage Syndrome". In a small shop, with a limited view, certain contours may look OK, and then not so OK from a distance. Tire placement in the fenders, continuity of body lines, and just the general impact of the car are best seen from another perspective. In fact, this might be a real good time to utilize the talents of your local opinionated hot rodder. Unless he's just a total pain, his critical eye may see some things that escape you. Don't forget to involve a lady, they have an artistic flair that many of us lack. It'll be easier to consider a change sitting on the picnic table now, with the car in the raw, rather than on another bench at a show looking at a finished car.

Hot rodding is all about breaking the rules, so please take the comments above as a gentle prodding to think your project through, not as preaching. The cars we remember 10 years later often ignore the latest trends, for a timeless look that reflects the owner's own vision. These cars begin new trends while the builder has already gone on to his next new idea. Who ever heard of building a fenderless '34 coupe until Jake Jacobs had the nerve to revive a forgotten hot rod style? Sometimes, the toughest decision is when to stop and exercise a little restraint. Will doing more make it any better?

Much time was spent referring to scale drawings and mocking up the shape of the top before welding took place when this '40 Ford was converted from an OEM 5 window to this phantom 3 window.

Design

Bracket Design Choices

Tensile vs Shear Strength

We make many joints between two objects when building our hot rods. Sometimes the joint is bolted on for later service, or welded for permanence or speed of fabrication. Structurally, there is little difference between the stresses for a bolted versus welded joint, assuming proper design features are used. Welds and bolts both have similar structural limits which need to be determined as part of the design. We'll not have space to get into those right now, but if either is assumed to have the tensile and shear strength no greater than that of the steel they are fastening, your design will be limited by the material, not the fastening method.

Normal hot-rolled and cold-rolled steel will have a tensile strength of around 60,000 PSI (pounds per square inch), and a shear strength of about 70% of that, or 42,000 PSI. That assumes a good clean grade of steel, which is often a problem with the foreign material often found in hot-rolled steel. When it is rolled into plate, debris and scale can cause inclusions which do not allow the rolling process to form a truly homogenous steel. I have seen hot-rolled steel plate completely delaminate into layers much like bad plywood. Examine any hot-rolled (HRS) for this problem, use cold rolled (CRS) whenever possible, and absolutely on critical items.

Specialty steels such as chrome moly (4130) and stainless steel require special knowledge of their characteristics before being used. Heat treatment of the welds is often necessary, and they are so strong in tensile strength that they lack the toughness (ductility, or resistance to repeated stress cycles) that are critical on devices used on public roads. The same goes for aluminum, but even more so. That is not to say these materials are bad, just as their use cannot be as casual as with mild steels. In general, on a Hot Rod chassis, any reasonably good design fabbed in mild steel with a thickness of 3/16 inch minimum will be OK. Since you are probably not a trained engineer with access to strain measuring equipment, look at similar brackets used in commercially available parts. Their experience will often be an excellent guide. Be very careful of using aircraft and drag race oriented parts, as they often compromise strength for extended mileage in favor of reduced weight. Our Hot Rods can stand a few extra pounds in favor of a greater safety factor. Those exotic parts aren't wrong, just designed for an entirely different environment and maintenance cycle.

It's important to understand the types of strain that our parts must withstand. Tensile force is that which pulls on an object, trying to tear it apart. Cylinder head bolts are an example of a tensile stressed application. In fact, the requirement for a torque spec is a good indicator of tensile strain. Compressive forces attempt to push parts together, as in a column holding up a front porch on a house. They are seldom an issue on a hot rod other than items like a brake pushrod, which must be strong enough to not fail as a column. Shear stress is usually the most critical to consider in design, since the material and fasteners have about 70% of their tensile strength, as mentioned above. Fender braces, brake pedal pushrods, and coil-over mounts provide good examples of how to understand these forces and design a strong and reliable bracket.

A fender brace typically has a bolt through the fender and a bracket, providing only one area in the joint where the strain pulls one way on one object, and the opposite direction on the other. That's exactly what happens with your sheet metal shears, and is what causes them to cut metal. To avoid the same shearing action when you want parts to stay together, the thickness of the materials and the fasteners in that joint must be large enough so that a stress of less than 40,000 PSI is generated in any component of the joint.

A ¼ inch bolt has a circular cross section of about .048 inches, and can therefore withstand a 1920 pound shear stress. If the bracket is 1/8 inch thick steel, it can resist a 1200 pound load. (.25 inch diameter times .125 thick, multiplied by 40,000 PSI) Remember that is a static load, without the dynamic accelerations caused by movement and that infamous sudden stop at the bottom. Doubling the steel thickness doubles the shear strength since it doubles the area under strain. Increasing the bolt size to 5/16 inch increases the circular cross section to .076, for a shear strength almost doubled to 3040 pounds. It's tempting to just use the larger bolt, but you can see that does no good without thicker material. That's why I made the statement above regarding using the material as the normal limiting factor, unless unusually small fasteners are chosen.

Since a fender won't usually see a 1900 pound load, light brackets and small bolts mounted in single shear are OK. A brake pushrod will need much higher strength. It takes brake fluid supplied to the wheels at about 1500 PSI to stop a car. A common one-inch bore master cylinder has a cross section of .785 square inches, so a force of 1178 pounds is

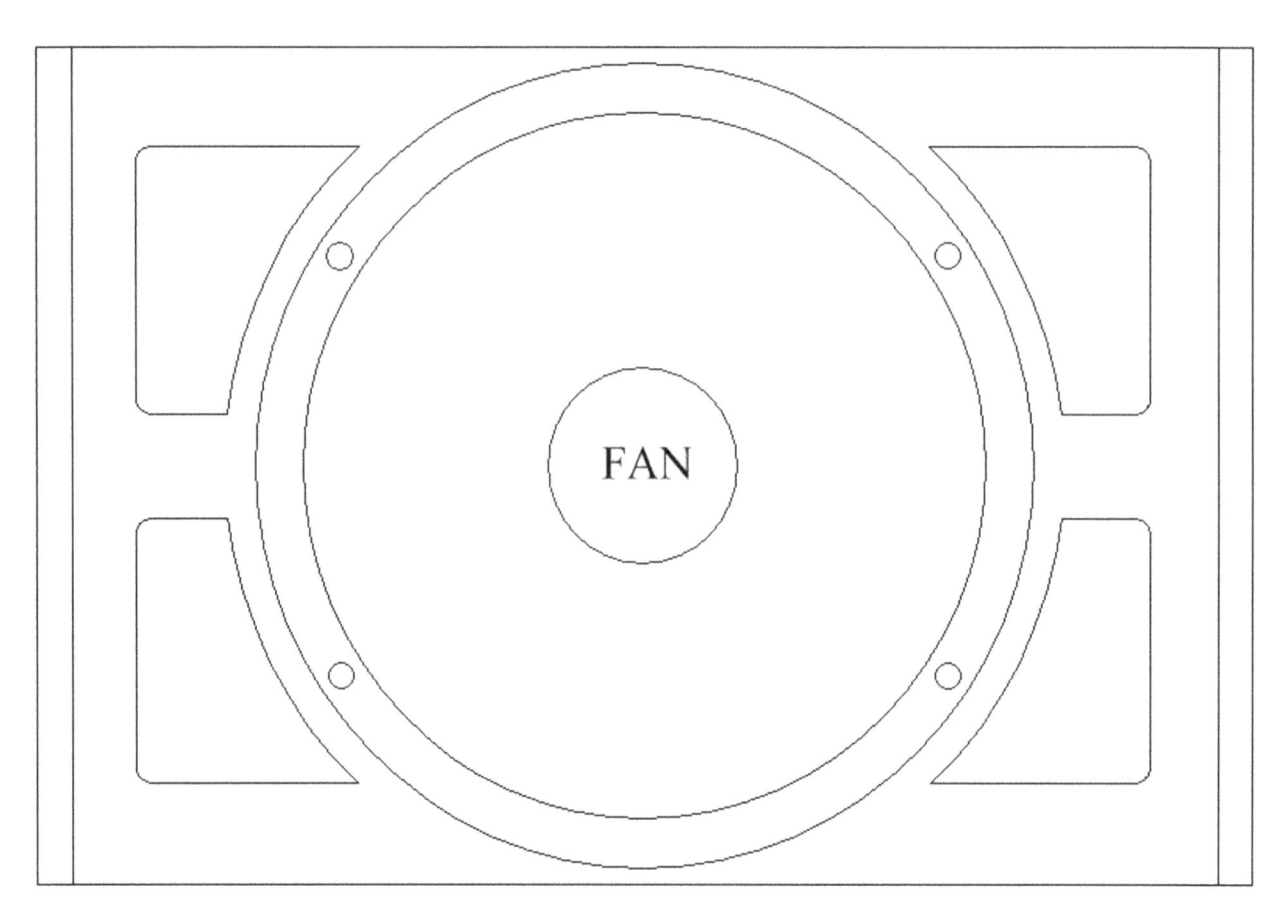

This fan mount design illustrates how the proper mounting holes for the fan are created and then simple cutout shapes are added to save weight, add interesting details and enhance free air flow.

required at the pushrod. A 5 to 1 pedal ratio gives us a foot pressure requirement of 235 pounds. That's why a 130 pound woman will need power brakes! Since our 5/16 inch bolt from above has a .076 square inch, the bolt must withstand shear stress of about 15,500 pounds. That is below the 40,000 PSI shear strength, so the 5/16 inch bolt is OK.

If we use a simple lever with a ¼ inch thick arm, we can resist a 3120 pound load, which is above the 1178 pound requirement. Common industry practice is 3/8 inch thick pedal assemblies with 3/8 inch bolts, for a comfortable safety margin. The bolt can be fatigued by repeated bending at the joint, work hardening the bolt and causing it to fail at a much lower level of strain. Consider that having the pushrod placed in between two ¼ inch levers (a double shear design) would provide a much larger safety factor, and prevent the bending that causes the hard-to-predict effect of bending stress on the bolt.

We used to see a lot of shock brackets made in a single shear design, and they were prone to failure. Thicker material and larger bolts help, but the nature of the rubber bushings in the shock ends allow the bending stress just discussed. It's far better to design a double shear bracket that covers both sides of the bushing. Another way is to weld in a short section of tubing that changes the nature of the single shear bracket. A bolt mounted in a cantilever design works quite similar to a diving board at the pool. As more of the board/bolt is kept immobile at its mount, it becomes stiffer and will bend less under stress. That's bad for a diver but good for our hot rod.

You will see this cantilever design quite often in rear coil-over mounting. Common industry practice calls for short sections of tubing welded in at one-inch centers to provide adjustment and mutually support one another while providing a secure bolt mount. Bending stress is nearly eliminated. Deuce Factory and Air-Ride make a variation on this theme that has the spacer necessary for keeping the coil-over away from the axle bracket made in such a way that two mount bolts are used, again eliminating the bending stress. It is critical that coil-over mount bolts must ALWAYS be perpendicular to the shock body. Any angle imparts a bending stress that can fail the bushing loop where it joins the shock body and shaft. Break a bushing, and the car drops right now. Check yours carefully!

Front coil-overs must always be in a double shear mount since they receive a much higher load. Not only is the front of the car usually heavier, but if an independent front suspension is used, leverage in the lower coil-over mount on the control arm may more than double the apparent load. If the coil-over is mounted half way between the inner pivot and the tire contact patch center, it sees double the weight of that corner. It will require a double shear mount, and is often fitted with a rod end style swivel bushing to allow it to accept the angle changes seen as the suspension moves. That swivel bushing prevents the bending stress we've been discussing.

There's no way this subject can be fully discussed in this space. Perhaps you are intrigued enough to learn more, think a little longer, and look at proven designs. If so, thanks for the extra effort that will keep our cars safe and our sport free from any more oversight from outside interests.

> **I have seen hot-rolled steel plate ... delaminate into layers much like bad plywood ... use cold-rolled whenever possible, and absolutely on critical items.**

Design

Shape Matters

Why a Birdcage can be Stronger than an I-beam

There are two primary ways to get strength in any structure. Our Hot Rods are simply a specific structure subject to the laws of Physics. The designer can get a strong structure by using simple design with heavy enough members to resist the applied stress. Around our shop, we refer to that as the "railroad iron technique". It's unnecessarily heavy and frankly looks a little crude. Boxing a frame with 3/8 inch plate, and the I- beam X-members in many '50s convertibles come right to mind as examples. The factory designers found it economical to simply add massive I-beams to their closed car frames in order to keep the convertibles rigid. If you have worked with one of these cars, you know how massive, yet inadequate, those frames became.

The other approach requires more thought, but can often be stronger, lighter, and certainly more elegant. By utilizing shape rather than mass, the designer can build a more efficient structure. A real good way to visualize this approach is to look at a highway bridge. An arched bridge uses many beams, primarily set in a way as to be in compression to support weight. A suspension bridge such as the Golden Gate uses cables in tension to do the same job. Both use much less material than a simple platform bridge, and can cross spans that would be unthinkable with a plain bridge.

When we box an open channel frame, we are using shape to achieve strength. It's pointless to use material any heavier than the rest of the frame. Even huge 8 inch open frame channels on big classics and trucks will flex until being boxed. This is why the simple ladder frames are improved with x-members. The next level of improvement is a roll bar cage. A simple hoop helps, and continues to add frame rigidity as front and rear legs are added to become four and six point cages. We're actually making our chassis resemble an arched bridge, with our roll cage adding frame stiffness along with roll over protection. As an interesting aside, the NASCAR guys here in Charlotte are doing a lot of work refining their roll cage fabrication. They find that even the sequence of welding the bars in the cage can pre-stress the chassis and add an element of spring rate to a corner! That may be one of the reasons a particular chassis out performs another. We don't need to be quite that careful, but that illustrates how much shape effects strength.

The ultimate extension of this concept is a full tube chassis. That idea showed up as early as WWI when the Fokker fighters pioneered welded tube fuselages covered with fabric. Probably the ultimate use in a car was the "Birdcage Maserati" which used very many tiny tubes to form an incredibly light structure. The Gull Wing 300 Mercedes had a tube chassis, which needed depth at the door area for strength, hence the need for a gull wing door to allow passengers to step over the very high door sill. A few hot rods have been built with full tube chassis, but do require tremendous effort and time (read money). For the needs of a street driven Hot Rod, we can get sufficient rigidity with a boxed frame and an X-member to feed corner forces into the center of the frame where stress is dissipated into the remaining three corners.

Extending this idea further led to a genius named Buckminster Fuller (an amazing life to read about if you enjoy clever people) designing a shape known as a geodesic dome. You occasionally see a home built in a dome shape, looking like a bee hive. The structure is made up from connected pentagon (five sided) shapes. They support one another for incredible strength with minimal weight and no need for internal supports. I've also seen a couple of fabricators build complex shapes for a car body with an incredible number of little triangles welded together to form the shape. As you can imagine, the smaller the triangle the smoother the final shape and less need for a smoothing filler. Pullmax and wheeling machines are faster and cleaner, but not everyone has one. I mention the above techniques to get your mind to the ultimate extension of using many small shapes to make a larger complex shape.

Monocoque construction (which is simply French for Unibody) first showed up in aircraft, where maximum strength and minimum weight are critical. The race cars guys have the same issues, so it didn't take long for that technique to show up on the track. The European road

The principles of triangulation are used to create a K member that strengthens the chassis structure while providing a mount position for the transmission.

racers led the way with foreign manufacturers quickly adopting unibody construction for their passenger cars. The complex stamped sheet metal parts are really an almost infinite number of small shapes bent and formed for strength, and then welded together to form an amazingly stiff structure. Once American Indy racers went monocoque, the old heavy Curtis style roadsters were toast. They sure do look cool restored though, don't they? Trend setting fabricators like Steve Moal are bringing a lot of aircraft and racer style to our hot rods now. There is something inherently elegant about clever and efficient design.

So, what shape is best? Round tubing has been demonstrated to be the strongest per unit of weight. That's why roll bars and Cobra roadster frames are built that way. The downside is the time and labor involved, along with a significant skill level. It's also more difficult to mount a flat floor too, as in a '40 Ford. Plus, an X-member with limited depth for ground clearance can be more difficult to get exhaust thru. Using 1x2 inch rectangular tube provides plenty of compressive strength yet allows more space than the 1-5/8 inch diameter tubing that is often used. You gain 1-¼ inch more space, which goes a long way toward avoiding rattles. When you box a frame, or use rectangular tube, that presents a parallelogram to resist twisting stress. The tube will be plenty strong in compression, but torque can still distort the shape. If the rectangle's material is sufficiently strong, it will be OK. Otherwise, supporting that parallelogram with gusseting will prevent distorting its shape. To be specific, an independent suspension loads the corner of the frame with torque, since the spring is mounted away from the frame. The shock tower and gusset serves to protect the rectangle shape, and is greatly aided by a gusset inside. We use a tubular style motor mount that carries the engine weight to the crossmember rather than the frame, and then reaches over to the top of the frame. The weight of the engine is therefore used to assist the frame in resisting the torque the suspension induces on the frame rail.

What we have really done is to achieve a triangulated shape. The strongest shape for an assembly of members is the triangle. Going back to our example of an arch bridge clearly shows how triangulation is used. Round tubing can flatten and rectangular can go out of square, but a triangular shape cannot be distorted unless an individual member fails. That's another reason why an X-member works so well in a chassis. Our tubular style motor mount triangulates the frame stress pints to eliminate distortion. Try to design any bracketry you need in such a way as to use this triangulation concept.

Let's say you need a shock bracket or an alternator mount. Start with two mounting points on the base of the bracket, the upper component mount being the third point. Then add a brace that extends back between the lower two mounts. What you have is a triangulated base with a similar face. The left and right hand sides also form triangles. This part cannot fail unless a bolt or bracket material fails. Vibration will be lessened since the shape cannot distort. Did you ever notice why a three legged stool is more stable than a four legged one? No matter the surface, the three legged deal will always be stable. That's why modern engine and trans mounts have three points as well. The triangle is the engineer's best friend, and comes in pretty handy out in the hot rod shop too!

> **By utilizing shape rather than mass, the designer can build a more efficient structure.**

Design

Fastener Tips

More then just Nuts 'n Bolts

Bolts and nuts are critical is keeping your Hot Rod together. Any part that must be installed and removed periodically will use threaded fasteners rather than a weld or rivet. The wrong choice or improper installation can create safety and reliability problems. Different materials, grades, and finishes are available to match the usage, and the subject of fastener selection and use has filled many a book. The discussion that follows is aimed at providing a few ideas to help you make that proper choice.

There are three basic grades of plain carbon steel bolts that we deal with every day. The Grade 2 bolts have a tensile strength of 74,000 pounds per square inch, Grade 5 are 120,000psi, and Grade 8 are 150,000 psi. The weakest point on a 3/8 inch bolt will be at the root of the thread, a diameter of around 5/16 inch, roughly the tap drill diameter. Doing the math tells us that a 3/8 inch bolt then has .076 square inches under stress. It will theoretically hold a tensile force (one causing elongation) of 5624 pounds in Grade 2; 9,120 pounds in Grade 5; and 11,400 pounds in Grade 8. A common assumption that works pretty well is to assume that the bolt can withstand a shear force (slicing across the bolt) of about 70% of the tensile strength.

Unmarked heads on bolts actually signify a Grade 2 common hardware bolt. These should only be used in non-critical strength applications such as fenders and other sheet metal. Grade 5 bolts have three hash marks on the head, and work very well for general chassis work. The highest tensile strength bolts commonly available are Grade 8, with five or six hash marks. An exception to this is socket, or hex head bolts, which may have flat, button, or cylindrical heads. Many people call these Allen heads, and all are Grade 8, even though not marked as such. Metric bolts will generally have an 8.8 marking on the head, which is roughly the equivalent of a Grade 5 bolt.

In actual fact, Grade 5 bolts are often preferred over Grade 8. A Grade 8 has very high tensile strength, but can be brittle. In applications such as suspensions, a very high number of load/unload cycles can produce work hardening, which produces an immediate, or catastrophic failure. It's often much safer to use a Grade 5 bolt which will bend, thus providing a warning, rather than a Grade 8 bolt breaking without warning. As long as the Grade 5 bolt has been sized large enough to take the expected load, we don't want to trade toughness (resistance to stress cycles) for the ultimate tensile strength of the Grade 8 fastener. Very highly stressed parts such as engine cylinder head bolts do see stress cycles, but use Grade 8 bolts that have been torqued to a certain value to maintain their fastening strength.

Bringing a bolt to a torque specification works by stretching the bolt until it gets to a tension force level known as its yield strength. That means that additional tensile stress will not stretch the bolt further, causing it to loosen. If a torque rating is specified, you also need to know whether the rating is listed with either dry, or lubricated fasteners. You may have noticed that really critical applications such connecting rod bolts are often set to torque by actually measuring the stretch. Proper torque also helps a bolt resist fatigue failure in an area with a high number of load cycles. Most of the time, on chassis, fenders, and general use, just tighten the bolts with common length wrenches and ratchets. The length of these is actually calculated to provide proper torque with normal human strength. That's why your wrenches get longer as they get bigger! Don't get carried away and damage bolts by overdoing it.

Based on experience and education, I'd recommend Grade 5 for anything other than engine bolts. Stainless is just dandy for fenders and engine brackets where the trick appearance is worth the expense. Special higher strength stainless bolts are available from the better hot rod fastener specialists for use on applications such as suspension and engine intake manifolds. Cylinder head bolts should remain as Grade 8 or better. Whenever stainless steel fasteners are used, liberal use of anti-seize compound is absolutely essential. Grease is NOT an acceptable substitute. Without it, these fasteners will actually undergo a microscopic welding process that will render them seized, and completely useless. If you don't have anti-seize all over yourself and your tools, you aren't using enough.

Nuts are normally made from a grade of steel that is equivalent to a Grade 2 bolt. The idea is no allow the nut threads to deform enough so that they closely conform to the mating bolt. Therefore, even regular nuts should not be reused. The thickness of the nut allows enough material under stress that full bolt strength can be developed. Stronger nuts are used as castle nuts with cotter pins, and also in special applications, generally having a flat washer made integral with the nut. Aircraft fasteners are expensive, but use higher strength nuts - if you have a use that seems to require more than normal security.

Nyloc nuts are extremely popular for use on hot rods, as they generally provide a nicer look than a split lock washer. They also work very well where much vibration is experienced. Throttle linkages are real good examples of this and the rotation of the fasteners cannot be tolerated well by any other type of locking device. Just be very sure that at least three threads extend through the Nylon, or the locking might not occur. When Nylocs are used with rubber or urethane suspension bushings, resist the temptation to over tighten. Use a flat washer, and turn the nut one turn after the washer stops turning. Never reuse Nyloc nuts, as the locking effect is greatly diminished after the first use. And don't even think about using them near heat! See you fastener supply house, or aircraft supply store for an all-steel locking nut that can take the heat.

It's important to think a little about how your bolts should be arranged in the joint. A little trick that I first heard of around airplanes is to try to have the bolt heads forward, and up whenever possible. The idea is that the bolt shank will stay in place and provide some security even if the bolt breaks or the nut vibrates loose. And, you'll have fewer problems finding another nut than another bolt.

To keep your Zinc plated Grade 5 bolts looking better, try making a simple mask from cardboard, and then spraying them with a coat of aerosol clear lacquer. This little trick works well on any metal surface, especially with cadmium plated air conditioning fittings, gauge sending units, and brake lines. A little quick polish with a 3M pad will bring up a nice shine that will last a couple years when sealed with the clear lacquer. We always keep a can of clear around when doing final assembly on a project car.

Another nifty trick for better cosmetic appearance is to use Nylon washers under plain flat washers in order to prevent damage to painted surfaces like fenders. While you are at it, buy flat normal SAE flat washers one size under your bolt diameter. They generally will still fit over the bolt, but are tight enough to stay nicely centered. USS Grade flat washers will also do this, but are more expensive, and harder to find.

On the next page is a fastener I.D. and torque spec chart for use where no spec is published.

> **Based on experience and education, I'd recommend Grade 5 for anything other than engine bolts. Stainless is dandy for fenders and engine brackets...**

TORQUE SPECIFICATIONS

BEFORE DRIVING YOUR VEHICLE, YOU SHOULD CHECK THE TORQUE ON ALL NUTS AND BOLTS IN THE KIT, INCLUDING ANY SLIDER BOLTS ON THE CALIPERS. RE-TORQUE CALIPER BOLTS AFTER 500 MILES. ALL SPECIFICATIONS ARE IN FT-LBS.

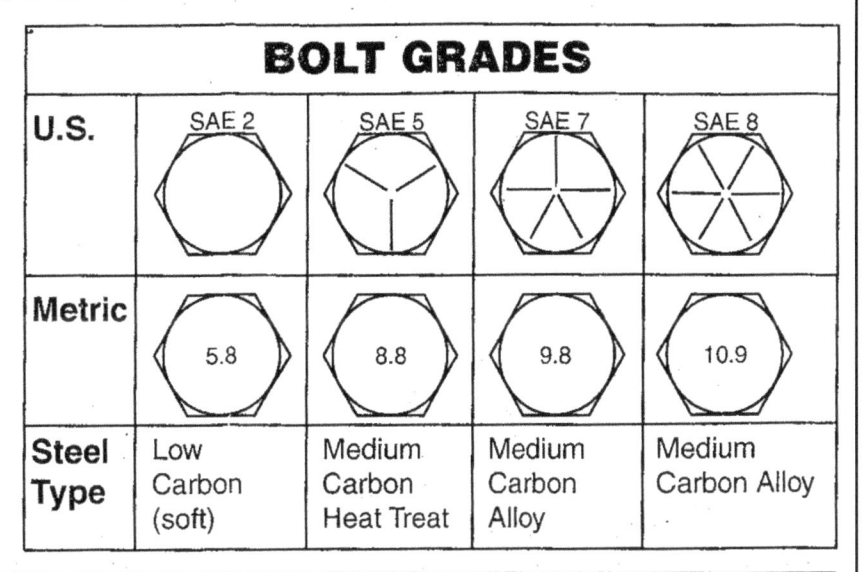

BOLT GRADES

U.S.	SAE 2	SAE 5	SAE 7	SAE 8
Metric	5.8	8.8	9.8	10.9
Steel Type	Low Carbon (soft)	Medium Carbon Heat Treat	Medium Carbon Alloy	Medium Carbon Alloy

SAE Bolt Grade		2	2	5	5	7	7	8	8	Socket Head Cap Screw	Socket Head Cap Screw
Bolt Dia.	Thread per inch	Dry	Oiled	Dry	Oiled	Dry	Oiled	Dry	Oiled	Dry	Oiled
1/4"	20	4	3	8	6	10	8	12	9	14	11
1/4"	28	6	4	10	7	12	9	14	10	16	13
5/16"	18	9	7	17	13	21	16	25	18	29	23
5/16"	24	12	9	19	14	24	18	29	20	33	26
3/8"	16	16	12	30	23	40	30	45	35	49	39
3/8"	24	22	16	35	25	45	35	50	40	54	44
7/16"	14	24	17	50	35	60	45	70	55	76	61
7/16"	20	34	26	55	40	70	50	80	60	85	68
1/2"	13	38	31	75	55	95	70	110	80	113	90
1/2"	20	52	42	90	65	100	80	120	90	126	100
9/16"	12	52	42	110	80	135	100	150	110	163	130
9/16"	18	71	57	120	90	150	110	170	130	181	144
5/8"	11	98	78	150	110	140	140	220	170	230	184
5/8"	18	115	93	180	130	210	160	240	180	255	204
3/4"	10	157	121	260	200	320	240	380	280	400	320
3/4"	16	180	133	300	220	360	280	420	320	440	350
7/8"	9	210	160	430	320	520	400	600	460	640	510
7/8"	14	230	177	470	360	580	440	660	500	700	560
1"	8	320	240	640	480	800	600	900	680	980	780
1"	12	350	265	710	530	860	666	990	740	1060	845

METRIC	5.8	8.8	9.8	10.9
Bolt Dia.	Oiled	Oiled	Oiled	Oiled
5mm	3.5	5	6	8
6mm	6	9	10.5	12
8mm	15	22	25	32
10mm	29	44	51	62
12mm	51	76	89	111

This chart will help you determine the correct torque specs for a fastener when no published specs are available for your application.

Design

Engineering Angles for Hot Rods

Remember Trigonometry?

A fabricator is constantly thinking of how angles affect his work, even if he's not really aware that angles are part of his thought process. Adding a gusset to strengthen a bracket is an example of adding triangulation for more security. But how can we determine the actual effect of a particular angle and whether a larger angle would provide more strength? Can we use a little simple science rather than making a seat of the pants or a TLAR (That Looks About Right) decision? Can we build sufficient strength into our designs without piling on bigger, heavier and uglier brackets than are really necessary?

I think sometimes it's unfortunate that our High School teachers are unable to interest students in their subjects. If that Trigonometry teacher could have understood your interest in cars and shown you how a few simple calculations would make you a better fabricator one day, I'll bet you'd have found a better place than class to catch that little nap. Actually, anything you can do with Trig can also be done by laying out a drawing of the shape you want to build and then measuring the angles and triangle lengths as we will show in the drawing below. I'm not a math historian, but I'd be willing to bet that Trig was invented as a much faster way to do the same thing. And with the cheap modern calculators containing the Trig functions, it's easier than ever to do the math. Please hang in there for a little math review, then we'll talk about how you can USE this information to build a purposely designed hot rod.

The drawing at right shows that for any triangle, there are corner angles with matching opposite, adjacent, and hypotenuse sides (hypotenuse being a long Greek word for the longest side). For simplicity, let's look at a right triangle (one corner at 90 degrees) with sides 10 inches long.

Taking first the method of actually drawing that triangle at full size, we'll find that for a triangle with two 10 inch long sides joined at a square corner, the long side will measure 14.14 inches long. If you want to save the time to draw it out full size or change the lengths of the sides, we can quickly calculate that the longest side is 14.14 inches long by using the formula H/squared= A/squared plus O/squared. That would be seen as H/squared=10 x 10 plus 10 x 10. Run the numbers by adding 100 plus 100, getting 200, whose square root is 14.14.

Or, we can do it with Trigonometry. That subject is WAY too much to cover in this little column, but I remember a helper I was taught to keeps all the terms in order. That Helper is called "Chief SOHCAHTOA" (apologies to our American Indian rodders). He helps me remember that for any angle, the SINE of that angle = the length of the OPPOSITE side divided by the length of the HYPOTENUSE (longest side). In this example, that means that the SINE of 45 degrees=10 inches divided by 14.14 inches.

If we don't know the length of that HYPOTENUSE, we can calculate it by using a little Algebra and rearranging the S angle=O/H to read H=S angle times the O. Before calculators you had to look up the Sine of 45 degrees in a table and do the Math. Today, modern calculators have memorized those tables so you just hit "45", then SINE, and finally multiply by the OPPOSITE side length. When you do that calculation, you get the same 14.14 inches we did when we actually drew out the triangle, but in less time with less effort.

Finishing up with our friend, Chief SOHC-AHTOA, we can also pull out that the COSINE of an angle =the ADJACENT side divided by the HYPOTENUSE, and also that the TANGENT of that angle=the OPPOSITE side divided by the ADJACENT side. The same Algebraic rearranging we did earlier will let you find the value of any one of the three factors when you know the other two.

Our example used a 45 degree 10 inch triangle, but I'll bet you have already figured out that you can change the lengths of the sides or the angle and do the same calculations to get your answers.

I have used a 12 inch normal height here to help illustrate how these angles affect the mounting and the action of a 12 inch center-to-center (at ride height) coil-over shock and spring, a size in very common use. For simplicity, let's say that the coil-over has a spring that will hold up 1200 pounds when mounted vertically. If you move the upper mount 2.08 inches inboard for a 10 degree angle, the same spring can support 1182 pounds, not much difference than vertical. If you move the top over 6 inches to 30 degrees, it can only support 1040 pounds. By dividing the 1040 by the original 1200, we find that we need a spring 1.15 times as strong, or 1380 pounds. Realize that all the mountings will now have to withstand the same 15% increase in loading, while you lose 15% of the available true vertical travel in the suspension. Since neither effect is a good thing, you can see why keeping coil-overs as close as possible to vertical is a more efficient design. They are often mounted with a one-inch offset for a 5% angle, giving a pleasing appearance with almost no affect on performance.

The same affect goes with normal shocks as well. On many cars such as my own '56 Ford Vicky, the stock design rear shocks are at about a 35 degree angle, and go to a 45 degree angle when dearched springs act to raise the lower shock mount relative to the frame. At that increased angle, stock shocks will only do about 71% of the work they could if mounted vertically! So, improved aftermarket shocks with stronger damping ability become almost a necessity, especially since we also need to decelerate the same amount of mass in half the travel distance, on a lowered car.

If you are faced with trying to mount a shock

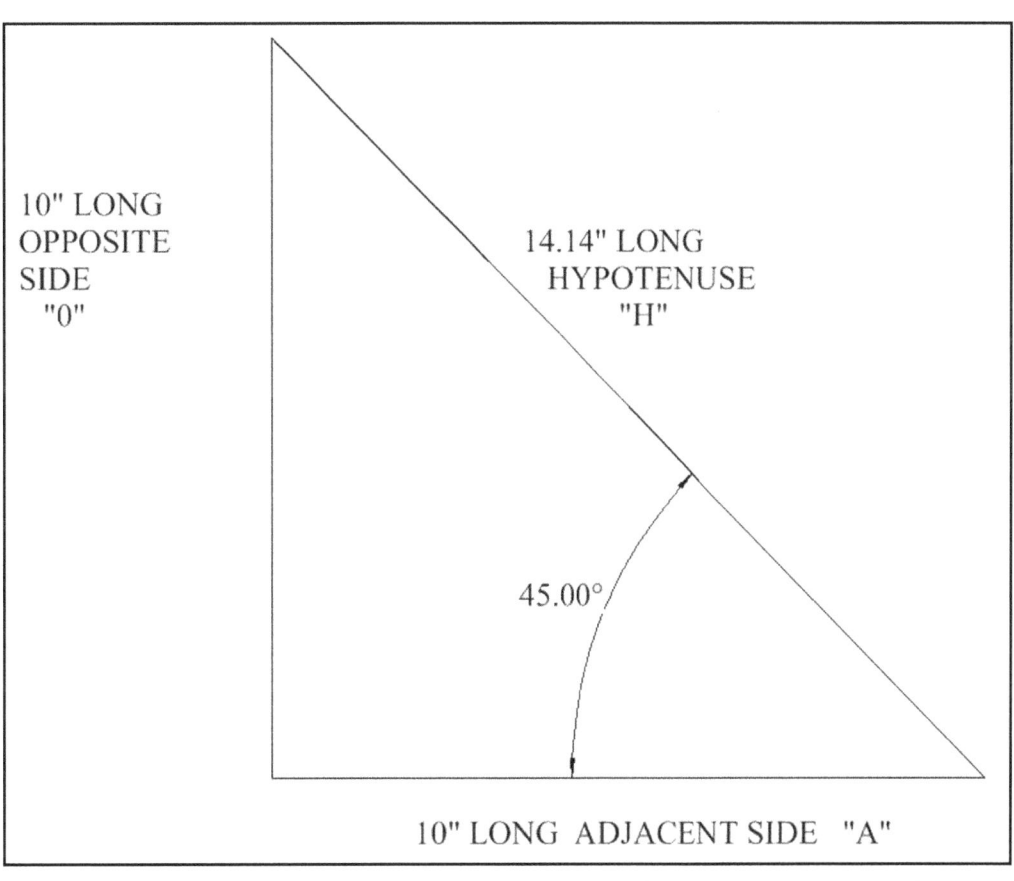

Mounting a shock at a 45 degree angle allows a 14 inch part to fit in a 10 inch vertical space, but also makes the shock 40% less effective.

in a space that is too short, this same angle effect can work in your favor. By leaning the shock, its compressed length will be shorter than if mounted vertically, but remember that a better quality shock will again be highly recommended.

Congratulations. You now understand all the Trig you'll ever need in the real world, and it didn't take an entire Semester.

OK, we can now find the DIMENSIONS of a part we need to build, but how does that figure into the strength of that part? The cool deal here is that we can change the "inches" of line length into other units such as "pounds" to calculate forces on our bracket we are designing. In Engineer speak, the HYPOTENUSE represents a VECTOR force. All that means is that if our triangle sees a 10 pound force acting vertically along with a 10 pound horizontal force, the two forces combine to put a 14.14 pound force measured along the line of the HYPOTENUSE. Let's say we are making a shock absorber bracket with a 50 pound load with the shock at 45 degrees. (I use 50 pounds because that's about all the strength you have to use to open or close a typical shock absorber) The frame rail must resist a 50 pound horizontal and vertical force where the bracket attaches to it, and the bracket must withstand a 71 pound load in both compression and tension, (50X1.41).

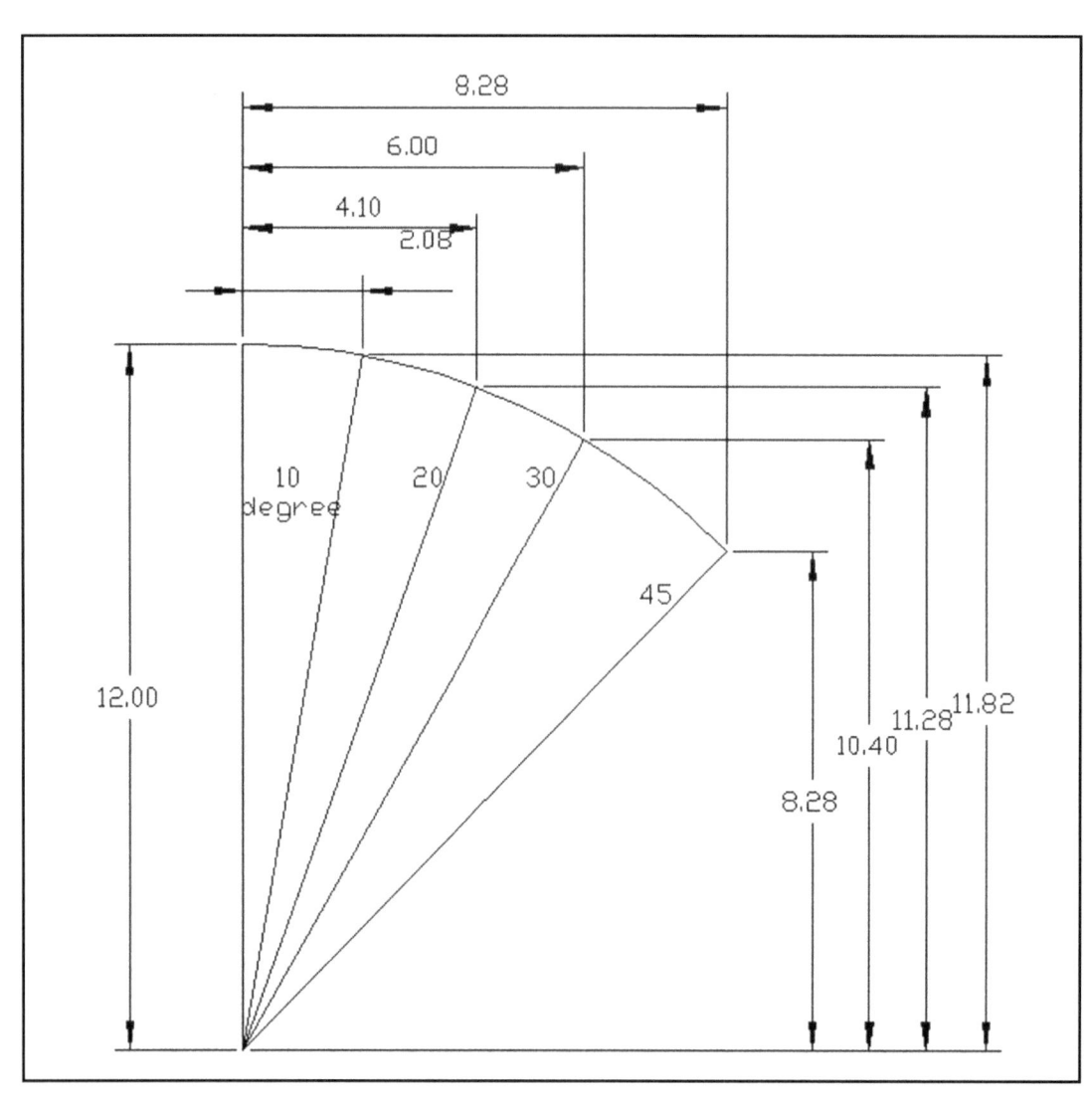

There's a whole lot more involved in figuring the actual force on something like our shock bracket. Leverage, total loads if the shock is bottomed or topped out, weight of the vehicle and so on…much more than we can cover here. Perhaps you now have a little more understanding of how loadings and design strengths are affected by mount angles, and can use that insight to continue the tremendously improved evolution of hot rod design and fabrication.

As you can see, the relationship between travel and function changes as the angle from true vertical increases toward the horizontal.

Drivetrain

Smoother Cruising

A Little Mis-alignment can be a Good Thing

Vibrations sneak up on you. They often get worse slowly so that we mentally adjust to them as normal. Your buddy may jump in the car and immediately feel the problem. Sometimes they aren't there in the morning and appear in the afternoon, Sometimes they are there all the time. Sometimes they come and go. Here are a few things you can do to get rid of these funny goings on - for free.

Let's first assume that your driveshaft is properly made. That means the yokes are in properly alignment to each other, and square to the tube. That tube needs to be straight, with no dents. You hopefully had the driveshaft built by a good shop that balanced it after the welding. Finally, the total length should be under 58 inches, since longer shafts often suffer from vibrations due to harmonics (which is why two piece shafts are needed on very long vehicles).

There seems to be two main schools of thought regarding U-joint angles between the transmission and the rear axle. The conventional wisdom, seen in many tech articles, is that the angle of the engine and trans driveline should be matched by the driveshaft. In practical terms, that means that if the trans is at a 3 degree downward rake, then the rear axle U-joint flange should be parallel, at 3 degrees rake up. The idea is that as the circle representing the rotation of the U-joint is tipped (at a 3 degree rake in our example), that circle changes to an elliptical shape. If the amount of tipping of the circle changes, so does the ellipse. That change of ellipse shape causes the distance around the ellipse (its circumference) to change. So, if the trans tailshaft ellipse has a different circumference than the one at the rear axle, the U-joints and driveshaft are forced to twist to accommodate this difference in rotational speed. That twisting stress can cause vibration and excessive wear.

I completely agree with that engineering concept, especially when there is a large driveshaft angle involved, as in a truck or four wheel drive where the rear axle is at a far different height than the transmission. However, on most hot rods, we lower the car by raising the rear axle. That raising of the rear axle can make the angle between the trans and the rear axle so small that the U joints operate at a very near zero angle. That nearly zero angle does not provide enough rotation to keep the u joint bearing needles rolling enough for proper lubrication. More importantly, the U joints will have a small section of their rotation at a point where the normal production tolerances will allow a little slop in the joint.

I think the easiest way to explain this is to think of the last time you enlarged a hole with

> **Let's first assume that your driveshaft is properly made. That means the yokes are in properly alignment...**

U-Joint Orientation

When two joints are used on a shaft, the forks of the yokes closest to each other should be in line, or "in phase." Premature wear or binding can result if the u-joints are not phased properly. Sometimes if the u-joints are at a severe angle, even if they are phased correctly, a hard spot in the steering may occur for no apparent reason. If this happens, index the u-joints two or three splines in one direction. The hard spot should disappear or be minimized.

CORRECT PHASING

INCORRECT PHASING

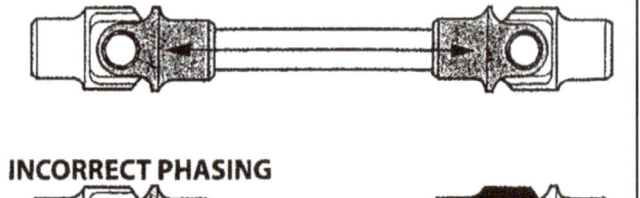

When looking for the source of a vibration, consider the driveshaft - are the U-joints in-phase?

your die grinder. Remember how you had to keep the tool firmly against the metal to prevent it chattering and making a sloppy hole? That side loading you put on the tool cancelled the looseness. Now apply that same concept to our driveshaft angle problem. Perhaps it's better to actually have a little MIS-alignment of the joint angles to provide just enough side load to prevent both joints hitting their "loose point" at the same time. And, the needles will roll more for better lubrication.

I think a proof of this can be seen with production auto steering connections. We are often told that steering U-joints should be held to equal angles and matched rotational angles. A quick look at some OEM installations will show you that they do NOT follow that advice. My theory is that they found that having all the steering U-joints hit their dwell "loose point" at once caused loose steering and vibration. I think they are willing to give up a little theory for a better real world usage, especially given the very low rotational speed involved in steering. We generally install our steering U-joints just a tiny bit off from perfect rotational alignment for this reason.

Over tightened driveshaft universal joint clamps can be an overlooked cause of driveline vibration. Too much torque on the clamp nuts can squeeze the bearing cap to the point that the needle bearings cannot roll freely.

In my shop and in personal hot rod experience I set my rear axles at dead zero angles. That is as measured with the chassis finished, setting on the usual 2-3 degree forward rake. The drivetrain angle can be 3-5 degrees, whichever fits well with the least interference with floors and crossmembers, 3 degrees being optimal. I never see any vibration, and when the rear axle winds up a little under acceleration, the U-joint angles are then at zero, meaning minimum stress when under maximum force. Whenever I used to set the car up at equal angles per the "common wisdom", I would often have a vibration until I changed the rear axle angle to zero. That's my opinion, based and science and practice…your mileage may vary!

Another very common cause of odd vibrations are the U-bolts that hold the U-joint in the pinion yoke. No one wants their drive shaft falling out on the street so most people over-tighten these bolts. A U-joint is composed of four bearings running on four journals. When you lay into that wrench you squash the bearings on the pinion side causing them to bind and generate beat. The greater the angle through the joint, the greater vibration created by the bound joint. Over time the two pinion trunnions will turn blue and may even burn up from the heat generated.

You'll want to adjust the tension on these U-bolts. Just loosen the nuts all around until you can spin the lock washers. Turn the nuts evenly on one U-bolt until the lock washers flatten. Then give each 1/8 of a turn. Then do the same thing to the other U-bolt. That's It. This will put the correct 14 to 17 foot pounds of torque on those U-bolts and allow the bearings to turn normally, If you think the nuts might back off, put a little lock-tight on the threads. You will not believe the difference this simple procedure can make in your car.

> **If you think your car runs better in the morning than later when it has warmed up, you may not be imagining things. Look at your U-joints.**

An unfortunate fact of life is tolerance stack-up. All manufactured parts are made to a range of dimensional tolerances, accounting for some cars in a production run being "sweeter" than most. This accounts for the "lemons" as well. If you are aware of a vibration that gets worse as you go faster, try this out. Remove the U-bolts and rotate the drive shaft (or pinion yoke) 180 degrees. Put the U-bolts back together as described above and go for a ride. The vibration will get better or get worse depending on whether the tolerances stack up or cancel out. The same thing can be done with cars equipped with flange mounts.

If you think your car runs better in the morning than later when it has warmed up, you may not be imagining things. Look at your U-joints. If you see grease fittings you may have found your problem. All serviceable, U-joints have some end-play. This should be .0005 to .0015 of an inch to allow the grease to flow around the needle bearings and be purged through the seal. We have found this style of U-joint with as much as .015 of an inch endplay. There is usually a stripe of grease on the bottom of the car also caused by this looseness. To convince yourself that you have this problem just grease the U-joints one afternoon and go for a test ride. Pay a lot of attention to how the car feels. Later in the cruise think about the feel of the car again and you'll notice a difference. You can cure this looseness with shim stock in all four bearing caps or you can install sealed for life U- joints made to tighter tolerances.

There are many causes for vibrations in cars. Many of them cannot be cured for free but try these before doing anything else. Remember that the simplest, most obvious possible cure can often be the most effective. Always go back to the basics first! (See the nearby Drivetrain Angles article for more on this topic.)

Drivetrain

Engine and Drivetrain Angles

Throw the Rulebook Away?

First we'll discuss the rules you've probably heard before and then we'll consider situations for situations where these rules do, and don't, always apply. As is so often the case with Hot Rods, your special construction can create situations which alter the "rules". My purpose is to help you understand the engineering principals which always apply.

Common wisdom says that the engine's crankshaft angle, often measured on top of the valve cover, should be about three degrees. This is based on the idea of keeping the carburetor level since most intake manifolds are machined with a three degree angle. It is true that carbs function best when the floats are level but we've all gone up enough steep hills to know that the floats are tolerant of some pretty extreme angles. The point is that engine angle based on carb angle can't be all that critical. For example, boats often run up to eight degrees of engine angle with no changes to the engine other than manufacturing the intake manifold with an eight-degree angle. With fuel injection having no floats at all, the engine angle becomes quite less critical.

It's often forgotten that this engine angle measurement assumes the vehicle is at its final ride stance. As mentioned, most Rodders instinctively but incorrectly set their chassis at the level front to back position when in the shop. A better idea would be to simulate the finished rake at about two-three degrees since the vast majority of hot rods have been seen to sit at that angle. The engine is then mocked up at a three degree true angle which adds up to be around six degrees relative to the frame. That six degree engine angle would look all wrong with a level chassis but would be totally correct in reference to the car's final stance.

Ford engines with their front mounted oil pump often need a little extra angle to clear the front cross member even when dual sump oil pans are used. It's not unusual to see Ford engines at a 4-5 degree finished angle. On some applications rear sump GM engines can benefit from increased angles which raise the fan and align the engine with slanted radiators common to the cars such as '33 to '37 Fords. The conclusion is that while a three degree angle is a worthwhile goal, shifting it a couple of degrees to get better engine fit really won't create any problems. It often works well to lower the front of the engine as far as practical, then raise the tail shaft of the trans to get as close to 3 degrees as possible. You may be saving yourself a lot of extra effort trying to achieve an engine angle that simply isn't as important as you may have been led to believe.

Similar confusion may exist with regard to rear axle pinion angle. The common wisdom is that the pinion should point up at the same angle that the engine points down. The purpose of this arrangement is to provide equal U-joint angles in turn producing equal acceleration/deceleration of the U-joints to cancel any vibrations. That change in rotational angular velocity can be visualized by holding a common diner plate in your hands. Keeping the plate vertical would represent a zero degree U-joint angle. When you tip the plate so that you see an elliptical shape you are simulating the angular velocity changes which occurs with increasing U-joint angles. Matching the front and rear U-joint angles is important in normal passenger cars and critical in 4WD trucks which have a large height difference between the transmission and rear end with the attendant relatively large U-joint angles. If we were concerning ourselves with those type vehicles we would follow the matched angle set up principle, but in fact a hot rod is typically a very different animal due to our lowered ride heights.

Lowering the rear of a Hot Rod is actually accomplished by raising the rear axle in the chassis. But if we follow the rule of equal engine and axle angles, we'll end up with the driveshaft in a straight line with nearly zero-joint angles. In that case the needle bearings won't roll enough to stay lubricated, causing greater wear. Vibration often results as there is insufficient side load to keep the needle bearings rotating smoothly. A few degrees of misalignment between the transmission and the axle will avoid these problems.

Aside from angle problems causing driveshaft vibration, over tightening the U-joint retainer straps can constrict the ability of the needle bearings to roll smoothly, as mentioned before. Some research will quickly show that most service manuals specify about 25 foot pounds of torque on the retainer strap bolts. That can easily be applied with a standard length wrench so don't get carried away leaning on those U-joint fasteners!

Drag Racers often set the pinion angles on their race cars down a few degrees. The spinning drive-shaft acts as a gyro, resisting being pushed forward as the pinion rises and helping to plant the rear tires. At my shop we generally set the pinion level while at the approximate final ride stance I keep nagging you about. The engine angle is disregarded as long as it is less than 5 degrees true angle as discussed earlier. This level maintains improved lubrication of the U-joints, cancels harmonic vibrations, helps traction, and extends bearing life by unloading the U-joint as the pinion rises under a full power launch. And don't we all like to stand on it once in a while?

If your hot rod has a vibration and you've explored all the usual wheel and tire issues and made sure all drive line parts are in good mechanical condition, it may be time to check and alter your U-joint angles. I have personally worked on cars with a vibration in the steering column you would have sworn were front suspension related, but turned out to be in the driveline. Four-bar cars allow easy alteration by simply extending the lower bar adjustment and shortening the top bar a similar distance. Leaf spring suspensions are easily altered with a wedge shim placed between the axle mount pad and the leaf spring. These are available at NAPA and other stores in their alignment products line. If the car uses lowering blocks we often mill an angle into the lowering block once the necessary change has been determined.

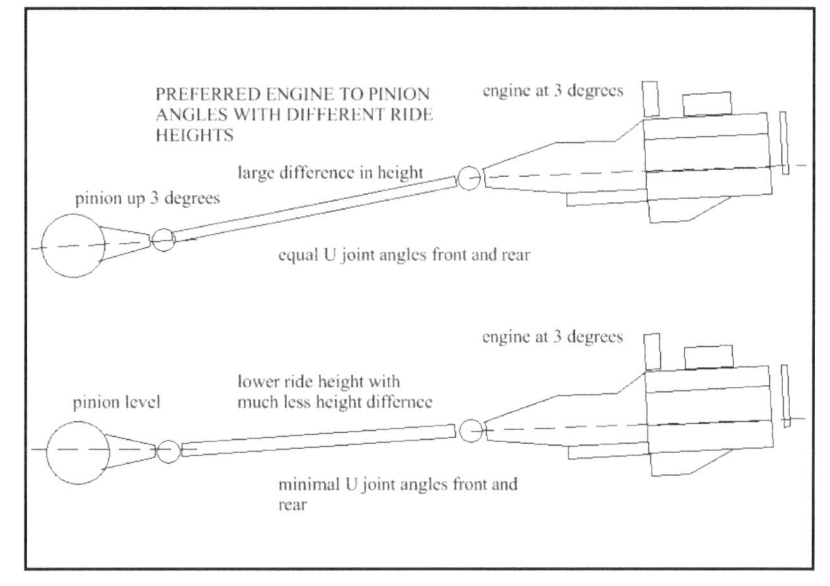

The "rules" of drivetrain angles are altered when a low hot rod stance raises the rear axle in the chassis, directly affecting how the driveshaft U-joint angles should be set to avoid vibration and needle-bearing wear.

Drivetrain

Mounting The Motor

Where and How to Place that Big V-8

The engine and transmission need to be mounted in the car pretty early in the build. You can't do plumbing, exhaust, or hook up the steering until the drivetrain is positioned. You've already decided what particular engine you want, hopefully based on an honest appraisal of the car's intended use, available space (and budget) and you personal brand preference. Now it's time to mock that bad boy in place.

We'll deal quickly with engine position and angles here, since you have read many articles, here and elsewhere, discussing that subject. The highlights are to begin by position the radiator, providing sufficient space for more fan and shroud than you think you need. The ideal engine angle is 3 degrees, measured with the frame mocked up on a 3 degree forward rake-not level. Use the top of the valve cover to measure this angle. The purpose of this is to level the carb so the floats will work at their best. If you have injection with no floats, or have noticed how a carbureted car can climb a steep hill just fine, then you know this 3 degree deal isn't sacred. If a little more tilt saves a bunch of firewall of floor work, go ahead without losing any sleep over it.

Engines are ideally mounted square in the chassis and centered left to right. Many factory vehicles (F-100/150 trucks and nearly every '60 up Mopar come right to mind) have the engine offset a little to the right to help with steering box clearance. You can even swing the engine a little out of square if needed. The driveshaft U-joints rotate and don't recognize any difference between the vertical and horizontal alignment and angles. I'll probably take a little heat for these opinions, but Detroit does it all the time. Just don't get so far out of square and centered that it starts looking goofy.

There are usually several options for oil pans on any engine. Crate engines always seem to come with the largest and least adaptable oil pan. Do some research at the dealer, salvage yard, and aftermarket if the pan already on your engine is causing interference with the steering or crossmember. A simple swap can make a tough job simple. A good rod shop or the kit manufacturers are also good sources of assistance. Just don't panic into cutting the pan or crossmember first. That may indeed be the final solution, but must be approached with caution and experience.

Do whatever you need to in order to provide clearance at the floor and firewall. Clearance should be at least a ½ inch to prevent rubbing and allow cooling air to pass. You may find out the hard way just how hot an automatic trans can get in July on the Interstate. NEVER start at the firewall and assume you can figure your way out at the front later. You will have no end of cooling problems, and will cuss the lack of working space as you continually try to rescue a bad set up. Been there, done that, and lived to regret it. Cut the firewall or pick a better fitting engine.

OK, so we now have the engine position mocked up using whatever devices you have on hand. A cherry picker tends to get in the way after setting the engine. We use cinder blocks, wood scrap, or whatever is lying around that will keep the engine in place and off your face when lying underneath. You can use a complete engine, the nifty plastic motors from P-Ayr, or gut a junk block to save weight if you do this stuff a lot. You just need an engine to provide the fixture to place the insulators. Then you will build mounts to keep the engine where you mocked it up.

Small block Chevys mount well using a '65 Chevelle type insulator, NAPA #602-1154. Big blocks use a '68 Vette deal, #602-1127. Actually, either mount will fit either engine. The small block unit is cleaner while the big block one will take more torque with its interlocking steel tabs. You can also go to urethane mounts for style, durability, and torque carrying ability, but at the price of more vibration transfer. In my experience, the higher durometer rating (measure of stiffness) of urethane simply shakes a little more since they hold the engine a little tighter. It's the "practical versus radical" trade off deal again. An old trick is to use either a torque limiting strap or chain that holds the left side of the engine down while having enough slack to let the insulators do their job. You can also drill thru the insulator and add a 3/8" bolt and Nyloc nut, set with about ¼ inch of slack. That also allows some movement but restricts large amounts of torque reaction. Any GM trans we've seen works well with a NAPA #620-1031 insulator.

Ford engines have a multitude of different style insulators with either a horizontal bolt or a stud. The stud types are a pain to deal with, while the '68 Mustangs and Galaxies all used the horizontal bolt type, kind of like the brand "C" above. If your engine was ever used in the '68 cars, use that insulator. Windsor engines use NAPA #602-1152, which can be shimmed at the vertical block attachment bolts if you miscalculate crossmember clearance. Ford transmissions typically use a # 620-1040.

Unusual engines can provide some challenges for a clean and strong mounting system. I believe the OEM designers spend a whole lot of time designing insulators for maximum NVH (noise, vibration, harshness) suppression, but they tend to be huge and ugly. The nice old flathead Ford biscuits continue to be an elegantly simple solution. In my personal opin-

A well engineered engine mount helps cancel frame twist due to engine torque, while allowing easy connection to the rack and pinion steering. A really good mounting system also adds style to the chassis design.

ion, I wonder about using an insulator designed for a heavy, slow turning but torquey, moderately powered engine. Just food for thought, knowing it has been well proven. We see some really cool looking motor mounts made using a 4 bar insulator bushing as the basis. The same precaution regarding NVH suppression as mentioned above should be considered.

We prefer to adapt Chevy insulators to everything from Hemis to 500 Cadillacs. Street and Performance pioneered the use of the LS-1, and offers a nice simple aluminum adaptor for standard Chevy insulators, while you can make your own or buy steel ones from Fatman. It's usually easier and cleaner to adapt the Chevy stuff to the block than to mount the stock insulators to the frame. We also adapt Chevy trans mounts to the Mopar trans with a rather simple plate with 4 holes rather than trying to use the goofy stock piece.

The actual frame mount can be built next. It is very important to be sure the insulator-to-bracket through bolt is tightened in place at the top of the slot in the insulator. If you aren't careful with this, the engine will fall lower in the slot and mess up your clearances. We typically use a 3/4 inch OD by 1/2 inch ID tube cut to length, fitting inside the insulator mount ears. A 7/16 inch fine-thread grade-5 bolt is used. By the way, have you ever looked at a drag car that uses common radiator hose clamps to retain a saddle mount over a frame tube? I couldn't believe it, but it obviously works pretty well. Just remember 500 miles is a whole lot of drag racing but not many highway miles.

That horizontal tube you just installed now needs to be supported to the frame. The common flat plate with a gusset underneath is the classic deal on '23-'34 Fords, and many others. It works very well, especially with a straight axle set up that supplies mainly vertical forces to the frame. Consider that any type of independent suspension has the spring outboard of the frame rail, which induces a torque stress in the frame rail. An unsupported mount as above adds more torque, in the same direction, which is tough on the rails. On the '23-'34 type chassis, a large gusset between the frame rail and crossmember will resist the stress quite well. You can also use the type of mount that passes under the engine, but they often interfere with oil pan access and are generally judged to be a little funky looking.

The '35 and later cars generally have the engine far enough forward that the mount can be supported to the suspension crossmember. At Fatman we use a section of 7/8 inch X .188 inch wall tube bent 80 degrees and welded between the top of the frame rail and the crossmember. This provides the triangulation strength of a rather large gusset with a more open appearance that also allows easier clearance for the typical Mustang IFS front mounted rack and pinion. Chevy and Ford pickups of the '60 to '90 era did the same thing. Strength nearly equal to a full engine plate can be achieved. You can even fab a vertical strut added between the flat style mount discussed above, and the crossmember. I've seen mounts that go to the crossmember without tying into the frame, but then you lose the valuable frame-triangulation effect.

> Many factory vehicles have the engine offset a little to the right to help with steering-box clearance.

The trans mount can now be added, although we often do it first just to stabilize the engine. We often buy a commercial trans mount kit like the excellent ones from guys like TCI, Pete & Jakes, and Chassis Engineering. They get you started right with a standard type installation, and are easily modified if you are doing something more adventurous. No Limit makes a really cool and affordable transmission crossmember that fits just about any '37 up pickup we've ever done. Universal usually means it doesn't fit anything just right, but Rob came up with a design that really is pretty darn adaptable, at a price that makes building your own a waste of effort. If you do make your own, be sure it fastens to a strong section of the frame. Use 1X2 X .120 inch wall tube, or 1/4 inch plate as a minimum to avoid strange vibrations messing up the "Good Vibrations" playing on the CD.

Electrical

Electronics vs Electrical Circuits

Don't forget the Ground Circuit

We are certainly in the modern electronic age, for many personal devices as well as some of our hot rods. Sure, there are nostalgia hold outs with points ignition and carburetors but each year we see more electronically controlled ignitions, fuel injection and even now, lighting and gauge circuits based on fiber optic and wireless modules. That is a big change from the old electrically based analog systems where a check with a test light was about all you needed to analyze any problems with that circuit. The electronic age brings that simplicity to a total halt.

That fact was recently brought to my attention while using the family late model truck and a small trailer to take household items to the daughter's latest new location. (Those of you with grown children know how THIS works.) All was fine until I heard a "beep" and I lost all brake, turn signal, and dash functions. This quite naturally always occurs late on a Friday afternoon, so needing to continue the trip and fearing some major computer based failure, I pulled into the local dealer for help.

The "short" version was that I had failed to pay enough attention to maintaining the condition of the battery terminals. The OEM positive terminal clamp had corroded to the point where reduced voltage was being supplied. A test light showed continuity but only 11.2 volts were arriving to the system computers. Since 12 volt systems really operate at around 14.2 volts, the computers are designed to tolerate voltage down to a true 12 volt, but shut down below that level. Just 30 bucks later and properly chastened, I was on my way again. In fact, several other weird erratic electronic gremlins "fixed themselves".

Clearly, actual delivered voltage through altered conductivity was the root problem. So when you cut down wire length of a factory harness you may be also creating a change in delivered voltage. Disabling ABS and anti theft systems may do the same. Running all the grounds on a fuel injection or digital dash to a common point, even when the directions CLEARLY state to use several separate grounds can be another cause of delivered voltage being out of spec. Now, in the old systems, low voltage may result in no more than a dim tail light bulb or an inaccurate temperature gauge, altered delivered voltage may be telling a computer a different set of sender signals than are expected. You may be chasing electronic gremlins of your own creation which will drive you nuts trying to solve.

Proper grounding of your hot rod's electrical system is essential, and even more important with a digital electronic system. Getting power from the battery through the switch and on to the particular function typically is our main focus when wiring a car, but it's only half the job. We often forget the ground completes the circuit, allowing proper function. It's kind of like a "round trip" that never brings you home. Either the component in question doesn't function at all, or acts strangely. We had this problem several years ago with our 'glass 32 Highboy Sedan where the gauges suddenly showed a hot engine and a lot less fuel than expected. We stopped and replaced the fan belt since we thought it might be slipping and causing low voltage in the system. That didn't help, but the lights were bright and the engine didn't act hot so we continued the trip. When a power window was activated, the gauges went right back to normal readings.

A firewall to frame bolt being used as an anchor for the entire dash ground wiring had worked a little loose and then gotten just a light film of corrosion. Since the gauges now had a ground with greater resistance, they read wrong until actuating the window switch and relay provided an additional ground path. We had noticed the door on that side wasn't latching just right, which gave us a clue about the ground bolt having loosened up. (Two seemingly unrelated symptoms often have a connection that can help your troubleshooting.) The gauges and the door worked perfectly with just a cleaned terminal and a snugged up nut.

British cars with the old Lucas positive ground wiring systems suffer from many electrical faults because the ground half of the circuit is much more prone to corrosion. You've seen that effect with your car battery. When those cars are rewired to Negative ground systems as used in this country, they work much better. Be sure to insulate and seal your ground connections just like the hot side.

Both analog and digital gauges, and fuel injection systems, work by measuring voltage through a sending unit. Since insufficient grounding can create resistance, those voltages will be altered and the function altered as well. Any sending unit with a single terminal must be installed without sealing tape that might interfere with grounding. If your gauge reads hot but the car isn't boiling over or detonating, you might have a sender installed wrong. Many fuel injection troubles are traceable to bad grounds. Try running a temporary ground wire direct to the battery if your injected engine is running poorly with a proven harness. The sensors may be sending faulty voltage info to the computer, which is controlling the amount of fuel flow based on that misleading data.

I recall a good friend (a 30 year electronic tech at IBM) who installed his first computer controlled engine. No start no way. Even though the instruction said to run multiple grounds, he didn't see the need for that. So, we reread (and actually paid attention to) the instructions, ran the multiple ground wires in the wire gauge required and fired her right up. Maybe the guy who wrote the instructions knew what he was doing after all.

Trouble starting a hot engine is almost always due to lack of good grounding. We've even seen cars that were burning up choke and throttle cables, since the engine didn't have a ground cable and the control cables were the only route available to the system. Always run a ground cable directly to the engine block rather than bolting it to the frame and counting on the frame as the conductor. Connect a large gauge ground strap from that same point to the frame and also to the body. If you are building a glass car you'll want to have a special bus bar to bring all the ground wires together here as well. Most wiring manufacturers have an option to accomplish this very important function. A simple ground wire to a screw will get you by in a steel car, but it sure won't work with glass!

It truly is the little things that drive you nuts. Take extra care with the ground half of your system the next time you wire a car, or try to sort out a problem. The stranger symptoms almost always come back to a basic problem that has been overlooked. It's so much easier to do it right the first time at home, rather than fix it in a hotel parking lot later.

Electronic circuits with demanding voltage control generally use Weatherproof connections to control losses thru connections that can corrode and alter system resistance.

Electrical

Wiring a Hot Rod

Easier than you Think

The wiring on a Hot Rod is a lot like the circulatory system in our own body. In order to communicate the condition and regulate the function of many systems that keep the body functioning, wiring is essential to the reliable operation of that vehicle. The battery must be kept properly, not over or under, charged in order for all the other systems to work correctly. The primary ignition circuit has the job of providing ignition power to a gas-fueled engine, and all the other circuits handle the lights, gauges, and all the rest to keep track of mechanical systems. The wiring must be in good condition, including the ground circuit (which is half the electrical circuit) for all this to happen.

If you are essentially restoring an older car, you may be so lucky that the original wiring harness can be reused. A careful check of the wire insulation and particularly the contact blocks at any and all switches must be made. If cracked insulation or corroded terminals exist you will have funky electrical gremlins that fail intermittently in order to deprive you of the fun of driving that hot rod. Aftermarket harnesses were created to alleviate those common problems and are generally easy to obtain and install. They also generally will allow you an extra circuit or two to cover the feeds to an Air Conditioning or power window upgrade. If you have a less common model of car, or have made enough modifications to the engine, gauges, and accessories it may be better to start over with a completely new wiring harness.

You could rewire the car the old way, using wire from the parts store and working thru the systems on your own. That's fine if you can find enough colors and know what you are doing. I think you will find that any hot rodder who has wired a few cars finds an aftermarket harness a better plan. First, the wire size and color variety they have is far greater, and all the better harnesses made today use a modern insulation first developed for aircraft, where the smell and smoke of a grounded wire can be a genuine hazard rather than a major inconvenience. The insulation is tougher to begin with, has a higher melting temperature, less acrid smoke, and is alone a major reason for using a new harness. You will also get new terminal ends, and often new switches, that really reduce your chances of those gremlins showing up. There may well be extra circuits available for added accessories.

As noted in another article, the move toward computer-controlled engines has really changed things in automotive wiring. The older cars generally worked fine if the system operated at the designed voltage, with minor raised resistance levels due to corrosion not causing much trouble. In the digital world of the computer, minor changes in resistance and delivered voltage can wreak havoc on the system, particularly in the case of fuel injection. Since the computer is receiving signals from all the sensors measured in very precise voltage levels, any unusual resistance will alter the computer's perception of engine and outside air temperature, air pressure, fuel pressure, etc and cause poor engine operation. You have heard the old computer adage "garbage in….garbage out", and that is just what you will have. As mentioned before, the ground circuits in particular are far too easy to overlook in this case, particularly with fresh paint or a fiberglass car. The computer simply requires far more precision in delivered voltage, so it is no surprise that most hot rod wiring companies also offer harnesses for fuel injected engines.

When your hot rod project is built from scratch, whether it's a car from the '30s or '70s, an aftermarket harness seems to be the only way to go. The better wire we discussed is often used, and generally clear instructions are supplied so that a novice can do the job. It's intimidating the first time you open all the bags of wire, but if you read thru the instructions a couple times it won't seem so bad. Some harnesses are wired from the fuse block going out to the engine and lights, while others begin out there and bring the wires in toward the fuse block. Opinions differ as to which is better in terms of ease of running the wires and how cleanly the wire looms will appear, but either will function equally well. Some harnesses will supply all the switches while others offer you choices. This again is a factor in the price and your choice of harness manufacturer.

Another factor will be how many circuits you need. A rat rod or a carbureted '66 Nova drag car will need very few circuits. Adding accessories, computer controlled transmissions and fuel injection will naturally require more circuits. I would always advise you to have a couple of extra circuits in case things get more complex in the future.

Complete short outs of wiring have become rare since the switch from ammeters to voltmeters because there is less chance for direct battery voltage shorting to ground. Even so, a harness with a main fuse has become a wise choice. A battery cut off switch certainly helps as a back up, but you may not be able to get to it quickly enough to prevent real problems. Some harnesses use the old glass fuses if an OEM type harness is chosen, but the aftermarket harnesses generally use the new plastic blade fuses. The only gripe I have with them is that it is much more difficult to see if they have blown. Some fuse blocks will even have the relays for horn, headlights, and other functions prewired. The more the manufacturer does the more the harness may cost, but it may be money well spent in terms of time spent and the all important job of making secure terminal connections.

Take those swap meet el cheapo terminal ends and crimping tools and throw them away. Invest just a few more dollars in good tools and parts. Auto parts stores are generally pretty high on terminals, but you can go to an industrial electrical supply house for a better deal on really good terminals in quantity and the proper crimping tool, as shown in the photo. Mine is Thomas and Betts brand. The difference in connection security, lack of resistance, and appearance are well worth the investment. Many harness makers will supply the good terminals, so you may well just need the good tool.

All the information above seeks to arm you with good questions to ask as you contact the various harness manufacturers. The size of an ad or the amount of hype in the text are not always good measures of the quality of their product. You will want to spend a little time on the phone with their tech guys, or better yet visit with them at the local Goodguys show. Doing so will help you understand the features and pricing they can provide, and just as important, the level of support you can expect. You will find that it is critical to find a supplier and even a particular tech who can answer your questions and clear your confusions while remembering that this may be YOUR first time at bat!

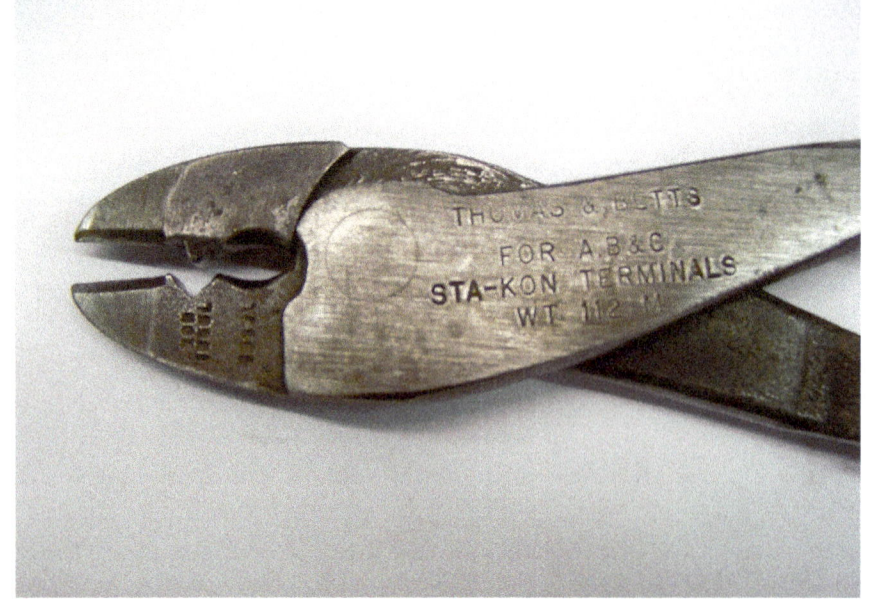

The correct tool always makes a job easier. In the case of wiring, the right tool also makes a much more structurally and electrically reliable connection.

Engine

Another Approach to Oil Control

Blowby be Gone

Like so many rodders, I get bugged by having oil drips under my hot rods. The Detroit factories have done an exceptional job reengineering their engine oil seals and gasket designs. Higher walls on cylinder heads and better gasket designs now prevent most leakage on valve covers. Full circle rear crank seals, improved PCV systems, fuel injection preventing premature wear, etc combine to make the newer LS GM and Ford MOD engine series excellent choices for these, and many other reasons as well. However, some vehicles just really need a more traditional engine for the "look", or just plain nostalgia value. The problem is that older engines return us to the days of yesteryear, days of higher maintenance and our current subject, leaking engines.

I love the small block Chevy with Ardun valve covers and Hilborn 8 stack injection in my '34 Highboy sedan. It makes so much torque so quickly that the crankcase pressure builds up and creates some blowby. It's taken a couple of tries to totally control the oil vapor, with the final solution being the direct crankcase vent system we'll be discussing. The 312 in my '56 Vicky runs great, but boy does it leak. Even after a rebuild by an experienced guy, I leak a quart every couple hundred miles. We now know that there is an improved rear crank seal available, but this one has the original rope seal. Coupled with the leaky original Ford ram type power steering system, this car has enough oil on the bottom to prevent much possibility of body rust. It's enough that I take some heat from the wife about parking it in the garage attached to the house.

I also have an airplane problem. I enjoy building and flying airplanes, and others similarly afflicted may remember the old adage to "never get in an airplane that isn't leaking oil…it stopped because it's out". Earlier on, we took a look at a homemade oil vapor separator that drops into the early style intake manifold mounted oil fill/vent tube. That works really well, but on the injected '34, the engine makes so much power so quickly that the crankcase venting seems to get overwhelmed. There is always some blowby of compression pressure past the piston rings, which then goes on to create a slight positive pressure in the crankcase. A functional PCV system helps, and the '56 312 has that, but we're still not totally out of the woods. The Hilborn injection on the '34 lacks any common plenum to install a PCV system so we're out of luck there. Any crankcase pressure is going to make marginal crankshaft seals leak a lot more than normal. How else can we prevent any excess crankcase pressure?

Some conversation with a racing buddy and a look at a modern Sprint car showed me that they run as many as 4 breathers on the oil pan itself. Those cars get pressure washed after every race, so a little oil under the car isn't a big deal. I got to wondering if direct venting of the crankcase would be workable. Then I noticed that the 312 has a rather unusual solution to this very problem. I have to suspect that the Ford engineers knew they had a leaker on their hands because there is a port in the left front of the engine block leading direct to the crankcase. It has a steel mesh filter cap and a road draft tube, so any oil vapor that gets thru the mesh passes down the tube and ends up on the car anyway.

The vent assembly replaces the original road draft tube on the Ford 312 and will allow excess crankcase pressure and oil vapor to pass to the reservoir.

Mounting the vent reservoir high on the firewall allows the oil vapor to condense and then drain back after the engine is shut down.

I had great success with the injected small block in the '34 by making a new fuel pump block off plate (electric fuel pump was used with injection) that was 3/8 inch thick to allow it to be tapped for a -8 ½ inch ID fitting and hose. That hose then plumbs to a reservoir mounted high on the firewall. I bought an aluminum power steering reservoir and drilled the cap for a vent of any leftover pressure. I can see that it has signs of oil vapor condensing and then returning to the engine at shutdown. The back of the car now stays totally dry.

I made a similar block off plate to replace the crankcase vent on the 312. A radiator overflow tank was used this time, 'cuz I had it sitting around. I did change the lower inlet tube to accept a 3/8" ID fuel line to use as the connecting hose. This cap needed to be drilled for passive venting as well. The car still drips PS fluid, but oil usage seems to be much decreased. We'll fix that later when I install one of our frame stubs with a Single Cam MOD 4.6 engine.

For now, it seems as though the combination of the new crankcase venting system and the use of an oil fill tube vapor separator has really made a difference. If you want to stick with an early style engine and would rather keep it cleaner, these tricks may be worth a try.

A base plate is fabricated to allow the vent system direct access to the pressurized crankcase, with a fitting added to connect to a reservoir.

Engine

Fitting Modern Engines

Say Goodbye to the Small Block?

Performance and economy have been combined in packages that make modern engines well worth considering for your next Hot Rod. By modern I'm speaking of the new Mopar Hemis, the Modular Fords, and the GM LS series engines. I discovered that unlike the traditional small block Chevy engine, the LS series is used in so many different GM chassis that things can get a little confusing.

I've not had too many problems installing the Mopar and Modular Fords in either our repro chassis or in the original vehicles. They are wider than traditional small blocks, but no wider than a big block. An exception is the 4-Cam Fords, which measure about 36 inches across the valve covers. An engine of that width creates difficulties in many chassis', and often fits better in a vehicle with a front suspension track width of 60 inches or more. Narrower cars tend to have trouble since the valve covers interfere with the upper control arm mountings. I have found that the more compact mounting used on a coil-over version of suspension in cars like the '55-'57 T-Bird should be used rather than shortening the upper arms to clear the engine since that generally ruins the front end geometry. McPherson strut suspension conversions eliminate the upper control arm entirely easing the way for a 4-Cam Ford. Maybe that's why Ford uses strut suspensions on the cars that come with factory installed 4-Cams!

Both the Mopar and Ford Mod engines have rear sump oil pans, the best Modular Ford oil pan being found in Lincoln applications. This works out fine in cars that have front side steering systems but poorly with rear-steer suspension system like in a '56 Ford stock vehicle. I have found that the easiest way to mount these engines is to make a simple plate from ¼ inch steel that picks up on at least three mount bosses on the original block. The Mopar version will then accept a conventional small block Chevy insulator for a '67 Chevelle (amongst many other applications), which by the way is NAPA part number 602-1054. The Ford Mod motor version will use a '68 Galaxie-type insulator rolled up to a new angle, seen at NAPA under part number 620-1040. The GM LS version of this mount is like the Mopar, using the '67 Chevelle insulator. Since these engines accept the familiar GM Turbo transmission, I at first thought I could simply make a mount adaptor that would locate the engine in the same location as the old 350 making it a bolt-in swap. But I quickly discovered that the low mounted alternator on the driver side of the '98 and up Camaro engines will not allow this to happen. I had to either put the frame mount further back than with a 350, or relocate the alternator. As you may know, relocating the drive accessories opens a real can of worms on a serpentine drive such as this. The best solution with a front steer application is to use a '97 and up Corvette engine which has a high mount alternator on the driver side, and a low mount A/C compressor on the passenger side. Aftermarket front drive systems can also be a viable solution to this problem.

The A/C compressor is most often mounted low on the right, which can create interference with some original frames, notably the First Generation Camaro and the '55-'57 Chevy. A notch will fix the problem as long as you can do it before painting. Most aftermarket frames allow more space in this critical area and your compressor will fit with less trouble.

You will find many differences in oil pans for the LS series motors because of their variety of uses in

Cadillacs, trucks, Camaros, and Corvettes. In fact, online investigation indicates that modified pans are often required for rear steer applications such as on the Camaros and the '55-'57s mentioned above. These pans are cast aluminum and can be easily modified by a skilled welder. The preferred Camaro rear-sump pan has now hit the market - reproduced by a number of companies.

Another little wrinkle is that there are three different crankshaft balancer lengths; on the truck, Camaro and 'Vette. The word is that the balancers swap OK but then you get into trouble having alignment problems with the rest of the serpentine drive.

All of these are great running engines with modern overdrive transmissions, self contained serpentine belt drives, and fuel injection; but more often than not they are kind of ugly with individual coils for each cylinder mounted on the valve covers. This is surely one reason for the recent popularity of engine covers which have been made specifically to hide all the topside plumbing and wiring. Of course the hardware can be relocated and the engines cleaned up but it is not an inexpensive process.

You'll want to do a lot more homework than usual before you buy an engine and then fit it to the chassis, or make mounts without the engine being on hand. This grey-beard remembers when the small block Chevy was really easy to mount since it only came in short and long water pump versions which were easily changed at that. But those days are over with the LS series motors. There are so many variables, what ifs, and exceptions that my chassis shop guys ask a lot of questions before fab work begins. Whenever possible, it's best to do the research first to find the combination with the fewest problems, and then have the engine on hand for the installation. When doing the work yourself, be sure to do the research and learn the details about motors. Many swap meet specials come with a murky past so you need to be able to spot them on sight rather than to rely on somebody else's description.

There are terrific sources of info out there in the aftermarket; mount kits, serpentine drives, oil pans and wiring kits abound. Review the magazine ads, talk to vendors at shows, and search the internet to get educated before putting up the bucks. At the risk of leaving someone out and/or offending them, I will mention that the real pioneers in the industry whose advice have been proven particularly trustworthy include Street and Performance, Vintage Air, Detroit Speed, The Detail Zone, and BRP Hot Rods.

Learning new things is an integral part of building a hot rod, and maybe one of the better rewards. New technology is a great way to break the "same old thing" mentality. The point here is that using these very excellent engines requires extra diligence on the part of the hot rodder, but pays major dividends out on the highway. And isn't that what hot rodding is all about anyway?

The Ford 5.4 Coyote engine is very wide and requires careful planning to fit, but provides remarkable power and torque.

Engine

Engine Oil Coolers

Another way to keep that V-8 Cool

When we talk about cooling a hot rod's engine, we tend to disregard the effect of the oil. In addition to its jobs of lubrication and cleaning the engine, the film of oil on engine parts also serves to carry away heat. Many heavy duty towing packages on our trucks include an engine cooler. Race cars and airplanes nearly always take advantage of this effect, so maybe we need to look closer as well.

We've discussed the difficulties of cooling the 500 inch Cadillac engine in my own '49 Chevy before. When preparing for another cruise across America, I added louvers to the hood to let trapped air escape, along with a metal shroud to replace the plastic one that actually sagged out of shape due to the heat! I also added an oil cooler, which seemed to have the greatest effect. Where the car used to run at 230 degrees at highway speed, it now runs at 185! The highest I've seen was 220 when shut down after a long, hard run.

It seems that as the day's drive continues, the large mass of the engine block and crankshaft picks up a lot of soaked in heat. Look at any block and you'll see that the water passages for coolant are concentrated at the top where combustion takes place. That leaves the oil to do the job on the bottom end.

It was pretty easy to pick up a cooler designed for engine oil at the local race car shop. Many sizes exist to fit your particular space. Don't try to use a trans oil cooler for the job as neither the fittings nor the cooler body itself are up to the pressures of engine oil. You'll want to get the cooler in a place where it gets direct airflow without sending waste heat into the radiator, which would be a self defeating location. On cars with a bulkhead mounted radiator, you should have room to put it to one side. It can be put under the car but airflow will be reduced and debris damage could cause a leak.

You'll also need an adaptor at the original oil filter location. Some simply screw on to provide ports for the hoses, but I really like the type made by Canton and some others that is held by a bolt, thus allowing the hose ports to be rotated to the most convenient angle. A few adaptors sandwich the hose section between the block and the oil filter which gives you the option of running two filters or adding only the cooler. I mounted mine with a simple adaptor (to help

> **Many towing packages on our trucks include an engine cooler. Race cars and airplanes nearly always take advantage of this effect ...**

with an accessibility clearance problem at the engine), and a separate oil filter mount on the inner fender panel. That allows easier oil changes as the filter is now the highest point in the system and little dripping occurs. It also puts the filter in the air coming through the radiator, carrying away a little extra heat. My system added almost a quart to the total oil capacity, which can only be helpful.

You can buy complete filter relocation kits and add the cooler in the lines. Just be sure to put the filter in line before the cooler to prevent clogging. These kits usually include black rubber hoses for connections. Be very sure whatever hose you use is rated for engine oil with its chemistry, heat, and pressure. I chose to use braided stainless steel covered hoses for their abrasion resistance, trick appearance, and the extra cooling the cover material supplies. The Nascar shop that helped me claimed an extra 10 degrees of cooling over plain rubber hoses. Reusable fittings are readily available to make your job of installing the hoses neatly much easier.

When you build your next hot rod, consider planning ahead for an oil cooler to avoid problems. It's not terribly expensive and provides a serious note to your engine's appearance. With winter downtime coming, maybe that's a good project for a road warrior too!

An engine oil cooler will perform admirably in reducing your engine's operating temperature and increase it's longevity as well.

Engine

Fuelish Choices or Carbs vs Injection

Simplicity and Nostalgia, or Precision?

Decisions-decisions-decisions! We all have to make many choices when building our Hot Rods. My own current project is a 32 Ford Highboy Sedan, with a small block Chevy disguised as a Hemi, complete with a fake Magneto (HEI guts) and a tunnel ram intake. I want it all - power, reliability, and good looks. Should I use a carburetor or fuel injection?

The carb is familiar and comfortable. I can work on it, with a little help. It's certainly good looking and nostalgic. The price is right, and all the linkages and connections are readily available and understood.

On the other hand, I've had plenty of carbs I wasn't in love with. Leaks, loading up, and poor idle qualities bug me. All the mechanical systems for acceleration and choke can be calibrated by an experienced, patient carb expert, which I'm not. The problem is that an automotive carb is limited by its design.

A carb can only meter fuel in relation to airflow, so it has to be set up at an average, compromise calibration. It cannot adjust itself for changes in humidity, temperature, and air pressure (altitude). A carb is often set rich to compensate, but that leads to less power with increased wear and pollution. The early Corvette fuel injection even has a hard time leaving the LA beaches for the High Sierras. Modern fuel injection can be more complex to install, needing a fuel return line, computer, several sensors, a special distributor and fuel pump. I've seen enough overheated, locked up pumps caused by our low Hot Rods. Mine's got to go in the tank, using the gas as a coolant (what a strange concept!), even though this adds a little more work to the installation. All this is unfamiliar, but enough tech support exists to put this new knowledge within reach.

> **A carb can only meter fuel in relation to airflow, so it has to be set up at an average ... it cannot adjust for changes in humidity, temperature, and air pressure.**

The injection is going to cost a little more than a carb, and I'm not too overly fond of computers. I'm remembering when HEI ignition and internally regulated alternators came along. We got used to them pretty quick, didn't we? Maybe the advantages of the injection will be worth the trouble too. These deals are "black box" hookups. I don't need to understand how the computer works. Just like A/C, I don't need to be a trained service technician to install the system. The after-market has plenty of support with linkages, cables, and wire harnesses to ease my re-education.

I'm not crazy about the look of many injection systems. Sure, they look trick on a high tech rod, but a Vette LT-1 looks so low it's lost in a tall hood line. There's a lot of sensors, wires, fuel rails, bells and whistles to hide too. (Maybe that's why a lot of these engines come with a full cover!) Perhaps I can get all the stuff on the passenger side of the engine that already is cluttered with A/C and heater hoses. For my nostalgia engine, maybe a throttle body injection mounted on a regular manifold will give me the look, but preserve the injection advantages.

I want the superior fuel atomization FI provides. To create a less powerful "trainer" division for sprint cars, they pull off the injection and install a carb. I want that extra power that injection provides. I want the system to run clean, giving me less wear and emissions. I like the fact that the computer automatically adjusts for temp, humidity, and pressure. I'll have a miniature tune-up expert constantly monitoring and adjusting fuel and ignition. His name is ECM (electronic control module) and he lives inside the computer. I also like the fact that every system I know of has a built-in back up closed loop system to get you home if part of the system fails. I've never yet seen a fuel injected Hot Rod overheat, due to the fuel mixture and ignition timing engine controls. We all like to avoid sitting in a pool of antifreeze!

I guess I've talked myself into it. I'm going to put a Holley digital control throttle body system on this 32. It should give me the look and performance I'm after. I'll let you know how it works out!

Electronically controlled Hilborn injection engineered by Imagine Injection Co. combines style second to none with amazing power, throttle response and mileage. It runs wonderfully well on the small block Chevy (disguised with Ardun valve covers) on my '34 Ford high-boy sedan.

Engine

Electric Fans

Why and How to Electrify your Fan

A proper engine cooling system is critical to the life of your engine and the enjoyment of your hot rod. Personally, I think that there are few things in rodding more stressful than sitting in traffic watching your temperature gauge rise, waiting for the boilover. Your air conditioning system has a hard time overcoming a too-hot radiator, and the condenser heat flow adds to the radiator's problems. You may have already invested in a top quality radiator that can take 15 psi in the system and added an overflow control system. The airflow has been properly routed, contained, and allowed a way out. You know that the best combination for top grade cooling is a big mechanical fan with a clutch and a shroud to channel the air, but there just isn't enough space without cutting up the firewall.

Or maybe you have a newer engine designed by the factory to run an electric fan. The question is; what type works best, and how do I mount and wire it?

As to fan type, let's first deal with fans designed to mount in front versus in back of the radiator. Yes, I know there are reversible types, but the more efficient blade airfoil shapes are very much directional. (more on that later) Model A and other early cars with an exposed radiator core just cannot run a fan in front. The fat fender cars like '37 Fords up thru the Fifties have room for an electric fan in front of the core, but there are downsides to that. The appearance can be less than great, but the real drawback is that they impede airflow. Once you get enough road speed that the air coming into the radiator has greater mass than the fan can move by itself, the fan becomes a blockage for that airflow. The A/C condenser gets blocked airflow, and is less efficient. Maintenance can be a real headache if you have to remove the grill to get to the fan. Front mounts certainly work, but are not the preferred position.

All those problems are minimized when the fans can be mounted to the rear side of the radiator. The condenser and the radiator receive fresh airflow in free air when at highway speed. It looks a little cleaner, and is much easier to service. At some speed, the fan cannot keep up with the ram air effect, which can be countered by having a thermostat and/or relay that stops the current supply when it's not needed. (We'll talk about that more when we get to the electrical portion of our program.) The better rear mounted fan units are built into a shroud that also mounts the fan, and have some clever rubber flaps incorporated. Those flaps open up at speed to allow the ram air to pass thru. A radiator with blocked exit flow is no more effective than one with blocked air entry.

Back to the blade design, the best and quietest fans have curved blades and are mounted in a ring with a mesh guard. We've seen tests where a fan with a ring around the circumference flows about 30% more air than one without the ring. Curved blades will be directional, with the blade shape optimized. Reversible fans have a blade shape that will work either way, but produce less flow. And, being a DC motor, they are perfectly content to run backwards if the power and ground feeds are swapped. You don't need the abuse your buddies will heap on you if they catch you with the fan running backwards!

You can buy fans with a shroud which provides both channeled airflow and a mounting surface. If they will fit your radiator core, that's probably the best way to go. The radiator suppliers often have their own line of electric fans proven to fit well. The fan can also be mounted to the radiator core using a metal bracket which is either screwed or Pop riveted to the edges of the core. Given the vibration that the fan works under, we find that stainless steel Pop rivets work best. They won't chew up like the aluminum rivets, or back out like screws will. Screws or Clecos will be fine as temporary fasteners during the fabrication of your car, but should be replaced by rivets on final assembly. BE VERY CAREFUL when drilling the holes!!! (voice of bad experience) You will be using a 1/8 inch drill bit for the holes, drilling along the narrow lip of the vertical steel band that surrounds the core. Before you drill, cut a short piece of 3/16 inch steel brake line to sleeve over the drill, leaving a minimum length of drill bit sticking out. Then the drill bit cannot pass thru the band lip and into your new, but now punctured radiator core.

Many fans come with easy to use and really ugly mount straps made from galvanized steel with multiple holes. The installation will look much better if you make a mount that picks up the fan body, and then fills the space over to the core side plates. A few holes or cutouts matching the mount outside shape adds a little class.

You'll often find that two small fans will cover the radiator better than one large one. It's also easier to work around a water pump nose with two offset fans. Another advantage is that one fan can be set to come on by a thermostat or manual/driver controlled switch, while the other is triggered by a higher set thermostat or a switch off the A/C clutch. The second then is only drawing power when needed.

It's also important to use a relay to power the fan. The bigger fans draw a lot of power, which puts too large a load on a direct operating switch and all the wire to get from the fan to the dash and back. Much better to use a relay, where the switching power signal comes from a manual switch on the dash, a trinary pressure switch on the A/C clutch, or a thermostat. Lighter gauge wire can easily handle the switching load, while 10 gauge wire can carry power from the battery post on your starter, through the relay, and on to the fan.

The relay also cures a couple of weird deals that used to come up when electric fans first came into usage. The high amperage draw of a cooling fan can overheat many common switches you might use while a relay limits that switch to carrying only signal amperage rather than the fan motor itself. The relay also separates the fan from the rest of the electrical system when it is not turned on. This is important because a DC motor becomes a DC generator when it is spinning without power input greater than the power output in its generator function. We used to have trouble with engines remaining running after the ignition switch was turned off. That was due to the spinning down fan continuing to supply ignition power to the distributor! Even stranger were the overcharged boiled over batteries which received excess charge from the unregulated electric fans. The fans would be spun by airflow at highway speed, and continue to pile power into the electrical system!

It can also be really handy to have the electric cooling fan relay wired to direct battery power rather than switched off with the ignition. This feature allows the fan to continue to run after the ignition is turned off and the key removed. If you have been caught in traffic and the car is running hot, it will cool down without having to keep the ignition on, leaving you time to get a drink and cool yourself down as well. It's easier on the radiator and hoses too, preventing a temperature spike or engine heat soak from a sudden shutdown. That's why new cars are wired this way. And just like the warning on the new cars, be aware that the fans can start without notice so watch your fingers.

Be sure your alternator is up to the total amperage load of the engine, A/C, radio, fans, phone charger, etc, etc, at idle speed. Check the specs and be sure that the idle RPM amperage is sufficient, as many of the cheaper imported alternators only reach their rated power at higher RPM levels. Belt diameter and the length of belt contact can affect the output as well, so you might want to stay away from "high performance" smaller diameter pulleys.

Like many jobs encountered in building a hot rod, adding electric cooling fans is fairly simple. With good attention to a few principles outlined above, you'll be able to select, install, and wire a set up that will make your rod a little more comfortable and reliable. You never now when the roads will be jammed with traffic back ups for construction on the way to your favorite rod run.

It's possible to fabricate a combination fan shroud and mount. In the case of this '40 Ford mount, the fan opening covers enough of the core to allow free air flow without extra holes. Note also that the fan is the best type with an exterior ring and directional curved blades for best airflow.

Engine

Out with the Bad Air!

Headers: Faster AND Cooler

Every system interrelates in a street rod, just like any mechanical device. The exhaust system can be an aid in proper cooling, maximum mileage, power, and that special "head turner" exhaust note. Done wrong, it can also have a negative effect, which we'll try to avoid.

It's important to fit the exhaust system while you're in the mockup stage. Along with wheel selection, chassis stance, air conditioning, and linkage, the exhaust system should be done early to check clearances, and to handle any welding or drilling necessary to mount the system. The muffler man won't be beating up your freshly painted chassis, and you'll have time to paint, polish, or ceramic coat the pipes while doing the paint and body work.

Some folks like headers for clearance, with hot rod looks and performance. A tuned set of headers looks really racy, but be aware that they're often a difficult fit, and tend to produce extra power only in a narrow RPM range they're tuned for. That's great on a racecar that runs, or is shifted at a specific RPM, but not all that useful on a streetcar. A healthy small block works fine with 1 5/8 inch primary pipes, but the 1 7/8 inch race headers will actually hurt torque production.

A lot of rodders prefer the common block hugger headers. Different manufacturer's route the pipes in number of unique ways, one of which may be just the ticket for your application. There is also a flat collector type, which arranges the primary tubes and collector, like the palm and fingers of your hand, for improved clearance.

Good old reliable cast iron manifolds are commonly used, with the '60s-'70s "Ram's Horn" center dump most popular on Chevy small blocks. A really handy variation is the '67-'72 Chevy PU manifold, which rolls the flange inward, and back at 45 degrees for much easier steering hookup. Cast manifolds tend to be quieter, and make decent power. Perhaps the neatest deal is cast iron headers, which provide improved flow along with improved clearance and a quieter cockpit.

> **The exhaust pipes themselves should be as large as possible, with a minimum of 2 inches on small blocks, and 2 1/2 inches on big blocks.**

The exhaust pipes themselves should be as large as possible, with a minimum of 2 inches on small blocks, and 2 1/2 inches on big blocks. Heavier gauge pipes sound better and bend with less kinking. Bends quiet the tone, but excessively tight bends or kinks really impede flow and cause heat buildup. Straightening out the over axle bends by going under the axle was worth about 10 degrees on my 500 Caddy powered '49 Chevy. A good muffler man knows to lubricate the dies and pipe, and to go slow to avoid collapsed bends. Even 14 gauge stainless can be bent on standard muffler machines using these tips.

Stainless pipes are still the ultimate, lasting forever and polishable, yet they tend to radiate more heat, cost more, and can sound "tinny" if too light at gauge is used. Most shops now carry aluminized steel pipe, which is coated with aluminum inside and out. They are simpler to weld, sound very good, and are inexpensive. You can also use standard pipe, and send it out for ceramic coating. The coating tends to hold heat in, releasing it out the tailpipe to help control under car temps.

Turbo style oval mufflers seem to be the most popular these days, with a nice tone and generally good clearances. Flowmaster pioneered the pulse reversion style oval muffler, which silences using carefully placed baffles rather than packing. These have a unique tone, often heard on your neighbor's kid's 5.0 Mustang. A great many folks also build straight through tubular mufflers, which provide the classic "glasspack" sound, although most use more durable packing today. They take up less space, and tend to produce excellent power. Smaller versions work well as tip resonators to civilize the exhaust note.

A nice set of polished stainless tips finish our system off nicely. I like a turned-down tip for quiet, and deflecting corrosive exhaust away from those expensive new bumpers. Straight tips and megaphone styles really provide a wicked hot rod tone, but can be a little ratty for more conservative rodders. To keep the inside quiet, be sure to exit the exhaust completely past the end of your car to avoid under car resonance. Side exhaust can get a little noisy, which is great if that's what you want.

A neat trick my local guy uses is to increase the pipe size a 1/2 inch for the last 30 inches or so. That increased cross section creates lower pressure due to expansion, which lowers the tone to that "Chriscraft" motor boat sound, and possibly creates some scavenging.

If clearances get tight, consider making simple aluminum heat shields, or wrapping the pipes with heat insulation from the racecar shop, both of which are retained with simple hose clamps. I've had great success with heat wrap decreasing floor heat transfer. The heat stays in the pipes and the exhaust actually feels hotter out back.

Be sure to re-tighten all the header and collector flanges after a good hard run, and repeat at least twice. Don't get carried away, just try for a good preload. When they're hot the bolts stretch, and will stay tight when cooled. Copper gaskets are now available for troublesome header and collector flanges, but be aware that constantly blowing regular gaskets is a good sign of excessive back pressure downstream.

Poor exhaust design is a strong cause of high engine or cockpit temps. Excessive back pressure can cause high speed cooling problems, shutoff heat soak, and poor fuel ratio through cylinder charge contamination.

You want the heat going away from the car to unload the cockpit, giving that neat new air conditioner a chance to work to its full potential on your next trek to a rod run!

> **Along with wheel selection, chassis stance, air conditioning, and linkage, the exhaust system should be done early to check clearances…**

Steering

Explaining Ackerman

Why you need Toe-Out on Turns

When front suspension design is discussed, the Ackerman principle seems to inevitably come up. There appears to be some confusion as to how proper Ackerman is designed into a system, and the effect that improper design has on the suspension function. Ackerman principle involves manipulating how the front tire's toe in changes when the wheels are rotated to turn the car's direction. We have seen improper use of this principle creating problems on some factory designs, and on Hot Rods with modified IFS (Independent Front Suspension) and lately with suicide perch straight axles on nostalgia themed rods.

This Ackerman guy was an Austrian carriage designer from the 1700s, who had a problem with the lightweight wheels of his sporting carriages folding up under heavy use. He realized that the excess stress on the wheels was generated when the wheels did not track smoothly through the turn. First one wheel, then the other had to slide sideways to "keep up" with the path of the vehicle. He found that the commonly used simple pivoting axle didn't work right, because the inner wheel has to turn tighter, or toe out, in order to track properly in a turn. The necessary toe out in a turn became his focus.

Mr. Ackerman's research showed him that a more complex linkage using tie rods, and pivoting spindles with specially designed steering was necessary. The outer tie rod end pivot must lie on a line passing through the center of the rear end and the kingpin (lower ball joint on an IFS). That means a front steered system requires the tie rod pivot to be outboard of the lower ball joint, and inboard for rear steer.

Some designs violate this concept, compromising the tire contact patch by creating toe in during a turn, causing loss of traction. Since the effect is greatest at extreme turn angles, skinny tires mask the effect while fat tires magnify the problem. Hot rodders get in trouble when we decide to swap steering arms to relocate the steering, such as normally rear steered Corvairs with front steer Pinto racks, rear steered Mustang II. This often occurs with nostalgia rods and T-buckets with early Ford spindles converted to a front tie rod, as is often used with a suicide perch mounting.

By swapping the spindles side from side with the tie rod in front, the suicide perch design allows the car to sit lower, avoiding the rear steer system problem where the tie rod interferes with the frame rail bottom, and often the radius rods as well. You'll find that these cars often exhibit a lot of tire scrub in a turn, and understeer badly due to that constant skidding of one tire or another. Harking back to Mr. Ackerman's problem with folding up front wheels, the early T buckets with skinny wire wheels often failed the same way. Stronger wheels, and wire wheels with a wider hub for better spoke triangulation helped. Even better, Total Performance, being one of the T bucket design leaders, redesigned their steering arms to greatly reduce this problem.

Although it's probably not possible to completely correct the Ackerman with commonly used spindles on straight axles, you can improve the situation greatly with a little work. Since most common axle spindles are forged, their steering arms can be heated and bent to get the outer tie rod end as far out as possible, without interfering with the wheels.

You will be pleasantly surprised at how such a small change will improve the car's handling.

We see this reversed Ackerman geometry causing trouble in some factory cars, notably the '64-'72 Chevelle and the '78-'87 G-body Monte Carlo/Malibu/S-10 suspensions. When pushed hard, these cars display pretty serious understeer due to the reversed Ackerman causing a loss of turning traction, as well as a very poor camber curve due to the too-short spindle height and improperly angled upper control arm. These are all front steer, and the designers had to limit how far outboard the outer tie rod end could be located and still clear the wheel. If your wheel and brake combination allows the space to heat and bend the steering arm outward as discussed earlier, you will be making a worthwhile improvement.

I was surprised to see that many Indy car chassis and some NASCAR designs exhibit reversed Ackerman. A suspension expert on A.J. Foyt's team explained to me that since steering angles were so small during normal racing that the reversed Ackerman presented less a problem than the spindle and shorter A arm design that would have been required for correct Ackerman. Further, I found that the NASCAR short track designs, where steering angles tend to be much greater, use a different design, since the performance requirements and relative importance of geometry features are different. In other words, those race car designers were faced with the same necessary space and design compromises made by the OEM designers and hot rodders working at home.

So, you can indeed drive a car with reversed Ackerman, it will not handle as well or be as safe in an emergency maneuver as one with correct Ackerman. Why not spend a little time checking out your ride and building it better?

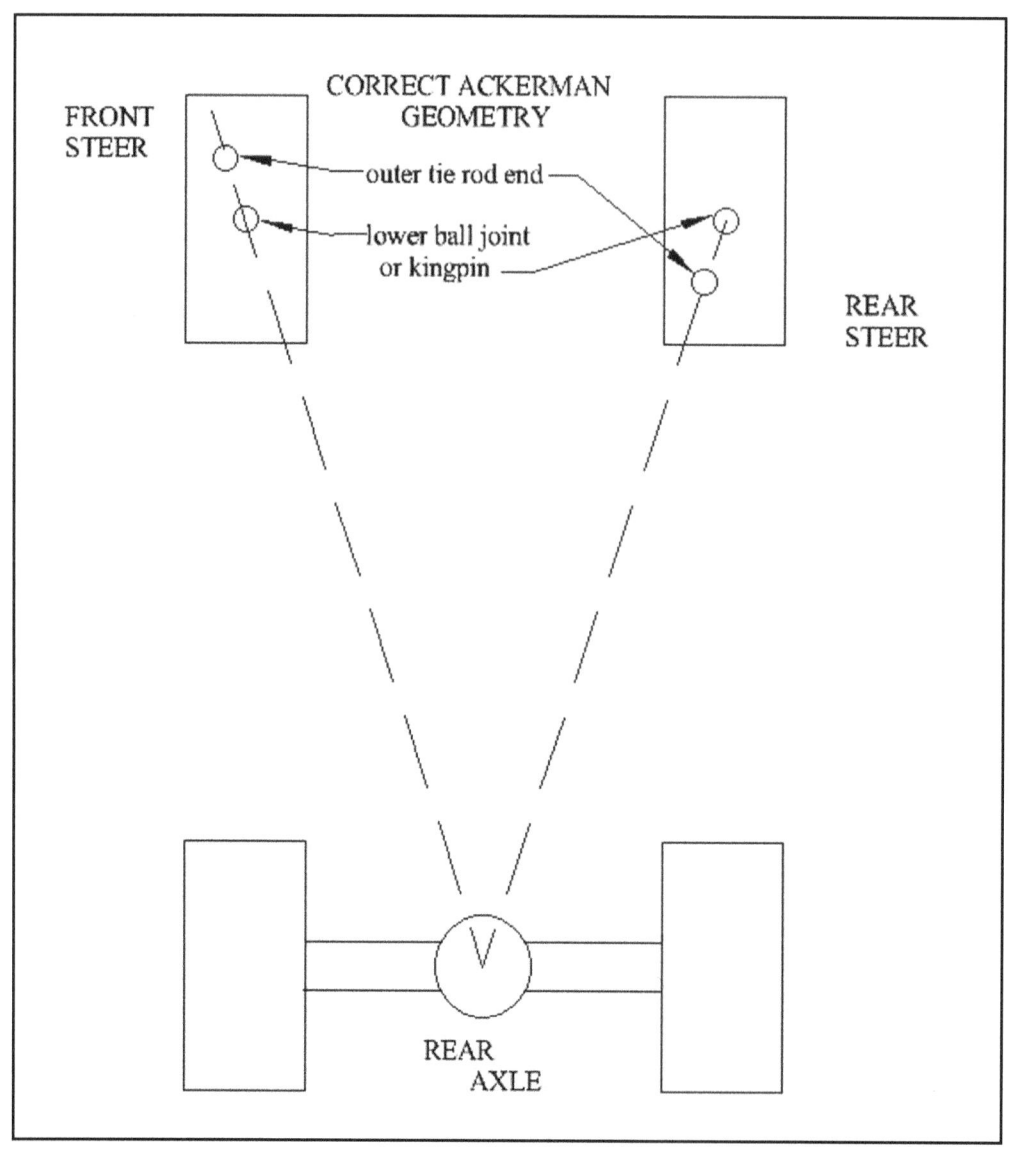

Proper Ackerman design allows your wheels to properly track through a turn without skidding thus enhancing safety and handling while minimizing tire wear.

Steering

What is Bumpsteer?

How to Avoid those unplanned Changes in Direction

Bumpsteer is a term that gets thrown around a lot when suspension designs are discussed. It is not a vibration felt in the steering wheel, but rather a change in the direction a car wants to go when a bump is encountered without the driver turning the steering wheel. It can also be felt as a "jerk" of the steering wheel if the road wheel changing direction force is strong enough. A real world example is a car that wants to dart left or right as it crosses the dips common to each end of a bridge on the Interstate.

The tern really describes a change in the toe-in (or out) that occurs when a suspension goes through its normal, and necessary, vertical travel which absorbs road bumps or body roll in a turn.

It is caused by a design which fails to keep the motions and effective lengths of the steering and suspension properly coordinated. To understand that statement we need to first be sure we understand how any bar that swings in a radius has a change in its effective length - the length as measured in a perfectly horizontal sense a vertical motion takes place. To boil that down in a more understandable way, think of any bar (be it a steering tie rod or a suspension control arm) as a radius that moves within a circle whose radius matches the true length of that bar. The nearby illustration is intended to make that point graphically.

Solid axle rear suspensions can exhibit roll steer, which is different from bumpsteer, and which we have discussed in another article, regarding the proper set up of leaf springs and radius rods. The roll steer that can result from an improperly designed four bar is actually a good example of this Arc Length Theory in action causing a rear axle to get cocked in the chassis as body roll develops (see the article in the Suspension chapter). That movement out of square causes an uncommanded steering effect similar to bumpsteer but caused by the improper design of the real axle control system.

Solid axle front suspensions can exhibit bumpsteer, especially in a vintage style steering system. As we relive the build styles of the past we also get to relive the bygone days of bad geometry. With cross steering (think Vega or original '40 Ford) or side steering (think original '47-'54 Chevy PU) the drag link connecting to the spindle has to have its length and angle carefully coordinated with those of the dual leaf springs or radius rods which position the front axle. The basic premise is that the steering drag link should be as long and as parallel as possible to the member that locates the axle. There just isn't enough space here to fully explain and illustrate that principle, but the Pete and Jake's catalog/website (as well as other websites) has really excellent drawings that will help you. The situation is slightly different for wishbone radius rods, four bars and hairpins and they do a great job detailing those.

Just to cover the idea of rack and pinion steering on a straight axle quickly, you will find that a frame-mounted rack will have major bumpsteer problems. That can be eliminated by mounting the rack directly on the axle but then you would need a sliding joint connecting the rack to the steering column. The length of the steering connection changes as the suspension travels, and getting a slide connection that is also very precise in a rotational sense has always been a problem. It has been tried, but without a lot of long-term success.

Independent suspensions have a more complex design that requires care to work properly with no bumpsteer. You cannot just put together any old combination of spindle, control arm, rack & pinion and tie rod length/angle and expect it to work right out on the road. Your arrangement may look good in the shop, but the first bump will let you know if a modified design is going to drive correctly. Changing rear steer spindles to front steer, adding rack & pinion to a suspension it wasn't designed for; and relocating control arm positions are just some of the common pitfalls that can cause bumpsteer.

The drawing below can be studied to help understand proper design for an independent suspension. It depicts an IFS (Independent Front Suspension) but applies to IRS (Independent Rear Suspension) just as well if you realize that an IRS - which uses a tie rod to maintain toe in (think C-4 and later Corvette) - acts the same in terms of bumpsteer as an IFS that is rolling straight ahead. The drawing also depicts an IFS whose control arm pivots are parallel to one another.

Many modern suspensions such as Classic Camaros and Chevelles have their control arms skewed inward to the rear. If you can mentally look in at an angle so that you are looking straight in at the control arm pivot axis, the drawing still works. You can also note that the labels of the components can change. The '57-'68 Ford Galaxie IFS has the lower control arm and tie rod positions switched without really changing how the geometry works. The critical point is to understand how the control arm and tie rod positions and lengths

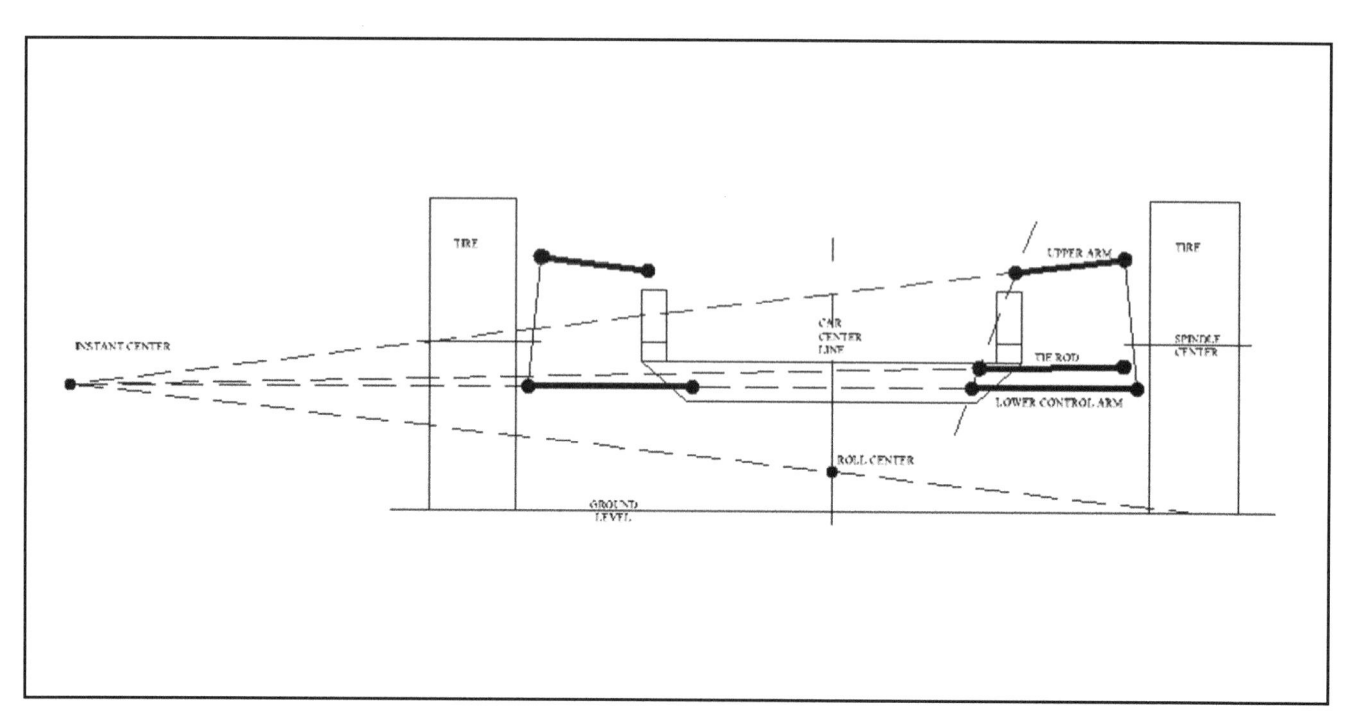

This drawing depicts the basic geometry needed to produce a "No Bumpsteer IFS" system: After plotting the positions of the inner and lower pivot points of the control arms and tie rod, those arm lines are extended until they meet at a point called the Instant Center. Note that the inner pivots of all three arms must be on an essentially vertical line. Those crossing lines will be used to find the correct location of the inner tie rod pivot if you are designing a rack and pinion steering system. After the IC is determined, you can find the height of the roll center by connecting a line to the center of the tire. The roll center is found where that line crosses the car's center line.

interact by applying the Arc Length Theory.

Begin by finding the lower control arm inner and outer pivot points. Then do the same for the upper control arm and tie rod. Next extend those arm positions as shown by the dashed lines. When properly arranged those lines will coincide at a point known as the Instant Center. That is the theoretical center of rotation for all three IFS members. Finishing that line of thought, roll center is found by connecting the Instant Center to the center of the tire patch on the opposite side of the car. The roll center height is where that line crosses the center of the car.

The next condition to accomplish zero bumpsteer is to have all the inner pivots of all three IFS members on the same roughly vertical line in order to coordinate their actions. It really isn't too much more complicated than that. But you can see that if a rack with the wrong inner pivot dimensions is used, the upper control arm shortened or angle changed, or if a spindle with a different outer tie rod end height is used, things go bad quickly. Any change that moves the 6 critical pivot points of this system will degrade its performance. Don't feel too badly if you have made any of these errors as many OEM designs aren't correct either. Our industry is full of companies who specialize in correcting the OEM deficiencies.

A lot of those design faults have to do with the advancement in tire technology. A 1965 Mustang has about as bad a suspension design as you could find, but with skinny bias ply tires and 140 horsepower this wasn't a problem. Add a couple hundred horsepower and some 9 inch tread width sticky 17 inch tires and you will experience the joys of major league bumpsteer very quickly as tire wear and drivability suffer as the greater tire grip magnifies the design faults.

> **The tern really describes a change in the toe-in (or out) that occurs when a suspension goes through its normal, and necessary, vertical travel.**

It is also true that many early IFS designs such as the first generation Camaros and Chevelles have problems as well. They use quite a short spindle that results in the upper control arm going downhill toward the wheel, making for some not too good geometry and roll center issues. GM fixed this with the second design versions of those cars largely through the use of a much taller spindle. The aftermarket has also responded with several manufacturers supplying a dropped spindle that is also taller in terms of ball joint height. This lowers the car, revises the roll center and transfers weight to the inside of a turn by leaning the tires into a turn rather than outboard. The lowered upper control arm positions used in the Camaro "Guldstrand Mod" and the "Shelby Mustang Mod" are other examples of good changes to the upper control arm angle problem.

That discussion is getting off the bumpsteer subject we began with, but we are trying to make the point that any modifications have to be clearly understood and accounted for in the IFS design. When you decide that a rack and pinion conversion is warranted for header clearance or weight reduction, be sure that the geometry will be correct. The inner tie rod end position is critical in both left to right and height in relation to the control arm pivot points. Forget the old racer's adage that tie rods need to be level to avoid bumpsteer. The drawing clearly shows that just isn't true. Don't lower a rack & pinion to clear an engine, raise the engine out of the way. It doesn't run any differently with a change of position but the steering sure does.

Finally, for the guys working with the first '40s to '50s IFS systems that used a two piece spindle with a kingpin, the drawing has to be altered in a sense. These designs typically have the outer tie rod end and the lower outer trunnion pin at the same height. Similarly, the inner control arm and tie rod pivots are at their own same height, which is not necessarily the same height as the outer pivots. Think of a sheet of plywood with a piano hinge on one side which represents the inner pivot axis of the lower control arm and tie rod. Since the outer pivot points match each others heights, they can be represented as being on the opposite edge of our sheet of plywood. If you erase the tie rod from our drawing above, our new situation is properly depicted. That plywood now serves as a plane that rotates the same way as the suspension and steering system, and since there can never be a relative change in the lengths of the lower arm and tie rod, no bumpsteer can occur.

This points out why it is essential to lower the outer tie rod end to match the raised height resulting from using a dropped upright to lower the car.

The steering arm is now bolted to a spindle that has been raised 2 1/2 inches, thus putting the outer tie rod end 2 ½ inches too high with regard to the suspension. The steering arm must therefore be replaced with one with the proper drop, or an original steering arm heated and bent down to return the outer tie rod end to its original height with respect to the lower control arm out pivot. That is confusing to read but will make sense when you think it through in light of the drawing.

One thing that should be obvious by now is that it is hard to fully explain suspension and steering geometry in a short essay such as this. But hopefully you have learned enough to want to learn more and to be in a better position to choose a suspension and steering system that will make your Hot Rod ride and handle exactly as you wish!

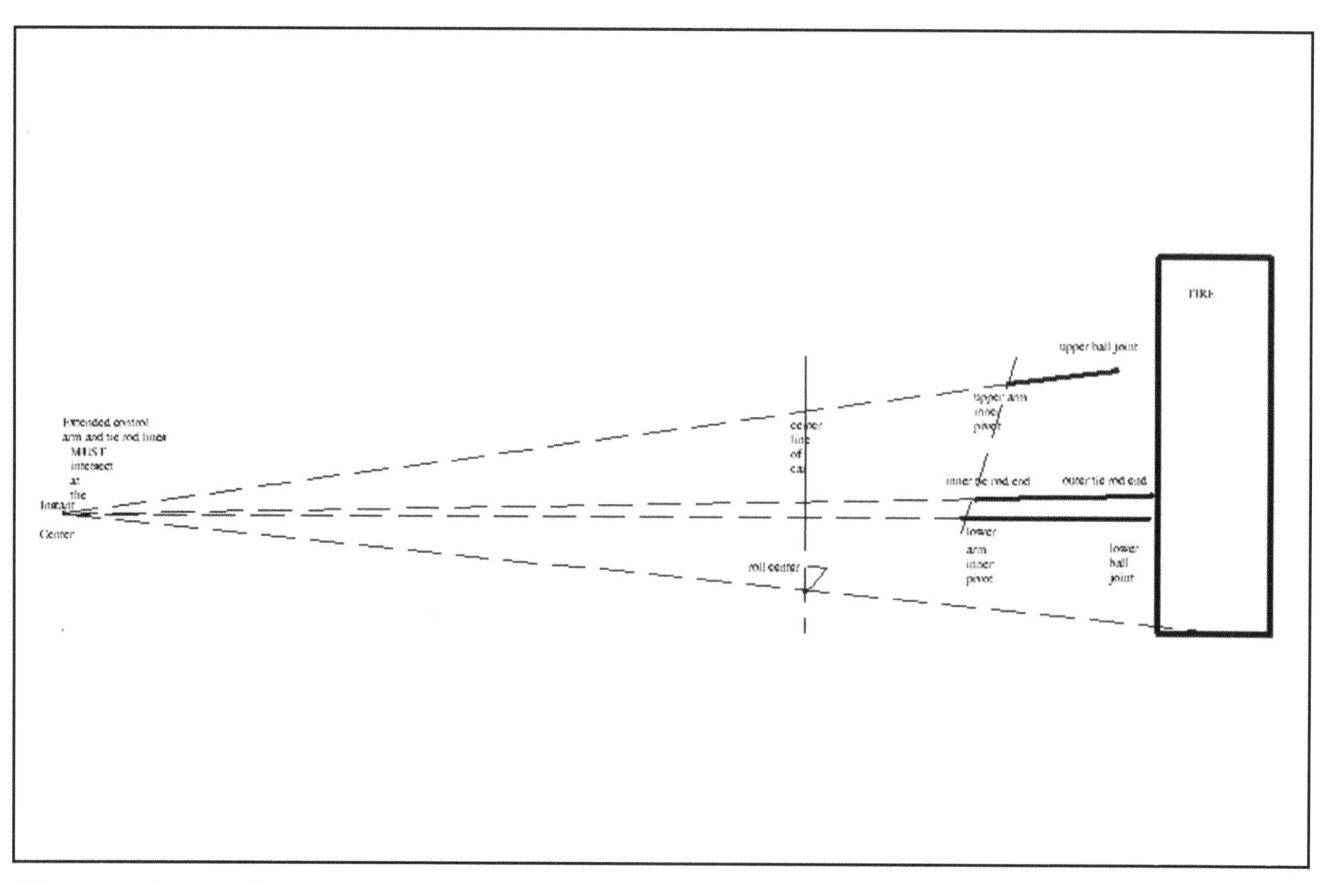

This somewhat simpler drawing depicts the basic principles involved in an IFS design that avoids bumpsteer in order to provide steering action controlled by the driver rather than the chassis.

Steering

Installing Steering Columns

Do it the Easy Way

This topic is very close to the heart of Ken Callison, our guest expert. Ken founded ididit, inc. and is widely known as the originator of custom columns for Hot Rods. Ken contributed a few ideas to pass along and make your tilt column installation as simple as possible. Adjustability in the column angle can really be an aid to driver comfort, as the best column position for fit and steering connection clearance won't always be the best for the driver. We'll provide some tips on selecting and mounting tilt columns.

Before we get into custom installations, remember that specially engineered column and mounting kits are available for most of the '55 and later cars. By making these kits with options for fitting to either stock or aftermarket steering box systems, your job of adding a modern and not worn out tilt column is much easier. The proper mounts and couplers make these a simple one-Saturday job in most cases. Why beat your head against the wall reinventing something that has already been done for you.

For a more custom installation on a typical earlier Hot Rod, you'll want a steering column that puts the steering wheel in a comfortable position, with the driver in the seat and the column head set straight. This means that you must have already mounted your seats and bought the steering wheel and adaptor you plan on using. Hold the steering wheel, with column adaptor mounted, and have a buddy measure from the lower end of the adaptor to the floor. Then add a few inches to get through the floor for the first U-joint. You generally want a minimum sticking through, but be sure to allow space if you're using a column shift. A sketch of the angle and mount positions will be handy later, as will digital photos.

Tilt columns are almost a necessity. Different drivers are easily accommodated, and proper fit can be had without settling for an awkward steering wheel position. Telescopic columns are not so good on smaller cars, since they do exactly the wrong thing. When collapsed, they're about the same length as a standard column, and then they get longer, not shorter. That can be great in a '40 Buick, but not too handy in a Model A.

There's quite a variety of dash mounts available. The ones that swivel for different column angles are particularly helpful. Your earlier mock up work can help you know how much drop is needed in the dash mount. You can also fabricate a mount with 1/8 inch sheet, boxed and welded to the column, and bolted to the dash. Be sure to allow a notch for the switch-actuating rod, and weld from the back side for a very clean installation. The original mounting lugs on a factory GM column are almost always too far away from the dash to use, making a cleaner and new aftermarket column worth a good look. If your dash is fiberglass, be sure to add a metal lower bar on the backside to handle the stress of turning the steering wheel. Tying the dash into the firewall with an additional bracket will be a wise move as well.

The simplest type of lower column mount duplicates the original column dust plate in 1/8 inch steel plate, and provides a tab to mount the column with a radiator hose clamp which is neatly hidden by your carpet. For a real clean mount, use a short piece of tubing that allows the lower end of the column to fit inside. Weld that tube to the firewall and slide the column into it. There are also some really nice aftermarket lower mounts which adapt the column to the toe board angle. The "eyeball" style, rotates to match the column angle, maintaining an excellent seal, and looking great.

GM-derived new and original columns are used most often, since Ford columns generally have lower ends that won't accept street rod U-joints easily. Common GM U-joints are 1-inch X 48 splines, 1-inch X DD (two flat sides) or 3/4 inch X 36 splines. You'll need to identify yours. Don't worry about your column having a shift indicator since screw-on or glue-on indicators are readily available in the street rod market. Be sure to identify the electrical connector for the turn signals, you'll need to know that to order the correct wiring kit. Ken says a common problem is misunderstanding the black horn wire. Do not put power to that wire! The horn is powered through a relay, fused separately. The black wire on the column provides a ground through the horn button, which activates that relay.

Another little trick Ken brought me up to speed on has to do with cancelling turn signals. After the column is mounted, the u-joint must be connected in such a way that, with the road wheels straight ahead, the blips on the horn cam must point to the 10:30 position, as viewed from the driver's seat. The horn cam is a plastic piece, somewhat funnel shaped, which has a flat brass ring on it to provide the horn pin contact. Correct position assures that the left and right signals will cancel equally.

It's not rocket science, but common sense with a little education - like everything on a Hot Rod. We'll try to keep steering you straight!

After you have measured the correct length for your new steering column, hold it in place to start the design of new mounting brackets.

Suspension

Air Ride Suspension Systems

In the Weeds and Good Handling to Boot

This sport has seen a major addition to our suspension options since the Mid '90s. The use of air suspension had been tried by brave pioneers before and since then, but it's a fair statement that Bret Voelkel and his gang at Air Ride Technologies have set the pace in this area. In fact, they have led so clearly that air suspension is generally referred to as "Air Ride" in conversation, as it will be in this column. It's like the brand name "Kleenex" becoming the generic name for a product. There are other companies doing good work with air suspension and control systems, so check them out too. The best companies have no problem being compared to worthy competitors. We at Fatman Fab have worked with Air Ride extensively since the beginning and have learned much by their input. As Bret says, "we have a dumpster load of ways we learned how NOT to do it."

That experience is really what you buy from any manufacturer, for any product, so that you don't have to reinvent the wheel on your own. Since this subject hasn't been discussed in this column for several years, with new rodders and new technology coming aboard, it's time for a fresh look at the subject. This can be the subject of a small book, but I think we can boil it down to some basic ideas. You are also encouraged to get ANY manufacturer's catalog and speak with their tech reps at the nearest Goodguys show.

There are some basic physics involved in any lowered Hot Rod. Factory cars are built tall with lots of suspension travel. That allows soft spring rates to be used for soft suspension deceleration rates and little fear of reaching the limits of the suspension, even with varying loads. When we lower that same car, we have to control (decelerate) the same amount of weight (mass) in half the distance. The inescapable fact is that our backs then are subjected to twice the "G" force, which we perceive as twice as harsh a ride quality. If the suspension travels far enough to bottom out on the bump stops or shocks, that suspension travel comes to an immediate stop, and "G" force becomes infinite. Big factory cars ride better than small Hot Rods because they have longer wheelbases, more mass, and generally more suspension travel. The facts of physics are immovable, regardless of opinions or advertising. Anyone who tells you a '32 Ford can literally ride like a Cadillac is engaging in exaggeration or self deception.

We can improve our chances of excellent ride quality through the use of proper design and construction. You must have sufficient tire to fender clearance and enough suspension travel. Air Ride will not cure poor design, nor help with harsh ride caused by overly stiff control arm bushings and short sidewall tires. Those are part of the suspension too. A bottomed out suspension won't work any better or worse with Air Ride, since it effectively has no springs at that point. Any suspension will work at its best within a certain range of its travel.

When Air Ride first came out, it was seen as a way to park a car at a stance lower than you would dare to drive it, or "frame surfing". It will still do that and do so safely if the guidelines are followed. Raising and lowering your vehicle are just a happy coincidence of air suspension. You must be certain to use a bumpstop on the sleeve type air springs to prevent damage to them and to keep the shocks from bottoming and being damaged. The double convoluted air springs used on independent suspensions have enough wall thickness to serve as their own bumpstop. You must not attempt to drive the car this way, as safe ball joint angles may be exceeded and alignment will be incorrect. Independent suspensions will exhibit negative camber due to the differences in control arm length and angles. Attempts to maintain zero camber with equal length control arms have been built, and will result in a car that looks better laid down at the expense of proper handling at ride height.

The real advances in Air Ride systems have come from its use to provide an adjustable suspension. We can draw an analogy to fuel injection, which constantly alters the fuel delivery and ignition curves to match the instantaneous conditions. The use of air suspension and adjustable shocks in either their separate, or combined Shockwave function allows the rodder to alter suspension damping along with air spring rate according to current conditions. You can quickly compensate for a load of luggage or a couple of friends in the back seat. I use Shockwaves in the back of my '34 Ford Highboy sedan to carry just me one day, and three guys and our weekend luggage another. Of course, all this adjustability also lets the less careful amongst us get out of the "window" of proper suspension ride height, a common cause of trouble.

Progressive coil springs; from pick ups to station wagons, including some coil overs and leaf springs, can provide a variable-rate suspension too, but cannot be quickly altered to suit. Air Ride does so at the touch of a button so you don't have to change springs repeatedly until you hit the right combination. That's expensive and a lot of work. Many rear coil springs are formed with a beehive-shaped end that cannot be trimmed to dial in ride height. An Air Ride conversion for the rear of any

Separate mounting of the air spring and an external shock makes for an economical front suspension with excellent ride and handling.

104

coil sprung vehicle is so easy to do that any other option is hard to justify.

This variability can also be used to alter handling qualities. You can make a cruiser-capable suspension act much more precise by working with the air pressures and shock settings, and then dial them back for the ride home. Air Ride has proven this dozens of time with their Autocross adventures. Cars never have equal weight on all four corners, this being easily handled by adjustments to pressure. You can preload, or "wedge" the chassis for a little drag racing. The point is, a turn of a dial on a shock and the push of a button lets you totally change the characteristics of your Hot Rod chassis!

Just as with any type of spring, improved shock absorbers and sway bars pay big dividends in handling improvement, especially on the nose heavy Muscle cars of the '60s. The very compliance that makes Air Ride work so well also requires better control to work at its best. The earliest control systems only split pressure fore and aft, not separating left from right. This could lead to pressure transfer from side to side during cornering, which actually increases body roll. You should not even consider a control system that doesn't separate each wheel's pressure with its own separate solenoid valve.

The ultimate evolution of Air Ride control systems combine separation of the corners with ride height control. By sensing and varying both ride height and air spring pressure, the proper driving (and aligned at) suspension height is preserved regardless of load. And they generally also allow other preset levels such as dumped for the fairgrounds and raised to get in and out of trailers. The really cool deal is that the four-wheel separate system can be upgraded to ride control or remote operation as a later "plug and play" option.

Shockwaves with their integral shock absorber make for a very clean installation without the need for separate shock absorber brackets.

You also have choices between separate air springs and shocks, or the unitized Shockwaves. The separate units are less expensive, but aren't as compact or attractive as the Shockwaves. The Shockwave offers unparalleled ease of installation, a very clean appearance, and a standard adjustable shock. Much of the air spring's capability over the hard riding old air shocks lies in the fact that they are high volume, low pressure to allow compressibility. Since the general rule is to use the largest air spring that will fit, it follows that the same air spring with a shock mounted thru it loses a little volume. That may actually tip the scale in terms of ride quality toward the separate units.

Another issue in air spring selection may be the total travel available. Independent suspensions typically have the spring of any type mounted about halfway from the lower control arm inner pivot to the tire contact center. That 2:1 leverage works both for and against us. A spring rate twice that of the necessary direct acting wheel rate must be used, but only half as much spring travel is required. A 4 inch stroke shock will allow around 8 inches of wheel travel. Not so in the rear on a typical direct acting spring, where 4 inches of travel is 4 inches at the wheel as well. If you are set up properly, you'll have about 2-1/2 inches of compression travel and 1-1/2 for extension. That is what you see on most coil-overs and rear Shockwaves, and is barely sufficient. The only way to get more travel is to lower the bottom mount, which generally violates scrub line limits. The upper mount can be raised in some cases, as we do in our 5-inch-travel '55-'57 Chevy chassis, but floor modifications and rear seat space limitations on other applications often make this difficult.

The problem is that the adjustability of Air Ride can allow you to run out of that proper travel setting. Run too low for style or a big load and you bottom out. Run too high and your shoulders feel the sudden stop. Both can break parts. You can see where careful manual control, or automated ride control, are important. Our '67 F100 shop truck works for a living and hauls trailers with Shockwaves all around. They have held up well, except for when we failed to add enough air for a load. With the Ride Height Control system added now, we can control the Shockwave mounted height and avoid damage. And we dial up the shocks for a load and dial them back when taking it on a cruise night.

The most important points for selecting and installing air suspension are covered in the literature in their catalog and instructions. Phone techs will always be happy to assist you. The MOST important thing is to actually READ the darn instructions! (Which is a common problem with many manufacturers of Hot Rod parts.) Be sure to select air springs that are rated for the weight of your vehicle, with the necessary travel. Build the bracketry to allow for that proper suspension travel. Be very certain that the air spring is mounted at the proper height at the driving chassis ride height so that proper pressures are being used. NEVER let the air springs rub on ANYTHING! Be sure to use DOT quality fittings, cut the plastic feed lines dead square, and use thread sealer tape on the pipe fittings to avoid system leakage.

Much of the fun in building a Hot Rod lies in learning to use technology to get the car sitting and driving your way. Just as gas, MIG, TIG, and stick welding all have their uses, Air Ride is another great option for suspending your project. It's not a cure-all any more than any other type of suspension, but it can do things no other choice can. The easy tuning allowed by the combined use of adjustable shocks and air springs will let you define, and change at will, the very personality of your ride.

> **Much of the fun in building a Hot Rod lies in learning to use technology to get the car sitting and driving your way.**

Suspension

Arc Length Theory

Why an Axle moves up - and Forward at the Same Time

Summer is almost here, with the Goodguys Nationals about to begin. One of the things I really enjoy (and hope you do too) is the opportunity to conduct Suspension Theory and Application Seminars at several events. We never use this as an opportunity to promote our products, but rather as a forum to discuss and teach Hot Rod chassis design, parts selection and usage.

There is one central concept to understanding nearly any automotive geometry question. Whether you're dealing with valve trains, throttle or shift linkage, or suspension, you must first clearly understand Arc Length Theory.

When a control link moves, it swings in an arc, whose radius is dictated by its length from the pivot point to the end in motion. As it swings it changes the effective length due to that natural radius, Depending on how the mounting points relate to each other, that length change can be equal in either direction, or longer one way and shorter the other. That's how independent suspension can be designed to lean the tires into the corner for better handling. Manipulating the changes in length, the pivot points, and how the links relate to each other, are how we can control the motion of the parts mounted on those links.

An application of that system would be '37 – '40 Ford hood hinges. That hinge is actually a four-bar system which often suffers from poor fit, especially on the passenger side. By lengthening the rear strap 3/16 inch on '39 – '40, and shortening it 3/16 inch on '37 – '38, the hoods fit properly. What we've done is use the arc length theory to raise the hood's motion, something that no amount of adjusting seems to cure. A similar change occurs when hood hinges get bent. Since bending the links changes their effective length, the hood no longer is controlled as the designer intended and the hood doesn't fit the opening as it should. That change in the control of a moving object's path is what a designer uses to get the effect he wants, whether for a hood or a tire in a turn.

Another easy-to-see example of this linkage length change is in rear, four-bar suspension. If the bars (links) are level, the up and down motion of the rear end actually causes the rear end to move forward slightly, equally on both sides (which is why driveshafts have slip joints). The wheelbase gets slightly shorter, but handling is unaffected since the axle remains square in the chassis. It is critical to understand that we refer to true level, with respect to the ground. As mentioned before, the angle of the bars with respect to the frame is not important. This is one of the reasons the finished chassis rake should

> **Whether you're dealing with valve trains ... shift linkage, or suspension, you must first clearly understand Arc Length Theory.**

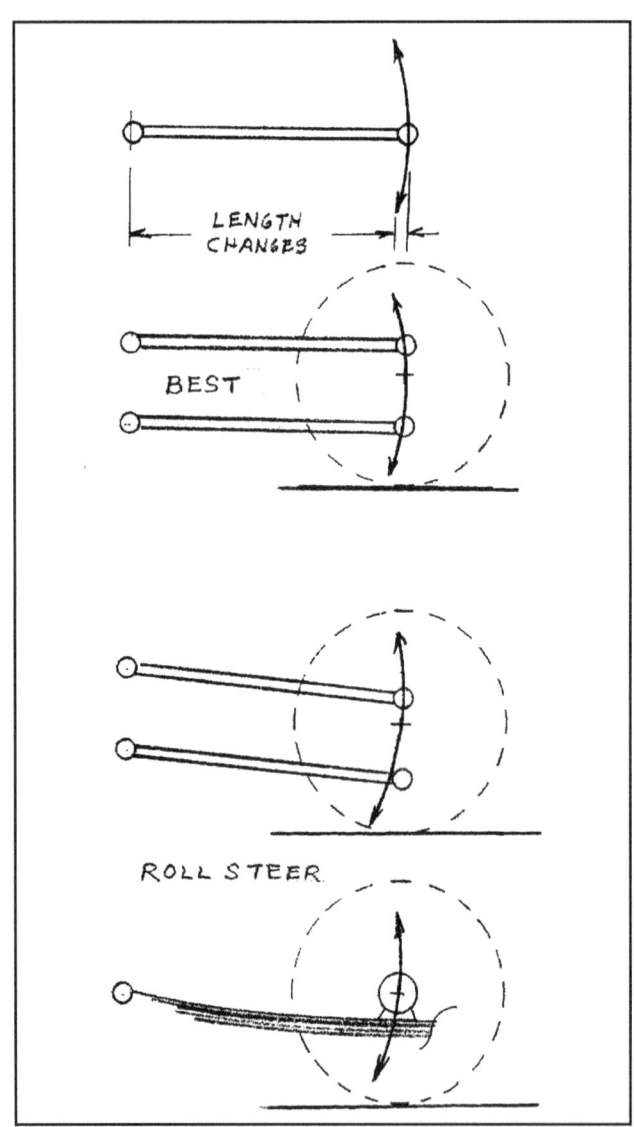

Left: See how a rear axle 4-bar or leaf springs can cause roll steer when the bars are not level to the GROUND. When bars are NOT level, the effective length change in the radius rod moves the axle out of square in the chassis and causes a roll steer effect. As drawn here, when body roll occurs in a turn, the non-level bars will shorten the wheel base on the inside of a turn and lengthen it on the outside.

be estimated, and set on jack stands at the angle before setting up your suspension.

Now let's say our bars run downhill 5 degrees to the rearend. As the suspension works, the wheelbase gets longer on compression and shorter on extension. That's not too bad until we get into a turn and the chassis leans. As the body rolls to the outside, the inner wheel goes down and the outer wheel goes up in relation to the frame. This doubles the length change, extending the outer wheelbase and shortening the inside! Cocking the rear axle this way immediately destroys handling by creating a rear steer, "squirrely" effect known as roll steer. The axle turns in a way that shortens the turn radius, which we feel as oversteer, caused by the roll steer. You will find yourself correcting back and

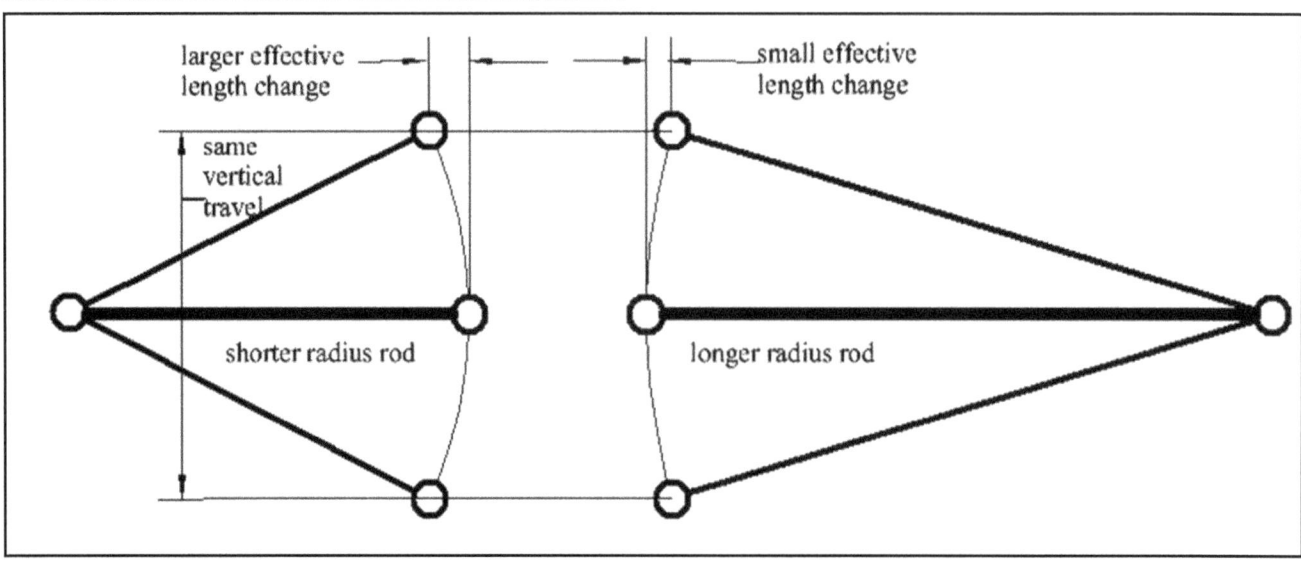

The designer's job is to use the changes in the effective length of a radius rod to control the movement of the object located by that radius rod. The length change can work for, or against his design. Trouble is the result when parts that should operate in unison don't!

forth, trying to catch up with the chassis, until you slow down or roll over. Not much fun.

You may have noticed that rods with leaf spring rears also move the axle forward as the car is jacked up and the wheels go down. When a line is drawn through the front perch bolt and the base of the axle saddle, it's apparent that the front half of the spring acts just like a four-bar link, and has the same roll steer problem. Lowering blocks and dearched springs help the handling by raising the rear axle and leveling the control link.

As you can imagine, rear sway bars are critical to minimizing this problem. Since the roll steer is created by chassis roll, higher center of gravity is a great problem. That's why sedans, coupes, and panels need rear sway bars and pickups do fine with none.

If your Hot Rod gets twitchy in a corner, this roll steer phenomenon is often at fault. You can often get the bars level by raising the axle in the chassis. Try raising the rear end and use a taller tire to maintain the original ride height. Sometimes it's easier to alter the height of the pivot points. The key is to maintain level control links. You can also look into adding a rear sway bar to make that machine handle as good as it looks.

Another example of this is in a throttle linkage made with solid rods. It is entirely possible to build a linkage where the actuating arm rotates below the link connecting to the carb. That condition is known as over centering and locks the linkage in that position. Your Vise Grips operate on the same principle. That's OK for a good grip, but not so much fun when the throttle locks in the full boogie condition. That is one reason that OEM designers and aftermarket Hot Rod companies use cable throttle linkages. They are almost immune to over centering and isolate vibrations as well. (By the way, if yours keep melting, add a ground from the engine to the body, 'cuz the cable is acting as a ground, causing the heat/melt.) With the popularity of vintage engine installations, old style solid linkages are being used again, so be careful with yours.

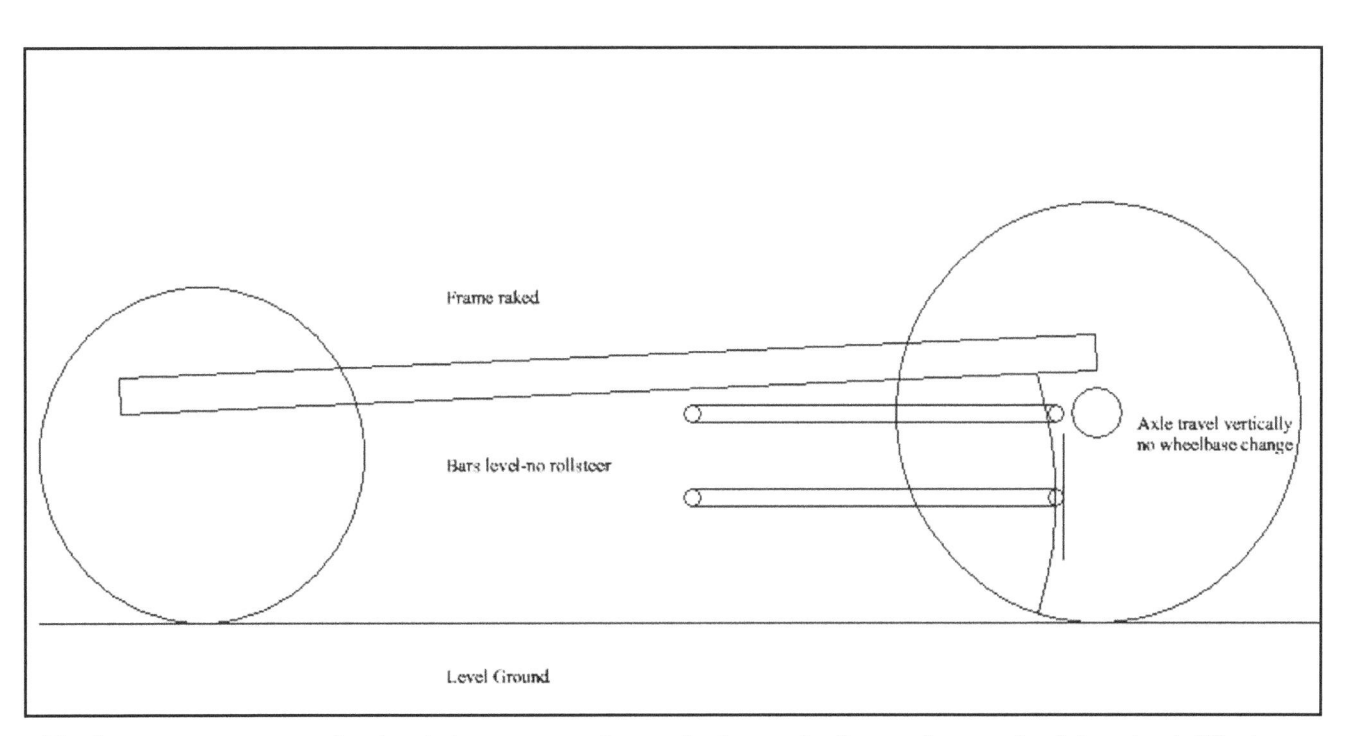

The better way to set up the chassis is to preset a forward rake on the frame, then set the 4-bars level. The bar arc is now vertical and the axle remains square in the chassis, thus preventing roll steer.

Suspension

Rear Suspension & 4-Bar Systems

Arc Length Theory in the Real World

The rear suspension on our Hot Rods has two primary jobs: to support the weight of the back of the vehicle, and to control the position of the wheels relative to how the chassis goes down the highway. Independent rear suspension is more complicated and less common than a solid rear axle, so we'll deal with that another time. Solid rear axle suspension is often called "live axle", and has to keep the axle square in the car so that a tendency to turn is not induced. You certainly would not intentionally install a rear suspension out of square, but that often happens accidentally due to improper design or installation.

Leaf spring suspension is probably more common on Hot Rods, but we'll first look at the equal length four-bar type to illustrate a critical design point. Four-bars control the axle by means of four radius rods. The term radius rods makes it clear that they operate in a radius, part of a circle, forming an arc as they rotate. In a Hot Rod, that rotation takes place as the axle moves up and down during normal suspension travel over a bump in the road. Travel also takes place in a turn since the body rolls outboard of that turn. What is going on during body roll is that the outboard end of the axle is moving up relative to the chassis, and the inboard side is moving down. And that's where problems begin.

If the bars are level, relative to the ground, the radius rods describe an arc that is perpendicular to the ground (true vertical). That motion causes the axle to move forward in the chassis an equal distance on each side, which is why drive shafts have a slip joint. The axle remains square in the chassis and no roll steer effect is induced. Notice that all this good stuff is based on the radius rod arcs being true vertical. What happens if they are not?

Let's say our intrepid Hot Rodder is the real careful type, and has real good equipment like a level, maybe even a digital angle one, or an angle finder. He most often sets the chassis on stands, carefully leveling it side to side and front to back. This is his first, fundamental, and possibly fatal error. If the chassis is not going to sit level front to back when it's done, why would you begin the setup procedure that way? Think about that a few minutes before going on.

If our builder made the common error and set the chassis level, he probably also set the bars level, being a careful guy who even reads instructions on occasion. When his Hot Rod is finished and does indeed sit on the predicted 3 degree rake, his bars will be down 3 degrees and the travel arcs will also be 3-degrees off true vertical. This doesn't sound like much until we realize that the effect is doubled in body roll. That outboard side of the axle is going up relative to the frame while the onboard is going down. A three degree error off vertical will give you about 1/8 inch horizontal movement based on 2 inches of travel. That means our axle suddenly goes from square to a total of 1/4 inch out. And, the effect of the body roll is to bring the axle forward on the inside of the turn and back on the outside, so we introduce oversteer, tightening the turn that the driver had in mind. Now he has to turn the steering wheel back to compensate, the body rolls, and the process starts all over again. These oscillations can be merely annoying and lead to the car being described as "squirrely". If all this occurs at high speed in a vehicle with a high center of gravity (read street rods and SUVs) it can get downright dangerous.

Our guy certainly would not purposely install the axle out of square it but ended up that way by accident. Sway bars would help by controlling the body roll that upsets the axle position and are highly recommended for any performance vehicle. Get them too stiff to compensate for bad design, and your back will complain as they damage ride quality. Experience has shown that a 2-3 degree rake is common to Hot Rods. Doesn't it make more sense to set it up with that rake? Then you don't have to be constantly making corrections for, or worse yet ignoring, suspension, engine, and drivetrain angles. Get this right and it all gets easier.

We've been discussing equal length four-bars here, since that is ideal for normal road use. You can also get good results from a four-bar which has shorter upper bars to fit under a floor which you'd rather not cut to clear equal length bars. There will be an increasing amount of pinion angle change as the difference in bar length increases, so watch before going too far. Turning on the opinion warning light, I would be very leery of an upper bar less than 70% of the lower bar length. Triangulated four-bars do have a shorter upper bar since it is angled to provide lateral axle location without the use of a panhard bar. The working length of that bar would not be its actual length, but rather the effective length as seen in a side view. That shorter upper should still be true level and parallel to the lower bar for best handling.

Another variation on the four-bar is the four link, coming out of drag racing. It uses upper and lower bars that are seldom parallel, or even the same length. Both ends of the bars can be raised or lowered in order to tune the system, changing the "bite" according to track conditions. What's really happening is that we have an adjustable length ladder bar system. If you make an imaginary line that extends the bars forward, those lines will eventually cross at a point called the instant center. As the angle of the bars are altered, that instant center can be moved up and down to change rear chassis rise, and forward or back to alter the weight transfer. All that is fine for a drag racer, but it doesn't answer the challenges of a street car as well as a more normal four-bar. It also tends to take up a great deal more space so you will often see the trunk area minimized or eliminated. It can be readjusted to have the bars level for the street and altered for drag racing, so it can work well for a dual-purpose Hot Rod.

Triangulated rear four-bars can work very well, especially with air ride. They eliminate the lateral locater (Panhard) bar by using the diagonally mounted upper arms to control side to side movement. In some applications this different mounting makes more room for exhaust, better floor pan clearance, or a perfect spot to mount coil springs or air springs. Drivability is excellent, as good as a "five-bar". The only real downside is that they are designed to mount to a weldable axle housing, so guys with 10/12 bolts, Dana, and Ford 8.8 axles will have a problem. Don't think that you can use some magic welding rod to weld suspension parts to cast iron axle housings.

I just mentioned the "five-bar", which is a term I use to describe a parallel four-bar system with an additional lateral locater or Panhard bar. The French Panhard cars in the pre WWI era used this bar to control axle side sway on springs, just as we do. It's probably true that each bar works at its best since the loading is all compression and tension with no side loads, but that doesn't seem to show up in drivability. The Panhard bar must be as long, as level and as high as possible to work at its best. That often causes problems with floors and exhaust as mentioned above. Too short a bar will see more sideways axle movement, as will an angled bar, for the same reasons we discussed all four-bars need to be level.

Since most older cars have a relatively high center of gravity (CG), it is better to have a fairly high roll center (RC). That sounds wrong until you realize

> **If the bars are level, relative to the ground, the radius rods describe an arc that is perpendicular to the ground...**

that it is the relationship between them (called the roll couple) that does the work. A high CG with a low RC will have severe body roll. Equal height center will have no roll, which is why tether cars have adjustable height cable anchor points. If you can get the RC above the CG, the car will transfer weight to the inside of the chassis in a turn. That is one reason why McPherson strut suspensions can handle so well. The height of the frame side attachment of the Panhard bar largely dictates the RC height. That's why you see the NASCAR guys adjust the rear bar to "tighten" or "loosen" a car during a race.

Speaking of NASCAR, to this day they use a trailing arm rear suspension very similar to GM pickups from the '60s and '80s. It has a front mounting point way forward and very close to the center line of the chassis. It works great for both traction and handling, and is very simple to install. I think the main reason you don't see them more is a space issue. Where the pickups have a lot of room under the floor, most Hot Rods and restomods don't. There are some excellent kits on the market, but you have to be willing to do the floor mods to get the needed space.

Finally, parallel rear leaf springs can be made to operate much like a four-bar. The GM engineers made a very clever mod to the '59-'62 Corvettes that added an upper bar to that system. The front half of the leaf spring acts as the lower bar, with the back half only taking vehicle weight rather than axle control. With the extra bar to absorb energy, axle wind up is eliminated. We have added similar upper bars to a number of Hot Rod rear leafs with much success. The "three-link" using a single long upper bar near the chassis centerline and a Panhard bar is a variation of this type that can work well if you have the space in the driveshaft area of the floor.

Going back to the whole discussion concerning the importance of a level bar controlling a rear axle, we can extend that concept to leaf springs. The point where the axle housing connects to the spring, or a lowering block, is connected to it's forward bushing center to determine the "bar angle". A highly arched spring with a tall lowering block will produce a steeply angled "bar". Major league axle hop often results. It would be better to dearch the spring or use a 2 inch tall maximum block to keep the "bar" more level. The real proof of this is seen on '34-'54 GM cars which originally used a high arch spring. When you jack one up, the axle moves way forward. That makes centering the axle in a Hot Rod fender more difficult. It also illustrates how important this entire level bar lecture is to those who think it's not important.

We used all the info above when we developed Fatman's Wonderbar rear suspension for the Early Camaros and Mustangs. It was our opinion that sufficient space was lacking for a proper length upper four-bar link, and not enough floorpan room for a trailing arm or three link system without major floor rework. Triangulated systems are out there that we have seen on the track, so they obviously can work OK. We have also installed systems which insert

This typical rear 4-bar incorporates a lower Z bar to control sideways axle movement while allowing easy tail pipe routing.

an upper bar link into a pocket welded into the floor. They allow a longer upper bar with little loss of rear seat space, and work really well with high horsepower drivetrains that really need help hooking up. We wanted to design something that would have all the handling and traction without the cutting.

Our Freightliner and other heavy trucks have used a single tapered leaf with Air springs for years. The spring is flexible enough to allow one wheel to rise over a bump while the other side stays in place, yet still enough to add a little roll resistance. It is mounted level to keep the axle squared, and provides chassis rise on acceleration to plant the tires. Coil-overs or Shockwaves are used to support the car's weight. Since the tapered leaf does not have to absorb energy supporting weight and serves only to locate the axle and absorb axle torque, it can handle wheel hop control easily. This design doesn't replace a four-bar in 500HP plus situations, but works surprisingly well in uncut Hot Rods with more reasonable engines. Our '34 Ford Highboy sedan is using this system with Shockwaves for excellent ride and handling. Please don't take this info as a sales pitch, but rather an illustration of how you can take all the theory and use it to come up with innovations.

When you have done a bunch of cars and found out what works well, it makes one appreciate the aftermarket kits more than ever. Most manufacturers have really done their homework on proper design. They wouldn't survive long in the market without good word-of-mouth advertising. Different designs exist for different purposes and opinions. We can talk over any question in the seminars offered at select events. Collect the catalogs, check the websites, and talk first hand to the vendors at the next Goodguys show to find the system that suits you best. See 'ya out there.

Solid length coil-over simulators are used to help get the angles dialed in before all the welding takes place.

Suspension

Choices in Radius Rod Types

Options, Options

You hear a lot of conversation about the different types of radius rods that are used on straight axle suspensions, with different types of axle construction. Nostalgic Hot Rods have made a huge comeback in the last few years, bringing this question up to a new generation of Hot Rodders. I love seeing the interest and respect the younger guys have for traditional cars, but it seems that the same learning curve we went through earlier is being experienced again as well. Maybe some tech info on this question will help prevent experiencing the more difficult parts of repeating history. What are the best combinations of split wishbone, hairpin, and four-bar radius rod systems versus the forged or cast I-beams and round tube axles?

The issue at heart is how the axle's flexibility, or the lack of that property, affects the action of the radius rods. If the axle and radius rod types are both very stiff, those parts will be overstressed, and failures may occur. Welds, brackets and bolts may fail, causing a very dangerous situation. If those parts are sufficient strong (or improved to that level) no failure will occur, but very stiff handling and ride quality will be the result.

This difficulty is caused by the need for each wheel to react to, and only to, the bump it sees on its side of the road. If it cannot react because the suspension has been built very stiff and heavily enough to not fail, the car will have to hop over that bump rather than riding over it. That will quite obviously cause the poor ride quality and poor handling spoken of above. This need for an acceptable level of flexibility is really the reason IFS (Independent Front Suspension) was developed, yet many cars just look better with a straight axle. So how do we get the proper combination of flexibility and strength?

Historically speaking, forged steel axles with an I-beam section were the first to be made. A very good grade of steel was used, combining strength with durability. I have a CD of the 1940 World's Fair, showing an original 1940 Ford I-beam axle being twisted three complete times around! This obviously took a good bit of force to accomplish, but the point for us to see is that the axle does actually have the ability to twist. Ford's wishbone design did not require the axle to twist when the suspension moved. Since both the axle and the wishbone were mounted to the frame at its center, the axle and wishbone assembly had the ability to rotate in order to ride over bumps. (some early rodders in England and the US saw this as the inspiration for adding a center hinge point, converting to a swing axle IFS, but that's another story for another time).

So when early rodders began installing modern V-8 engines, the original radius rods began to be split to the side of the frame rails rather than remaining in the triangulated wishbone shape of the Ford design. With the wishbone leg now converted to a solidly mounted radius rod, the axle now needed to twist for one wheel to react to a bump on its side. Proof of this need to twist is the experience of users of any type of radius rod, whether split bones, hairpins, or four-bar, where the rod end jam nuts are difficult to keep tight at all times. The axle became an enormously stiff anti sway bar, which resulted in pretty good handling on a smooth road, but a quite stiff ride. That same stiff ride would also cause a loss of wheel adhesion to a bumpy road, then losing traction for steering and stopping. You see this same effect on excessively stiff modern suspensions, especially those lowered to the point of riding on the axle travel bump stops. All this worked pretty well for a number of years on both road and track driven Hot Rods.

As the early dirt track racers sought higher speeds and better handling, they found that the quite stiff roll resistance of the split radius rod set up was working against them. To get a more freely articulating suspension, the hairpin radius rod came into use. Note how one style is called the Kurtis style, named for the very successful builder of Midget, Sprint, and Indy cars from the '30s and 40s. The hairpin itself has the ability to flex in torsion, thus freeing up the assembly and not requiring the axle to twist. Then the lightweight '37-'40' Ford tube axle from the V8-60 cars began to show up. It not only looked good, but reduced unsprung weight and helped handling. Since it would not twist like the forged I-beams, the more flexible hairpins became more important. I cannot prove it, but I think that this very stiffness of the early Ford tube axles led directly to the use of the four-bar system. Since fabricated round tube axles have the same attributes and problems as the early 60-horse Ford axles, the same logic applies to them as well.

A four-bar system is probably the ultimate in controlling the axle's position in the chassis while allowing free motion. Since the axle doesn't need to twist at all, the axle caster doesn't change with travel, as it does with split bones and hairpins. It's also very handy to have such an easy way to adjust caster, also an advantage of hairpins made with

The Classic Early Ford tapered oval radius rods can be safely used on modern high speed hot rods when their strengths and limits are properly considered. (Note: Be sure to check the radius rod illustration farther along in the Straight Axle Tech Chapter.)

adjustable clevis ends at the axle. Since the four-bar does not attempt to twist the axle at all, the stress on the four-bar itself is reduced. Very good handling with quite acceptable ride quality often results. Broken links, mounts and damaged axles are a rarity with a four-bar for the same reason.

When the reproduction Bell style dropped tube fabricated axles first came on the market in the '70's, there were some occasional failures. Those early axles had ordinary cast iron ends arc welded to a steel center tube. They normally held up fine when painted as produced. What happened in actual use was that when an axle was chrome plated, the weld was typically ground for a better appearance. The reduced weld cross section naturally had less strength, further reduced by Hydrogen embrittlement occurring during the plating process. That embrittlement could actually cause a crack to begin, and gradually spread over time until one day it would fail. As long as the weld was not ground nor the axle plated, I'm not aware that any failures occurred.

Since we all like smooth plated axles, the manufacturers switched to ductile iron cast ends. Welding ductile iron to steel is seldom a problem for any qualified process. Spicer type rear axles such as GM 10 and 12 bolts have been done this way for years. Properly done, TIG welded with a nickel based filler rod, this is an accepted way to join cast iron and steel. Hydrogen embrittlement can only occur in high Carbon metals such as spring steel and ordinary cast iron, so the ductile iron ends and mild steel center tubes avoided this problem altogether. Leaving the weld at full cross section would be a safety precaution, but since the two greater problems just discussed no longer occurred, grinding the weld for a smooth look has not proven to be a problem is actual use. I'm not aware of any manufacturers that use anything other than ductile iron ends today.

> **A four-bar system is probably the ultimate in controlling the axle's position in the chassis while allowing free motion.**

I-beam axles are available in both cast and forged versions. As you can imagine from the earlier discussions, the forged axle is more able to resist stress. The cast axle will be much more rigid. We are also seeing aluminum axles, which should prove to work quite well, given the properties of the alloy being used. I would expect them to act the same as a forged axle in use. Drilling the axle, unless taken to an extreme, shouldn't affect the axle much. If anything, the forged axle will become a bit less stiff, as well as being lighter and cool looking. But be warned, drilling a forged axle will take more time and better tools than you probably expect! Drilling wishbones shouldn't be a problem as long as good judgment is being used in terms of hole size. I'm going to make the dangerous assumption that no one who is smart enough to read will be dumb enough to drill a wishbone without welding tube sleeves back into the holes! Those WILL fail in short order!

In my opinion, the flexible forged I-beam axle with a four-bar is the best riding, handling, and safest combination. That forged I-beam will also work well with hairpins or split bones, but the added stiffness will detract from ride and handling. A more stiff cast I-beam or tube axle will certainly do well with the four-bar, and less so with the hairpins. Split 'bones with the more rigid axles will be the worst case, and need sufficiently strong bolts and brackets to prevent failures, while likely riding hard and handling pretty stiffly. A historically correct Hot Rod or personal taste may point you to a less than ideal combination, just be sure to take the added stresses into account in your fabrication work.

An excellent set of drawings and another explanation of these concepts can be found in the Pete and Jakes catalog (as well as many on-line sites). You'll find some very good info regarding many aspects of axle suspension explained and illustrated very well.

Suspension

Tall Spindle Technology

Good Geometry nets Good Camber Change

You have been hearing a lot more about improved IFS (Independent Front Suspension) geometry in the last few years, undoubtedly fueled by the interest in improved handling for Autocross work. A particular improvement to the first generation Camaros and Chevelles has been the introduction of a spindle which is taller than stock in order to improve camber angles throughout suspension travel. The meaning of this idea has been made a little murky because what is intended is to improve tire contact patch through altered upper control arm angles, achieved through that taller spindle. Let's first define the problem.

Looking at the nearby drawing you can see that most IFS are designed for a level lower control arm. The difference is in the angle of the upper arm. When the upper arm runs downhill to the wheel. The wheels camber OUT of the turn, minimizing the tire contact patch, transferring the CG (Center of Gravity) outboard, thus increasing body roll and under steer. Typical spindle heights are around 9 to 10 inches. Consequently these cars require very stiff springs, shocks and anti sway bars to control the body roll, at the expense of overly harsh ride quality and poor tire to road compliance.

You have surely seen Indy cars on TV where the upper control arm runs uphill to the wheel. As shown in the second example, more capable suspensions will generally have this design. Modern examples will have spindle height about 1-1/2 inch taller to achieve that upper arm angle. In fact, I have seen spindle heights in the 14 to 15 inch range on NASCAR and Mercedes, among others. Now the CG is transferred inboard, tire contact patch is maximized with less body roll and understeer. The car handles well with softer springs, shocks and sway bar rates producing a better ride and keeping the tire on the pavement. If the IFS design already has this geometry, say the second generation Camaro and the Mustang II, little is to be gained by increasing spindle height further.

Let's divert for a moment to the idea of level and/or equal length control arms to eliminate the camber change seen when an air suspension is let down. That goal is achieved but handling is very poor due to camber changes that are detrimental to the car's road grip. That idea died quickly in the evolution of air suspension.

Another terminology difficulty makes this concept harder to understand since in some circles it is referred as "positive camber gain" while others call it "negative camber gain." It is actually both; it just depends on whether you are referring to the outer or the inner tire.

I first became aware of this idea from an article in HOT ROD magazine from about 1973. Hotchkiss developed a kit to put the taller Second Gen Camaro spindle on the First Gen Chevelles. A special length upper control arm and modified lower ball joint were required but this simple swap achieved a measured 20% improvement is skid pad numbers. Since both cars are front steer this worked out great, but could not be applied to the rear steer First Gen Camaros without creating major Ackerman problems. For whatever reason, this brilliant bit of Hot Rod engineering seemed to not really catch on until we started looking at Hot Rod handling as well as acceleration.

At Fatman Fab, we were selling dropped spindles that had the downside of using the smaller Metric brakes and stock geometry. They were the best available but all they did was lower the car. In 2004 I began the design of a new dropped spindle that lowered the car but was improved by using the OEM larger disc brakes (as well as any aftermarket upgrade) and the taller height of the Second Gen Camaro spindle. Since the First Gen Camaro and Chevelle share the same spindle with different bolt on steering arms, it is possible to use the new spindle on either car by using their correct steering arms. I did have to relocate the upper ball joint tapered hole to allow use of standard length control arms, but that actually improved the scrub radius with wider wheels. An analysis of the bumpsteer showed that since the upper control arm angle change affected the steering arc, a lowered steering arm position was needed to achieve minimized bumpsteer. We got the drop and vastly improved handling with a simple bolt-on part.

After introducing the new spindle to the Hot Rod market, I found out that I had rediscovered a concept that had been around NASCAR since the Sixties. Some of you may know that until the 1980's NASCAR IFS design was essentially a beefed up version of the '57-'64 full sized Fords (similar to how the modern Hot Rod Mustang II IFS has been improved). I was watching the "American Pickers" TV show when they went to Pete Pistone's shop right here in Charlotte. He showed Mike and Frank a '57-'64 stock Ford spindle that had been modified by welding on a gusseted and raised upper ball joint mod. The '67-'69 Penske Trans Am Camaros also swapped to the taller Corvette spindle for this reason, along with the larger brakes. I remember reading that they had a little trouble getting their necessary special length upper arms past Tech, since those guys thought it was about weight savings rather than enhanced handling. Those guys back then often lacked the benefit of an engineering education but their amazing common sense often told them the same things!

This idea of getting the improved upper control arm angle can also be achieved by the "Guldstrand Mod" for First Gen Camaros and Chevelles and the "Shelby Mod" for Mustangs where the inner mount of the upper arm is lowered. Racers now can choose special ball joints with taller studs to achieve the same benefits. You cannot get the effect with tubular control arms that have differently curved tubes but don't alter the ball joint position. That's marketing, not engineering.

If I had a First Gen Camaro or Chevelle this would be my first step toward enhanced suspension performance. Lowering the CG and transferring it inboard in a turn and maximizing tire traction will allow your better, wider tires and brakes to perform at the best of their ability. Stock springs and control arm bushings in good shape will work fine. Shocks and sway bars can be upgraded without resorting to such gonzo rates that your CD player skips. It will be capable of putting in respectable Autocross numbers without having to become a race car. By fixing the REAL design problem FIRST, you'll have a much better handling car that is fun to drive on the road to the next Goodguys event.

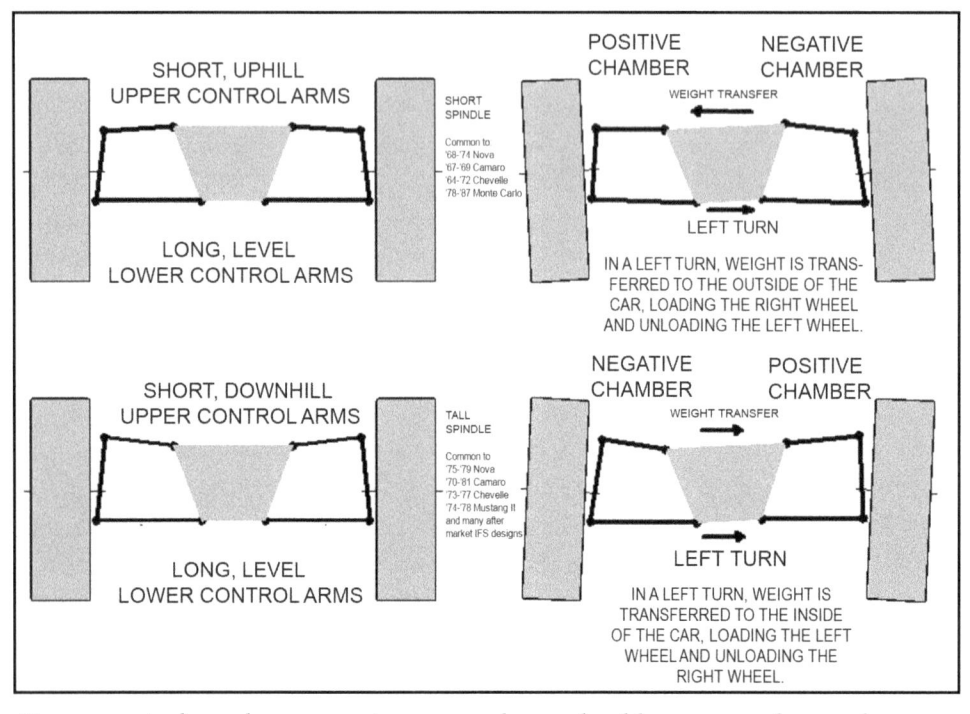

Since most independent suspension systems have a level lower control arm, the upper control arm angle and direction of that slope will control how the wheel camber changes with wheel travel and body roll.

Suspension

Understanding Coil-Overs

The Angle *does* make a Difference

Adjustability is a very important advantage in building any Hot Rod. Since all our cars are essentially one-off prototypes, the ability to fine tune various systems is really a big deal. Coil-overs in particular offer the advantage of dialing in our spring and shock combination to achieve the stance and ride we planned early in the project. This is a great example of reverse engineering where you start with a plan and choose components consistent with that plan. Coil-overs are not necessarily a device to lower or raise a car, although that can be done if you carefully choose the shock length, spring and mount style.

Always choose the shock length first, then the spring. Set your car at ride height (you did mock that up so you're not just guessing, right?), try to arrange for as long a mounting distance as possible. One of the really neat things about using coil-overs is that they can be replaced by a simple bar stock strut during build up in order to hold the design ride height and prevent damage from weld spatter and overspray. The most common shocks used in street rods have 11-1/2 inches center-to-center length, with 5/8 inch diameter eyes at each end. This shock will have 4 inches of stroke, and should be mounted to allow 60% of that stroke for compression, and 40% for extension. If you can engineer your mountings for a longer unit, the ride will improve because a lower spring rate can be used. A 20% longer spring can do the same job with a matching 20% reduction in rate. That softer spring rate will result in a better ride. The longer stroke shock will allow more travel and avoid bottoming or topping out, which will always hurt ride quality and be unsafe as well. When mounts or coil-over parts fail, the car is coming down!

The problem is, our low stance Hot Rods run out of room for taller shocks. Factory cars allow more space with a higher stance, and drag cars use a much higher kick up in the rear frame rails to get the extra space needed. If you can give up some trunk space for a taller shock, you'll be better off. Attempts are always being made to lay coil-overs down horizontally and operate them with a pushrod and bellcrank system. This works well as long as low friction bearings and beefy rods and mounts are used. In actual practice, all that linkage creates its own space problems, so this technique has seen limited use.

We tried to come up with something like this for our own '32 Ford sedan. After drawing it all up and seeing the practical space problems, we ended up using Air Ride instead as a replacement for coil-overs. The system is compact, and the spring rate is infinitely variable to allow for varying loads. If you have a sedan or coupe with a large trunk, your variable spring rate needs may be better suited to Air Ride as well.

Some general rules for mounting coil-overs include keeping them close to vertical, and as wide apart as possible. We lean the top in one-inch from the bottom. Any more just makes the shock less effective in damping and the spring rate requirement higher due to the trigonometry involved. Check it yourself by drawing a right triangle with the long side (hypotenuse) representing the shock (or just check out the article in the Design Chapter). The longer that side gets with greater angles, the more force must be exerted to end up with the same vertical component (length). Your High School Trig teacher was teaching you how to engineer a Hot Rod without either one of you knowing it. Naturally, a wider stance provides more stability just like you do with your feet further apart on a rocking boat. Pickups can often have their coil-overs mounted outboard of the frame and still have plenty of tire space.

End mountings must be much stronger than regular shock mounts since you are supporting weight, not just damping motion. Make your bracket support both sides of the bushing if you can (this is called a double shear bracket). If the bolt must be cantilevered (supported on one side only) be very sure enough of the bolt goes through a tight fitting tube for support. The mounting bolts must ALWAYS be perpendicular to the coil-over's vertical axis (centerline). Any angles induce a torque which can, and has, snapped off the shock mounts and ended a day unhappily. This is a good argument for the use of bearing style mounts rather than urethane bushings. The bearings will accept some angle without harm, and are especially useful with independent front or rear suspensions.

Choosing springs is much easier. You want a spring which will hold the vehicle at the designed ride height, with around 1/2 inch to 1-1/2 inches of thread exposed on the adjuster. Anymore or less indicates incorrect spring rate, and can easily be swapped for the correct spring. Your dealer should have enough experience to get you pretty close. The more unusual vehicles and more scientific owners can weigh the car front and rear by borrowing a buddy's race car scale or finding a sympathetic truck scale operator. With a solid axle, half of that end's weight must be supported. Independent suspensions have a leverage involved which requires a stronger spring. The coil-over manufacturer can help once the above information is available.

As mentioned above, coil-overs work best with a load that doesn't vary much, as in small coupes and pickups, front suspensions, and race cars, Bigger cars with varying loads can benefit from the use of a variable rate spring. Some manufacturers have these, as can be seen by a changing distance between the coils. A '34 sedan would really like a 250/500 pound rate to ride well loaded or empty. Honestly, since leaf springs and Air Ride are inherently a progressive rate, I like them better on the rear of bigger cars.

SPRING RATE CORRECTION FOR ANGLE MOUNTING

Spring rate correction factors for shock mounting angles measured in degrees.

Shock Angle	Correction Factor
10°	.96
15°	.93
20°	.88
25°	.82
30°	.75
35°	.66
40°	.59
45°	.50

Changing the mounting angle of a coil-over has a direct effect on stroke length and spring rate that must be accounted for in the mount design and parts selection.

Suspension

Suspension Tuning with Sway Bars

Anti-Roll Bars to the Rescue

The best guitar ever made cannot sound right if it isn't tuned properly. A Hot Rod suspension is really no different. Assuming that a decent basic design was used to build that suspension, it must still be tuned to the taste of the driver and to the purpose for which it will be used. Suspension travel, spring rates, tires etc all need to be coordinated. Even less-than-ideal original suspensions can be improved tremendously with taller spindles for better camber change and tubular control arms with revised geometry. Once the basic system has been assembled, proper selection of shock absorbers and anti-sway bars can be the easiest and most cost effective way to optimize suspension performance. We've discussed shock absorbers lately, so let's take a look at sway bars this time around.

Much confusion as to the actual function of suspension components comes from the fact that we often use improper terminology. Just as shock absorbers are dampers for suspension travel, rather than absorbing shock, sway bars would be better termed anti-roll bars. Rather than engage in a futile effort to change old habits, we'll call them sway bars for this discussion. They function by resisting body roll, through links that connect the rear axle or IFS control arms to the chassis. The central part of the sway bar acts as a torsion bar so that one side of the body cannot roll (changing its distance to the ground contacted suspension) without twisting that bar. As you can imagine, factors such as bar material, bar diameter, length of the lever end of the sway bar, all affect the relative stiffness of the anti-sway system.

If both wheels on an axle hit a bump at the same time, the sway bar simply rotates in its mounts and should theoretically have little effect on suspension travel. In the real world, bumps in the road tend to be less cooperative than that. Since there will always be some difference in the action of one wheel than the other, it is reasonable to expect that connecting those wheels by adding a sway bar, or increasing the stiffness of an existing bar, will tend to lead to a more harsh ride. That is a good argument for being cautious in adding roll stiffness this way. If the car gets too stiff, the tires will bounce over road irregularities. If the rubber is off the road, it cannot give you traction for turning, stopping, or acceleration.

We want to control body roll because it is uncomfortable for the driver and passengers, while causing a possible loss of tire traction in a turn. When weight transfer occurs during a turn, tires on the outside of the turn can become overloaded while the inside tire becomes ineffective. Suspension design generally assumes that the car stays pretty level in a turn, but body roll acts to move suspension mounting points in regard to the road, thus altering roll centers and messing up what might have originally been a capable design. Poor suspension geometry generally gets much worse when body roll is not controlled.

The body roll we are trying to control is caused by the relationship between the car's central of gravity and its geometric roll center. The center of gravity (CG) is the point at which the mass of the vehicle would rotate if you could spin it on a stick. An old rule of thumb says that most front wheel drive cars have a front CG that is about the height of the engine camshaft. The rear CG can be higher or lower based on the design of the car. Pick ups are light in the back and tend to have a low center of gravity while a panel truck CG will be much higher.

Connect the front and rear CG, and you find the car's roll axis. It's kind of like having the car on a barbecue spit, turning at those points.

The problem is that the suspension generally has an entirely different idea of where it should rotate. Suspension attachment point locations, ride height, and basic geometry design all serve to alter the geometric point of rotation referred to as its roll center (RC). Again, join the front and rear roll centers and you find the car's roll axis. Using our barbecue analogy, when the RC axis and the CG axis are different, your dinner will flop over as the spit revolves. You've seen that happen. And that is exactly what happens when your car's CG and geometry fight against each other. (you can find excellent drawings and discussions of these principles in many suspension books, and in the excellent seminars at Goodguys events, given by experts in the field such as Detroit Speed, and your truly from Fatman Fab).

A low roll center is often perceived by rodders as being a good thing, but that is generally quite incorrect. It is the difference between the height of the CG and the RC (referred to as the roll couple) that causes body roll. Think of a car running in a circle, attached to a string at the center of the circle. The car CG will be a given height based primarily on its distribution of mass, and actually changes slightly with the speed around that circle. The RC (roll center) is dictated by the height where the string is attached. If the RC is below the CG, the car will roll outward, loading the outboard ties and unloading the inboard. The car also rises a little and the CG moves outboard, making the body roll worse, limited only by the string. In a real car driving in a circle, tire adhesion is eventually exceeded and the car spins out.

If the RC string attach point is above the CG, the car will actually roll toward the inside of the circle. This loads the inside tires and minimizes the outward migration of the CG due to the constant turn. In a real car, you'll go faster with a lot less drama. So, the goal is to use sway bars to control body roll and if possible, raise the roll center enough that a lighter sway bar will do the job. That is one way that good suspension design can also offer superior ride, since a gonzo sway bar that will kill ride quality need not be used to overcome bad design.

So it all comes down to using sway bars to balance the handling of a car. Just because someone makes a sway bar that will fit your car, or one larger than it came with, doesn't mean you always want that sway bar. If you prefer a nice ride over killer handling, think about using just enough sway bar to control body roll for good handling and passenger comfort. If Autocross is in your future, the game changes. You'll be wanting larger sway bars at the expense of a cushy ride. Most likely, you'll really want to be somewhere in the middle. Rodders have found out that too much rear tire and too much sway bar will not allow power to be used to throttle steer the car through turns. Bigger is NOT always better.

> The best guitar ever made cannot sound right if it isn't tuned properly. A Hot Rod suspension is really no different.

As a general rule, the roll stiffness should be increased on the end of the car that is misbehaving. If the car understeers (pushes, in NASCAR speak) add more front sway bar. If it over steers, (loose, as said by the TV race announcers) add rear stiffness. A general rule is that the newer the car, and the larger the engine, the more front sway bar will be required. Engines have moved forward over the years, having the same effect on weight distribution as a heavier engine. A big block '69 Camaro needs a lot more bar than a small block version. And way more than a '34 Ford Coupe with a small block Chevy. The engine on the '34 probably sits 6 inches farther back off the front axle centerline than the Camaro. Since the car's weight distribution and other physical dynamics are so different, you would not want to approach the '34 the same way as the Camaro.

As a point in fact, we just worked on a '34 Plymouth sedan for a customer. He had added sway bars front and rear in an effort to make it handle well, but strong oversteer was the result. The body roll was excessive and the driving experience was very "nervous". We removed the front bar, and the car handled much better. The week earlier, we did a '64 Impala for another rodder, adding sway bars at both ends (and fixing some of the factory designed in bumpsteer) to make for a much improved driving experience.

As a general rule, we run a rear sway bar on everything other than a pick up truck. Panels, sedans, and coupes of all years are included in that list. Front sway bars are used where front end loading increases. Assuming that a small block engine is used, pre-'34 rods seldom need or want a front sway bar, while '55 and later cars nearly always need one. Adding a big block of any flavor, or going to newer cars as the engine mounts get very near the front axle centerline will make a front bar more desirable. On muscle cars in particular, it is generally necessary to increase the rear bar and front bar stiffness together.

Talk to other rodders, as well as the vendors, to get good info. Just as you have to do when asking questions in online forums, you'll soon learn to sort out good info from blather. And when testing your own car, don't be afraid to experiment by temporarily disconnecting sway bar links to see what the effect is. The change, plus or minus, will tell you if you are heading in the right direction. Hopefully, this short discussion will help you wrap your head around what is happening, and pique your interest in learning more. Why drive a car that is less than it could be? Why spend thousands to build it, and then not spend a few hundred more to get it right?

A well considered selection and mounting of your sway bars will provide a well balanced chassis that doesn't exhibit over- or under-steer.

This '66 Chevelle features a heavy duty sway bar made by Ridetech. It couples a tubular design to save weight with nearly infinite adjustments to allow a rodder to fine tune his suspension to personal taste, or for an occasional day at the track.

Suspension

Why Suspension Travel is Important

Half the Travel = Twice the G-force

Have you wondered why it is so difficult to get a lowered Hot Rod to ride as well as a modern production car? I always did too, and then really got focused on this problem after riding in Gary Meadors '29 roadster. You know, the yellow one with the track nose. I was in Pleasanton early enough to get into the Hot Rod Week shop tour, but couldn't drive my car due to an ornery early-style fuel injection system. (They are MUCH better now.) Gary was kind enough to offer me a seat in the roadster while we rode around the Bay Area. Now, I am a good bit larger than Mrs. Meadors, and I wondered if my bulk might cause some ride issues on the beat up roads common to San Francisco, as well as any large city.

I was thoroughly impressed with how well the chassis worked as we travelled. Not a sign of bottoming out with an amazing ride for a car that short and light. When Gary opened the deck lid to put away the windbreaker that became unnecessary later in the day, I saw the "secret". Steve Moal built the entire car and had engineered it with more travel front and rear than is commonly seen, yet with a low stance so important to a Hot Rod stance. That did require raising the trunk floor but the trade off of ride versus luggage space was well worth it!

The idea of Hot Rod ride quality really begins with some High School Physics. Don't worry; we'll need some common sense rather than a calculator. The teachers taught us that force equals mass times acceleration (F=m X a). If you work through the definitions of mass and acceleration you can quickly see that when the same mass has to stop more quickly, due to less travel, you will feel twice the G force in the seat of your pants. In other words, the same total Hot Rod weight with half the suspension travel will ride twice as hard. It's pure physics and no amount of pretty fabrication work or advertising copy will change that fact.

If the travel is short enough that the suspension instantly stops due to bottoming or topping out, the G force can become very high with the only cushioning left due to the seat, tires, etc. You will find that about 75% of ride quality problems result from this travel problem when either shock absorber length or bump stop contact limits wheel travel. Total available suspension travel also has an effect on the spring rate needed to support a vehicle, which naturally affects ride quality as well. Before we get into spring rates, let's talk about shock length.

For simplicity's sake, let's look at solid axle suspension first. It is very common to have about 4 inches of total travel front and rear. We'll deal with coil-overs as an example as they make it simple to calculate spring rates. A car that weighs 2000 pounds on each end will need a spring capable of supporting 1000 pounds at each wheel. With a 4 inch stroke that requires about a 300 pound spring rate. If we can design the suspension to allow for a 5 inches of travel we can support the same weight with a 250 pound spring rate. With the 17% reduction in spring rate the suspension will ride better and react to road bumps better, allowing improved handling as a bonus. That 25% increase in travel also nets a larger "window" for coil-over height adjustment with less risk of running out of travel.

What about shock mounting angles? With a vertically mounted shock each inch of axle travel equals one inch of shock travel. If you lean the shock at 45 degrees, the laws of Trigonometry tell us that the shock now moves only .71 inches with each inch of suspension travel. That also means that the shock loses about 30% of its effectiveness. It is therefore best to mount shocks as close to vertical as possible, although we often mount coil-overs with the upper mount moved an inch just for style, with minimal effect on function. When dealing with coil-overs, the same lean requires an increase in spring rate to do the same job, which adds to the stress on the mountings with no benefits at all.

When we look at an independent suspension, whether front or rear, there is also a leverage effect to consider. As mentioned earlier, if the shock, spring, or combined coil-over is mounted half way from the control arm inner pivot point to the center of the tire contact patch, a 50% ratio exists. That makes a 4 inch stroke shock allow 8 inches of wheel travel, but the spring must be twice as strong. If our sample car weighs 1000 pounds per corner a spring mounted to a straight axle would need to support 1000 pounds, while the same car with the 50% ratio independent suspension would need a spring that can support a 2000 pound load. It is tempting to design a trick IFS with an upper coil-over mount that is in line with the upper control arm pivots and the lower mount out near the lower ball joint. If that combined coil-over angle exceeds 45 degrees, the spring rate will actually DECREASE and the car will really wallow when a bump is encountered.

So how can you achieve a low ride height, while preserving proper scrub line clearance? Once you have determined your desired final ride height by mocking up the car, you will need to raise the upper coil-over or shock mount enough to prevent bottoming. Remember to place either shock type so that 60% of its total travel is available for compression. Use a shock on straight axles that allows more than 4 inches of travel if at all possible. Recall also that independent suspension actually multiplies shock travel, and that a more vertical mount will nearly always be best. While you do that planning also be certain that the axle travel will not be limited by the bottom of the frame, the trunk floor, or any other object. Modifying those will be extra work, but it will always pay off.

These concepts can be used to build a new car or improve an original. If you simply cannot add travel to a car that bottoms out, look into premium quality aftermarket shock absorbers, maybe even those with an adjustable shock rate. The more expensive and more sophisticated valving found in these shocks will do a great job of controlling suspension travel without undue harshness. A new set of four premium, adjustable aftermarket shocks can be installed in a half day's work for around $500 to $600. That just might be the very best single improvement you could make to a finished Hot Rod!

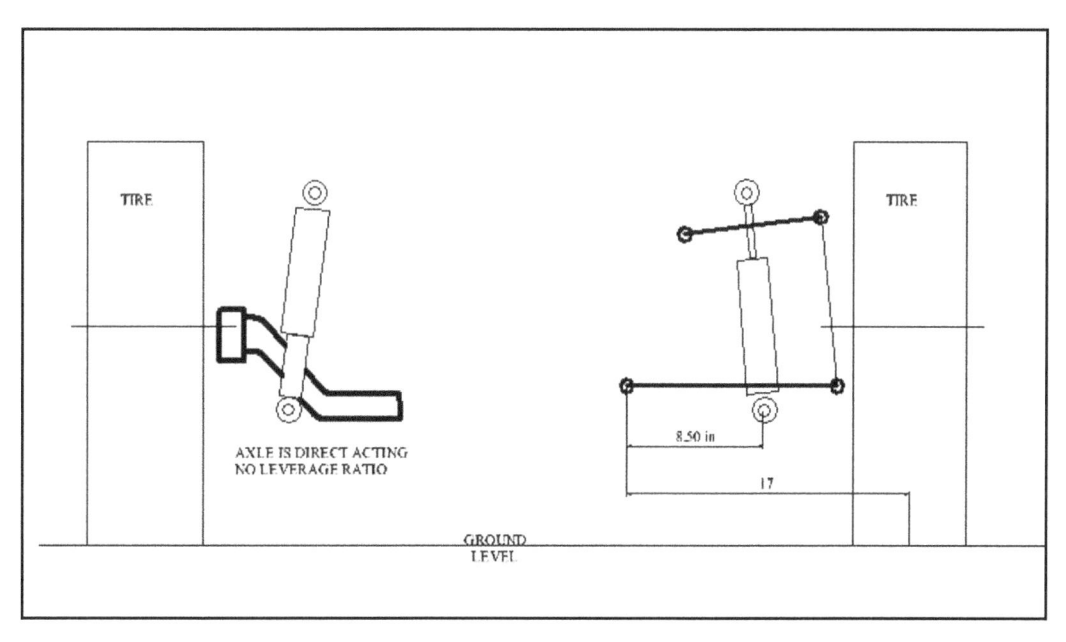

Whether you are considering a coil-over or a conventional shock absorber, the presence of a leverage ratio on an independent suspension alters both shock travel and spring rate. This ratio does not exist with straight axle suspension so the major factor becomes shock angle of the vertical as it affects shock travel and spring rate.

Suspension

Leaf Spring Suspension 101

Simple and Very Effective

Leaf spring suspensions have been in use since the first carriage builder thought he could improve ride quality on his buckboard wagons. It's no surprise that the first cars used an extension of that technology. Many other systems such as coil springs, torsion bars, and Air Ride have been developed to provide various advantages, but it's still hard to beat the leaf spring for a simple, clean way to provide suspension and axle control.

The simplest system was Ford's transverse, or "buggy spring" used from 1906 to 1948. It is very rugged, and saves weight, but requires a torque tube or radius rods to locate the axle fore and aft, as well as in rotation. When used with the original unsplit wishbone, the axle is free to rotate about the driveshaft axis, allowing easy travel over the rough roads of the day. On modern, smoother roads, the ride quality often suffers due to the single spring requiring a higher rate than two parallel leafs doing the same job. Ride quality can be surprisingly good when the steps we'll mention later are taken to reduce friction between the leaves.

Later GM, Ford, and Mopar cars used a dual spring parallel leaf system. This type is very common for street rods today, both updating the original system as well as complete modern kits. The major advantage is their simplicity. The spring controls both axle rotation and position, and only needs locating help with extreme use due to high horsepower engines and sticky tires. Traction bars of different types and panhard bars are often used to supplement the positioning ability of the leaf springs themselves. Good handling results as the leaves themselves resist body roll, and can easily accept sway bars for more roll control.

Leaf springs work particularly well in larger, heavier cars with a variable load. By that I mean sedans and panels where the load may be the driver alone one day and four people with luggage the next. We actually prefer rear leafs on most fat fender sedans, coupes and panels with their load carrying capacity. The leaf spring naturally has a variable rate spring in both multi and mono leaf styles. As the spring is deflected, the spring rate increases, giving the ability to carry heavier loads without bottoming.

Coil-overs work great on short, light cars like '32 coupes, but have a hard time dealing with the variable load we're discussing. If you don't change the vehicle's load very often, you'll be very happy with coil-overs. Some companies do offer variable spring rates on their coil-over springs, so these are well worth looking into when dealing with a heavier car. We use them on our '55-'57 Chevy chassis with great results.

On some cars, such as '32 Fords, leaf spring length is limited by space available in the chassis, so Air Ride with a four-bar is a good solution for sedans of that era. I have personally used The Cool Ride version on a '32 sedan, and Shockwaves on my current '34 Ford Tudor. We cruise these cars with just the driver one day, and then load three guys and luggage for the weekend the next. The Air ride lets us maintain ride height for the stance we want, and then we can bump the air pressure to carry the heavier loads. My personal opinion is that in a variable load situation, the extra cost of Air ride is well rewarded.

The tunability of a multi leaf spring can be a real advantage with our Hot Rods. Mono leafs and fiberglass springs are very attractive due to their easy action with no internal friction, but they lose the ability to be fine tuned by adding or subtracting leaves. That opportunity to match a spring to an exact application with a simple leaf change can be critical with so many variations in our cars.

It's a simple matter to lower a leaf suspension, provided you have enough axle travel. A spring shop (look in the phone book under truck repair) can reverse the eyes or raise/lower the arch to change the ride height. Aftermarket companies offer a great variety of brand new springs that are already designed to provide a drop. Lowering blocks can be used but should be kept to no more than 2 inches in height. Any more will create access problems to brake adjustment and can cause cornering and wheel hop problems. Blocks do have the advantage of being an easy way to slightly adjust the wheelbase for proper wheel to fender centering. This is really helpful on '37-'48 Chevys and '35-'40 Fords where the fenders themselves are not made consistently.

A few simple details make a huge difference in ride quality with leaf springs. First, be absolutely sure that the shock travel neither bottoms nor tops out. That is still the major cause of problems in any type of suspension system. Individual leaf spring length must be properly staggered for smooth action. Anything that will reduce the springs interleaf friction will also pay off in a better ride. Aids include Teflon buttons or strips, which are available with molded lips to help keep them in place. The GM cars use a 1-3/4 inch spring like early Fords, so just get two kits to do both springs. Lubrication is also helpful, and the spring must then be sealed or wrapped with a top quality vinyl tape which will stretch as the spring moves. In fact, most original springs came with a galvanized tin cover, while Ford added a hollow center bolt with a fitting and grooved leaves to allow grease to flow between the leafs. Many of these cars have received replacement springs over the years that lack these features, but what a difference they make. Around here, the Ford V-8 restorers are always after us to save those original springs for them!

This Chassis Engineering Co. parallel leaf spring kit incorporates all the features of a good design with the shocks and sway bar mounted to accomplish very good handling and ride quality.

Another very important feature in reducing friction is the configuration of the ends of the leaves. The very best springs have a tapered thickness with a rounded shape. Diamond cut ends and square cut ends are cheaper to manufacture, but have increased friction at their tips. Teflon buttons or strips will be very important with those style ends.

The tapered style makes an easy transition of load between the leaves for smoother action. This little detail makes an amazing difference in how smoothly the spring works. You can spend the time to grind your spring adding this important detail, or simply buy a spring made that way from the beginning. (They look nicer too.)

Shackles are required to allow the spring to change length as it flattens under compression. It is important that the loaded shackle angle be about 15 degrees from vertical, leaned toward the fixed end of the spring. The length change of the spring is then accommodated by the horizontal swinging of the shackle. If the shackle is too horizontal at ride height, it will restrict the spring travel and hurt ride quality. When that happens, the shackle has to rotate in a vertical mode, and the car will actually have to lift to allow the length change. You can easily imagine how that will hurt ride quality. When the shackle is too long it can hit the perch, again making the spring act like a solid bar. This advice applies to parallel leafs, as well as transverse Ford leafs. It's another good argument for using adjustable perches on a Ford dropped axle; allowing the shackle angle to be adjusted without changing the spring.

Speaking of dealing with length change, too many rodders struggle needlessly with mounting their transverse spring on dropped axle set ups. The original springs had the eyes on the bottom side, and were stretched enough to allow the shackles to be installed by using either a screw jack or hydraulic mechanism. Reversed eye springs don't allow that, and it's really hard to compress the spring enough to get enough length to engage the shackles. A better way is to disassemble the spring and just mount the main leaf to the shackles. It is easily compressed, and the rest of leaves added afterward by use of a temporary long center bolt, and a pair of C clamps to compress the spring stack. When it's all in place, replace the temporary pin with the original center bolt. This is an old and simple trick that seems to need relearning. In fact, we often mock-up a chassis with a reduced spring pack so that we can approximate final ride height with a car not yet fully loaded.

Some early cars like Buicks and Packards use parallel leafs with a shackle on each end, since a torque tube was used to locate the rear-end. We like to make a solid front perch on the stock spring and retain those when adding a late rear end, shocks, and sway bar. If the original springs are in good shape, I'm a big fan of using the springs that you already own, and that are already mounted, and designed for the car.

All in all, parallel leaf suspension makes a simple, affordable, and easy to tune suspension for the vast majority of Hot Rods. Many kits are available for specific applications, as well as universal kits that a reasonably skilled rodder can adapt to unusual cars. Today's rodder can buy a kit that will install right the first time without experimentation or the help of a spring shop to modify parts, like in the old days. You are buying someone else's experience instead of getting your own the hard way. Hopefully you've learned a few things that will help you select the kit you want. You can get fancier and more adjustable with other options, but sometimes "simplicity is still the ultimate sophistication."

> **We actually prefer rear leafs on most fat fender sedans, coupes and panels with their load carrying capacity.**

Suspension

Straight Axle Tech

A Series of New/Old Tricks Smooth out the Bumps

Independent suspensions have become very popular in the past few years, but many rodders still prefer the elegant simplicity of a straight axle. With the recent interest in "newstalgia," axles are being considered as a viable front suspension design which looks good, and can approach the ride and handling of independent front suspension when set up properly.

What you do get with a straight axle suspension is basic simplicity and a clean appearance. Many cars will accept a modified axle with a minimum of work, especially cars like Model T's and fenderless cars where IFS (Independent Front Suspension) often doesn't look just right. If you vary the paint style (paint vs. chrome), and technical options, a very individualized suspension can be built. A very basic, but stock rebuilt, undropped, drum brake suspension can be a very inexpensive first step for a new Hot Rodder. More upgrades can be added later as your experience, goals and budget grow. You'll often want to add power steering and disc brakes. If taken to the highest style and technical levels, you'll easily spend as much as most IFS systems, without gaining all of the ride and handling advantages, but it sure will look good!

What you don't get is related directly to the limitations imposed by an axle's need to have each front wheel react to any road surface contacted by the other side. Your ride and handling are unavoidably affected, although Teflon bushed springs such as those from Posies ,or monoleafs, can help. You can greatly improve the smoothness of the spring action by minimizing the friction between leaves. Multi-leaf springs have the ability to be turned by changing the number of leaves.

Any suspension reacts well to top quality aftermarket shock absorbers. Our British friends call them dampers, which more correctly describes their function in damping and controlling the motion of the suspension. The more modern tunable shocks will improve beam axle suspension ride and handling to a level that would have been impossible 40 years ago. This is a great way you can preserve the vintage style you love, while upgrading to modern performance levels.

The most basic of axle types is the good old original forged I-beams. These things are tougher than nails and about as attractive! Dropped versions are available for many cars and trucks, in both modified stock axles and aftermarket pre-dropped new forgings. Cast iron dropped axles are available too, as are composite steel tubing/cast-end axles. These last types are jig welded together, and should really be painted in an "as fabricated" condition. As mentioned earlier, excessive grinding and chrome plating can lead to failure in the weld since the joint has been weakened, especially by the hydrogen embrittlement often seen in plating a high carbon material such as malleable cast iron.

Fabricated tubing axles can look very clean, and are often used on T-buckets and full-fendered T's where a single-bend axle compliments the T's angular styling. This type of axle also works well on dual leaf suspensions, such as early GMs and Mopars. Since the dual leaf stock axles already have a pretty deep drop, be careful not to go too low with a dropped axle. The extra leverage of the dropped axle can cause

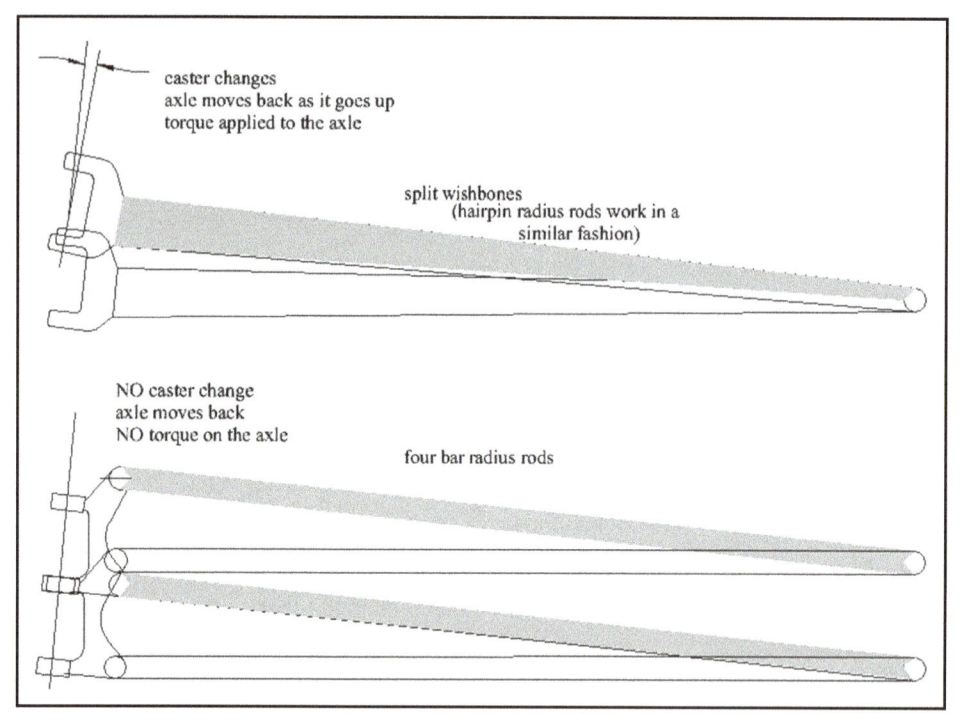

Here you can see how and why a bump encountered by one wheel, with split wishbones, puts a twist on the axle; while in the same situation a set of 4-bars allows one end of the axle to go up without putting any twist or torque on the axle.

wrap-up under heavy braking and steering. A cross-steering set-up is usually best with dual leafs.

Mounting the axle is very basic with dual leafs, but more complicated with transverse, or "buggy" springs. A wishbone, like a stock Ford, is actually one of the best set-ups, but usually leads to problems with oil pan access, transmission mounting and V8 engine exhaust. A 4-bar works really well, although it lacks a true nostalgic look. Split wishbones actually turn the front axle into a very large sway bar, since the ends of the axle try to rotate as the wheel on that side rises and falls. That leads to very tight handling, and often a rough ride. The twisting can lead to rod end or bolt failures, as well as problems with any axle type other than a forged I-beam. The forged I-beam allows a flexibility the others lack that helps to accept the twisting forces.

One of the best ways to assemble the necessary components for a good straight axle set-up is to review the various rodding advertisements and catalogs available. An enormous variety of axles, springs, mounts, steering and brakes are offered. Get the catalogs, read them thoroughly, and ask questions until you understand fully what's available. Once you sort out the different opinions and advice, you'll be a smart rodder who's ready to put your suspension together right, the first time.

Set up properly, a straight axle can give you ride and handling nearly as good as that of an independent suspension, but with the simplicity and The Look that only a straight axle can provide.

Suspension

Urethane Versus Rubber

NVH Suppression vs Improved Control

As we continue to search for ways to improve the function and appearance of our Hot Rods, the question often comes up as to using stock type rubber bushings or urethane in our suspension systems. A little history of how bushing technology works, and the history of Hot Rod suspension may be helpful.

Original factory suspensions nearly always use rubber bushings. For one thing, urethane chemistry hadn't even been commercially available when many of our cars were built. The cars from the pre 1930 era generally used bronze bushings at wear points. Those bushings often wore out fairly soon given the dirty conditions under the cars, and tended to produce an overly harsh ride, with a lot of suspension shock feedback to the passengers. Rubber bushings were steadily improved and began to appear in leaf spring shackles in the late '30s, and the front suspension pivots going into the mid 50's. It was expected that they would be replaced as necessary due to normal wear, which is just as important today. You can't expect dried out and cracked rubber to act as designed.

Engineers continued to improve ride quality, often giving up some handling precision in the quest to isolate the driver's senses from what the chassis was doing. This property is now called NVH suppression, which stands for noise, vibration, and harshness. Bushings began to be designed with larger and larger wall thickness in the '70s when cars started getting smaller in response to the first gas crisis and the quest for a "big car ride" continued. Proof of this evolution is steel bushings in '49-'54 Chevys, 3/16 inch wall rubber bushings in '57 Chevys and '67 Camaros, with the '79 Camaro having nearly 3/4 inch wall bushings in the front control arms.

As the oval track racers began to use the front steer ('70-'81) Camaro suspension, they quickly found out that changing to urethane bushings eliminated the very compliance (flexibility) that was designed in to provide better NVH suppression. Since a racer isn't concerned with ride quality this worked out well. Drag racers also like urethane bushings since they enhance front end rise by generally rotating easier than the rubber ones which are vulcanized to serrated inner steel sleeves. Those toothed sleeves bite into the mountings and the bushings act like miniature rubber torsion springs like we see on some trailers today.

Pete and Jake deserve credit for really making the front four-bar axle the standard it is today. The first units were made using bushings designed for '64 Chevy rear panhard bars. Under extended use, the early rubber bushings could come apart. Urethane bushings were developed as a replacement and were more durable, leading to their universal use today.

What we've seen is that rubber provides better isolation from road shock, but can be less durable. Urethane compounds have been developed with graphite impregnated for easier rotation and less squeaking, but will transfer motion more directly from the chassis to the driver. Where the bushing simply rotates on it's center axis as on front suspension control arms, urethane works well. It will tend to be harsher in some cases, but rodders can't usually detect much difference. When the new big wheel/short sidewall tires are combined with urethane bushings, the ride will usually be appreciably harder. How much is tolerable is a case of personal preference.

Urethane can be trouble when the bushing relies on twisting and changing angle as it operates.

Urethane can also be molded to provide a coil spring mount that will replace some of the NVH suppression lost with urethane pivot bushings that are less compliant than OEM rubber parts.

Urethane bushings are often used on performance oriented aftermarket control arms to enhance control and steering response, although at the expense of some NVH suppression.

Caution should be exercised using urethane in strut rod bushings on front lower control arms. Examples of this include Mustangs, both early and the Mustang II, '62-'67 Novas, and '63-'70 Buicks. The bushing can be so incompressible that the strut rod brackets may fail.

The very first four-bars were seen on sprint cars, using tie rod ends for an adjustable, replaceable, pivoting, sealed yet greasable, and readily available rod end. They are just about perfect but don't look trick enough for the smoothie kind of Hot Rodder. Urethane bushings have therefore become pretty much standard on front and rear four-bars. They hold up well, and actually add some roll stiffness to the suspension due to their resistance to being twisted. Many folks find their jam nuts won't stay tight since the bushings force the bar to twist and back off the nut. A good cleaning and a coat of Loctite generally cures that problem. We have seen tremendous innovation from the guys at Air Ride Technology, who have recently gone to a special rubber bushed rod end which provides good location ability, yet twists more freely for a more compliant suspension. This technology first appeared on Detroit cars, using an hourglass section bushing to provide proper component location without undue roll resistance. We use them and have excellent results. The bushing is larger than usual but provides a good compromise of stability versus flexibility.

Like so many choices in building a Hot Rod, it boils down to a choice of radicality of response and sleek appearance in our suspension, versus a more compliant yet comfortable practicality. Before you change, try to get a ride in a car changed the way you are considering. Then you can make an informed decision - that's always better, isn't it.

Fabrication Skills

Blind Rivets

One more Fastener Option

Different types of welding processes have long been the preferred way of joining metal components on a hot rod project. Lately, an even older process has gained acceptance whereby rivets are used to make the joint, that technique going back to the age of armored warriors. Solid aircraft-type rivets have also become quite popular for the highly functional style they present in addition to their strength. Special tools are needed for those solid rivets but the technique is easily mastered.

You may also find occasions where a pulled rivet is a good answer to a metal joining project. Commonly called "pop" rivets from the name of a very popular brand. They vary from import swap meet super soft weak ones to aircraft types that are as strong as a driven rivet. Naturally, the very soft cheap pulled rivets cannot be trusted to hold up under much stress. They are useful for installing window rub strips and glass channels where their soft alloy is less likely to chip installed window glass.

Good hardware and home improvement stores will generally carry the better quality "pop" brand pulled rivets. These are available in many diameters and grip lengths. Aluminum, steel, and even stainless steel materials allow choices of increasing strength where a load must be carried. Different colors available can be an aid to hiding these fasteners. We find the aluminum ones especially handy for mounting brake line and wiring clamps and the like where they are easy to drill out should you need to make changes. The steel and stainless items are handy for more highly loaded uses like mounting AC condenser brackets to the side of your radiator core. Just be VERY sure to limit your drill depth to avoid drilling into the core! Some stores and race car supply shops carry a large headed pop rivet that works well for attaching soft items like inner fender flaps on the muscle cars.

The very best type pulled rivets are available from aircraft supply houses like Aircraft Spruce and Specialty. As they are made from aircraft grade aluminum alloys they offer high strength and are quite resistant to damage through vibration and fatigue. A steel inner mandrel allows the stronger alloy body to be pulled tightly and is retained inside the rivet body, greatly enhancing the finished fastener strength. Conventional raised heads can be used or a countersunk version provides a smoother appearance. As these are a legal repair substitute for even certified aircraft, you can count on these rivets for reliable joints.

The conventional-head aircraft pulled rivet can be a part number such as CR3212-04-02. Decoding this tells us that the -04 means 4/32 or

> Good hardware ... stores will generally carry the better quality "pop" brand pulled rivets. These are available in many diameters and grip lengths.

1/8 inch diameter, described as how many 1/32 of an inch diameter are actually present. The -02 means 2/16 or 1/8 inch reach, expressed this time as how many 1/16 inch material thickness can be assembled. The actual grip range will often be stated on the package and for this size ranges from .063-.125 inch stack of material. For the countersunk type head, merely substitute CR 3213 for the prefix. There are many diameters and grip length combinations for these pulled rivets, as well as for the more common pop rivets discussed above. If you want to experiment with the "aircraft seat" style, these pulled rivets can be a good choice as they are faster to install and require fewer special tools to install than the solid driven-style rivet.

Recently I made a repair using the good aircraft grade countersunk aluminum rivets. While chopping a 1950 Ford, it became necessary to remove the front vent window lower pivot bracket to weld a failure in the bracket. A driven rivet might have worked as well but I was concerned about the force of setting the rivet causing damage to the fragile pivot bracket. The pop rivets replaced the originals quite nicely and are strong enough to keep the bracket functioning as it should.

There are some recommended rules for rivet spacing and edge distance. Keep your rivet centerlines 1-1/2 times the rivet diameter from the material edge. In other words, an 1/8 inch rivet must be drilled at least 3/32 from the nearest edge. Spacing seems to work out best in the ¾ to 1 ¼ inch range. Closer is a waste of rivets and farther apart makes for a weak joint. Aircraft supply houses also carry a rivet spacing tool called a "rivet fan" which is a big help in marking evenly spaces holes in straight lines. It is made with a series of bars joined in a parallelogram fashion which can be extended for different lengths and spacing. If you prefer the style of the countersunk head pulled rivet, the same supply houses will have tools to either stamp a receiving dimple in metal less than .060 inch thick, and countersink bits for thicker stock.

Have you noticed that pop rivets often seem to hang up as you install a common 1/8 inch rivet into a 1/8 inch drilled hole? That is because a 2 flute drill will drill a slightly 3-sided hole in thin metal (I can't explain that, nor can any one else I have asked, but I'll bet you've noticed this effect). Also, rivets are actually designed to be installed in a hole slightly larger than their generic name.

Blind rivets work really well for fastening brake line clips that will later be removed for painting of the chassis. On final assembly the holes can be tapped for screws or the blind rivets simply replaced for a secure and easy way to permanently mount items such as brake and fuel lines.

The most common 1/8 inch rivet really needs a hole .129 to .132 inch in diameter, which calls for a #30 drill. To complete the set you would also need a #40 drill for 3/32 inch, #21 for 5/32 inch and #11 for 3/16 inch rivets. Those hole sizes apply for all types of pulled rivets.

If you are going to install more than a very few rivets, invest in a better river pulling tool than an import copy. The better ones are made of cast aluminum construction and store the four different size mandrels right on the handles. When pulling the more common pop rivets with aluminum center mandrels as well as bodies, the mandrels will begin sticking in the tool head. Keep the tool head well lubricated with a kerosene based spray like WD-40 to prevent the galled aluminum particles from causing this annoyance.

Pop rivets have gotten a bum rap over the years as an unreliable way to attach parts. If the proper type rivet is installed in the right size hole with the correct tool, you will find this bad reputation can be undeserved. Like so many techniques, cheap copy parts poorly selected, and installed wrong, lead to trouble down the road - but isn't that like most short cuts we get tempted to use when fabricating a hot rod? Building a hot rod will help cement the realization that you generally get the quality you are willing to pay for.

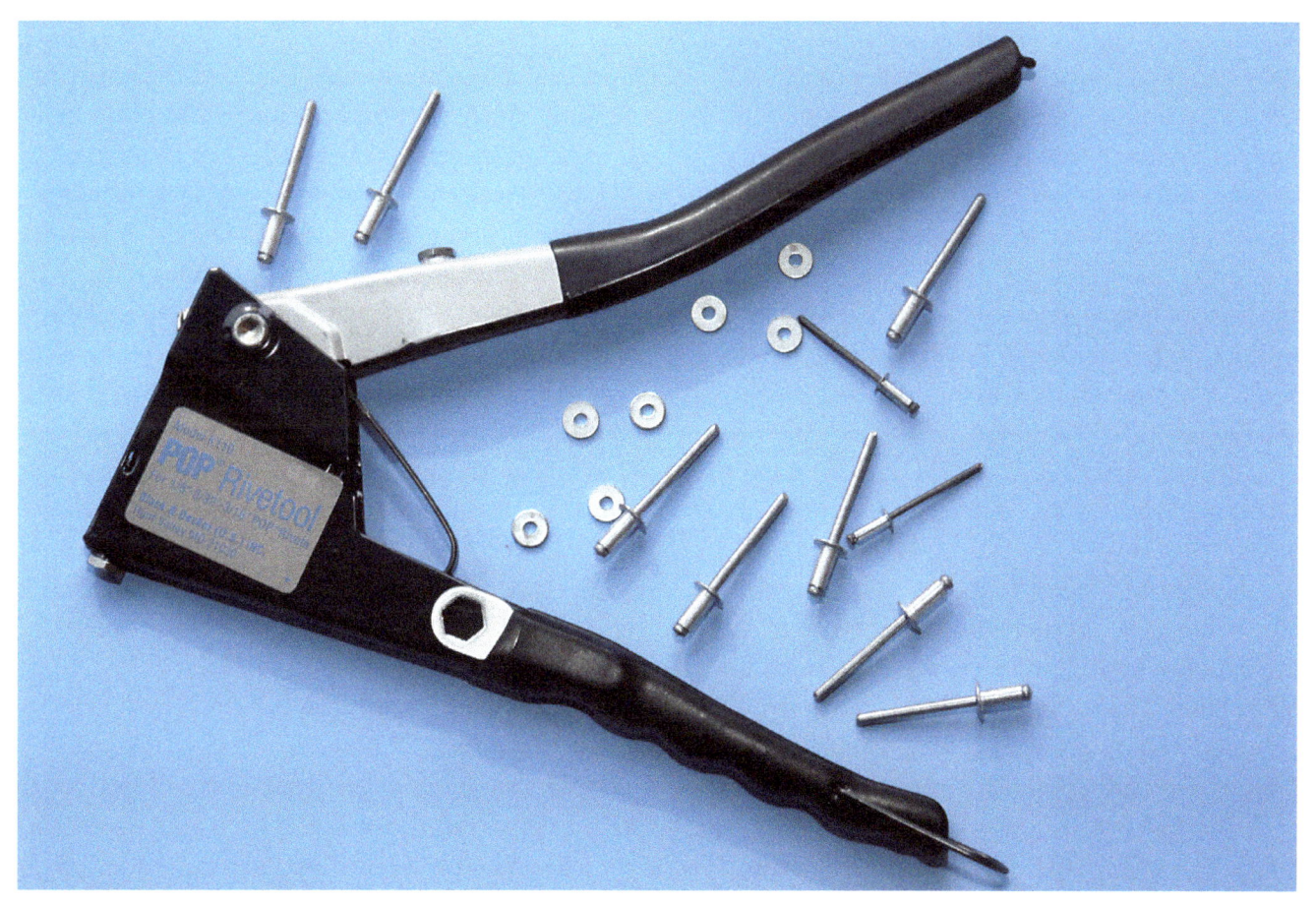

Sometimes called Pop Rivets, the rivets themselves are available in a wide variety of sizes, and from a number of manufacturers.

Fabrication Skills

Hammer Welding

Perfect Butt Welds require a Perfect Fit

A real mark of craftsmanship is using the hammer welding technique for repairing sheet metal. The smooth finish on both sides, and nice surface for finish body work, are a delight to see. Many nice cars have been built using the MIG-and-Mud body work technique, which is fine when performed well, but metal finishing is the ultimate goal. Although, several excellent videos are available, we'll discuss the basics here, since you really end up teaching yourself as you practice.

Heat control is the key, and requires the right equipment. You'll want the smallest tip available for your welding set, or buy a jeweler's torch set. We are especially fond of the Henrob/Dillon torch you've seen advertised. Its ability to concentrate and control heat gives you TIG quality welding without the complication. It will remove many hours from your learning curve in hammer welding. Whatever torch you use, be sure to keep your tip clean and well adjusted. Build a simple stand to keep the torch lit as you pick up your hammer and dolly.

Find some 1/16 inch thick steel scrap from the local sheet metal shop to practice on. Learn to control the heat, limiting warpage while achieving full penetration. You don't want a bead on the reverse, just good joining. As you improve, progress to thinner material like an old fender from the forties or earlier. Later model tin is just too thin and soft for the apprentice. The nicely crowned shape in that torn up practice fender will hold its shape as you weld. Dead flat panels will give you fits and might make you give up in frustration.

Filler rod is generally 1/16 inch in diameter, copper coated to resist rust, which would inhibit flow within the weld puddle. We often use 1/32 inch or .045 MIG wire for an even smaller bead. Don't even consider brazing. The smaller your weld bead, the less warpage, hammering and grinding. A perfectly fitted joint, flowing together without any filler rod, is the ideal.

The panels should fit perfectly, ground to butt up without gaps or overlap. Use as many clamps as possible. We've even used a bandsawn 2 x 4 to hold a surface contour from both sides as a clamping aid. MIG welders also work great to tack the edges together, being sure to grind each tack as you gas weld that section. Never allow an overlap, rather sneak up on a perfect joint by grinding to a scribed line.

Select a flat face hammer and a dolly with just a little more crown than the piece you're repairing. Tap lightly, as heavy blows will stretch the metal. Resist the temptation to hammer the metal when it's red hot. Despite what you may have heard, hammering red hot weld beads will only frustrate you, as it is actually the technique used to shrink metal.

If you are right handed, start finish welding at the left hand side of the panel. Weld a 1 inch section, welding right to left. Then leave a 2 inch section to the right, skip a 1 inch seam and repeat the 1 inch weld. You are welding right to left, but progressing left to right. This backwelding technique avoids welding on preheated sections. You should never begin to weld an area that is too hot to touch. Heated areas will be warped, and welding them will lock in that warp. Be patient and have faith that cool metal properly aligned at first will be right again once the heat is removed. A few light taps will perfect the joint once completely cooled. The metal will have shrunk via the heat, and a few light on-dolly hammer blows will stretch it back to the before welding condition.

Although this technique requires practice, it pays dividends. You'll know you're doing good work, and enjoy advancing your craftsmanship. Your wiring will get neater, and your panels straighter as the quality ethic carries over. We've all had to redo work that lacked care and cussed the workman's lack of skill. Be the guy others praise 20 years from now when your Hot Rod is passed to the next generation.

The key to any successful hammer weld is first creating a precise fit between the two panels to be joined. Any gaps will increase warpage tremendously when the weld is completed.

This real steel '34 coupe was in a severe rear end collision but rescued by careful dolly work and installation of new panels hammer welded for a nearly metal finished surface.

Fabrication Skills

A Few Tips on Welding

MIG, TIG or Gas, Parctice makes Perfect

Welding is one of the necessary skills needed in building hot rods. Many of us will remember the "Tool Time" episode where Tim Taylor (Tim Allen) taught his son Brad to "cut steel with fire" as part of his passage into manhood! Even though some really nice kits are available in a bolt-on version of a bracket, it's pretty likely that sooner or later a welded example will be preferable. It's often easier, cleaner looking and faster to accomplish a function with a welded bracket, even though bolt-on stuff is great where parts are already painted or changes are being made to a finished car. It's just so cool to see a bracket whose design flows with the car, and maybe even serves a couple different purposes. Some say it's one of the signs of a real top notch fabricator.

Very affordable welding units now exist for the hobbyist. You are not likely to work fast enough to need the type of high duty cycles on expensive professional equipment. In fact, many a frame has been ruined by too much welding without proper attention to weld spacing and cooling time. MIG units are by far the most common, just be sure it's capable of 3/8 inch material with at least a 20% duty cycle. The 110 volt units are fine for sheet metal use, but you'll want the punch of a 220 volt unit for chassis work. Some very nice air-cooled TIG units are out now at quite attractive pricing. A nice TIG weld will look great painted as is, saving the time grinding and finishing welds. For the duty cycle on a hobby level, the air-cooled torch will do OK, and can be upgraded to a water cooled system as usage and budget require.

You will actually be teaching yourself to weld through practice. The basics are learned by taking classes at the weld supply house and community colleges. You can also get help by attending the seminars offered at Goodguys events as well as by working with a friend with proven welding skills. If you are unsure of your skills, there's nothing wrong with tacking parts in place and later finishing them with supervision. You can even hire a guy to finish the welding, or collect on an exchange of favors with your buddy the experienced welder. Many builders will leave everything tacked until the entire chassis is done, and then finish all the welds once all design details are settled. You'll often wish you had waited!

The most common steel thickness used in hot rods is 3/16 inch. Racers often use 1/8 inch in a quest for weight savings, which aren't very important in the average hot rod. Strength must be achieved through careful geometry and design to avoid flexing, work hardening of the steel, and failure. Many brackets step up to 1/4 inch for higher-stressed suspension parts with the small increase in weight providing an extra safety factor.

Steering components are the only place where heavier 3/8 inch is commonly used. In fact, welding 1/2 inch plate to an 1/8 inch frame can actually cause problems in addition to being no stronger than the thinner material. For instance, a Mustang II strut rod bracket must be 1/2 inch thick in order to get proper crush on the bushings. A better way to build it is by using a 1/4 inch main plate welded to the frame with another 1/4 inch doubler added in the important area. This avoids the overheating and crystallization of the thinner metal which can lead to failure at the frame.

Learn to control the heat and use it to your advantage. Any time steel is heated, it shrinks. That's one reason why a bracket has to be tacked with the pull in mind, and preferably welded on both sides to equalize the shrinkage. You may have noticed that most rear four-bar axle brackets are made with a 3 inch hole for the axle tube. You do not have to saw off the ends of the axle to add these brackets. Simply saw them into two half circles to fit over the axle, and then weld all the way around. TIG welding will look best and cause less warpage due to the slower heat up/cool down cycle and smaller bead as compared to MIG welding. You are not welding all around for strength, but rather to equalize shrinkage and keep the axle reasonably straight. You can even straighten a bent axle housing by welding or heating on the "long" side in order to shrink it back straight. In fact, before the days of "no weld" heat treated truck frames, this shrinking effect was used to put a slight arch in flatbed truck and trailer frames to help carry the weight, as well as to make repairs.

Try to think a little first about how to design

Structurally sound welds can be ground to smooth a joint or left exposed to be an attractive feature of a new chassis for your hot rod.

your parts and welds for maximum strength. A compression joint is always the strongest since the weld merely serves to position the members. That's why round tube construction calls for fish-mouthing the tubes so that each member fits snugly against its supporting partner. A weld in tension is quite strong, as we discussed in the truck frame deal above. The entire cross section of the weld and the part are equally stressed, spreading the load. A shear joint will be the weakest due to a "peeling" effect that concentrates the stress to a small area. Gusseting is a big help here, and is usually done on something like a Vega steering box mount. Weld all around a bracket wherever possible. If you can't, at least wrap the weld around the ends a little rather than simply along one edge.

The wrap around trick avoids the creation of the source of weld failures. When a feature of a weld or bracket concentrates force, a stress riser is created. This causes less cross section and fewer molecules available to resist stress. In a strange way, I think that's kinda like all the trailer/driver, high buck/homebuilt controversies. If we all work together, we're stronger than putting our stress on somebody else's back.

Correct selection of wire speed and amperage combines with a sure hand to produce welds that are not only strong but a pleasure to observe.

Pro Builders And Home Builders Agree;
Fat Man Is The Quality And Value Leader

Fat Man Hub To Hub Suspension Apps

- 1933-48 Ford Cars
- 1928-89 Ford Trucks
- 1939-48 Mercury Cars
- 1934-54 Chevy Cars
- 1928-87 Chevy Trucks
- 1928-87 GMC Trucks
- 1953-62 Chevy Corvette
- 1933-37 Chrysler Cars
- 1935-37 Desoto Cars
- 1933-38 Dodge Cars
- 1933-64 Dodge Trucks
- 1933-38 Plymouth Cars
- 1933-36 Buick Cars
- 1934 Olds Cars
- 1934-36 Pontiac Cars
- 1940-41 Graham Cars
- 1937-64 International Trucks
- 1934-47 Studebaker Cars
- 1936-64 Studebaker Trucks
- 1933-37 Hudson Cars
- 1933-37 Huppmobile Cars
- 1933-41 Willys Cars
- 1946-54 Willys Truck/Panel
- 1934-41 Nash Cars
- Nash Metropolitan
- Austin & Anglia
- 1961-63 Olds F85/Buick Special

Nobody Can Fit More Cars & Trucks!

- Three A-Arm Options Available
- New High Quality Spindles & Springs
- New Low-Ratio Manual Rack & Pinion
- Big Diameter OE Style Disc Brake Kit
- New Premium Quality Gas Shocks
- QA-1 Coilovers On Stage 3 Package
- RideTech Shock Wave On Stage 5
- Thickest In The Industry 5/16" Steel Crossmember* & 3/16" Spring Mounts
- Precision Plasma Cut Components

Build Your Suspension Your Way!

Standard: Fully jig welded steel tubular a-arms. We've sold thousands of these proven, FatMan front suspension packages. They are the value leader for your daily driver!

Upgrade 1: If you want brute strength and beauty, our new nickle plated big-tube arms are the way to go. Add $225 to any stage setup shown to the left.

Upgrade 2: For show quality looks we offer these beautiful polished stainless arms for any of our kits, full chassis and sub-frame packages. Add $400 to kits shown at left.

All ISO 9002 Compliant Engineering

Upgrade Any Stage Kit

Polished Ball Joint Caps
Stainless Bolt Kit
Plated Steel Cross Shaft
Polished 17-4 Stainless Castings

NEW! Nickle Plated Big-Tube Steel A-Arm Option

Upgrade Any Stage Kit

Graphite Impregnated Urethane Bushings & Spring Seats

Formed, Machined & Welded In Our Own U.S.A. Shop

Upgrade Your Existing FatMan Setup For Just $805

Big Diameter 1 Inch x .188 DOM American Steel Tubing

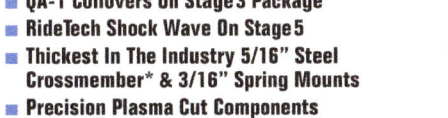

Made In The USA

Stage 2
$1,895 Hub To Hub Kit
Jig welded tubular steel A-arms. Manual rack, NEW spindles & shocks, OE style big brake kit. Why pay hundreds more elsewhere?

See Our A-Arm Upgrade Options At Right

Stage 3
$2,395 Hub To Hub Kit
Ultimate IFS! Jig welded tubular steel A-arms, genuine QA-1 coilovers. Manual rack, NEW spindles & shocks, and OE style big brake kit. There's NO comparable deal!

Compressor Systems Available

Stage 4
$2,395 Hub To Hub Kit
Fatman air ride IFS. Jig welded tubular steel A-arms, Firestone IV air spring set. Manual rack, NEW spindles & shocks, and OE style big brakes.

Stage 5
$2,995 Hub To Hub Kit
Jig welded tubular steel A-arms, RideTech Shock Wave system! Manual rack, new spindles & adjustable billet shocks, and OE style big brake kit. The ultimate in comfort and ride height adjustability!

704-545-0369
Mon-Thurs 7am-6pm EST - Fri 7am-12 noon
www.fatmanfab.com

FAT MAN
FABRICATION™

Wolfgang Books On The Web

http://www.wolfpub.com

SHEET METAL FAB FOR CAR BUILDERS

Thousands of Cobra and Lotus Super 7 replica owners dream of one day turning their fiberglass tribute cars into genuine metal machines, like the originals, but don't know where to begin. Many more car guys would love to customize their hot rod, or restore their classic without paying the stiff fees charged by custom panel shops.

Now, for the first time, they have a guide that goes into graphic detail on how to build complete metal bodies, not just patch panels, for any car project without the need for expensive tools, years of training, or paying for professional help. Some of the world's greatest panel crafters share their tips, techniques, and experience to get the home builder up to speed quickly.

144 Pages $27.95   Over 400 color images - 100% color

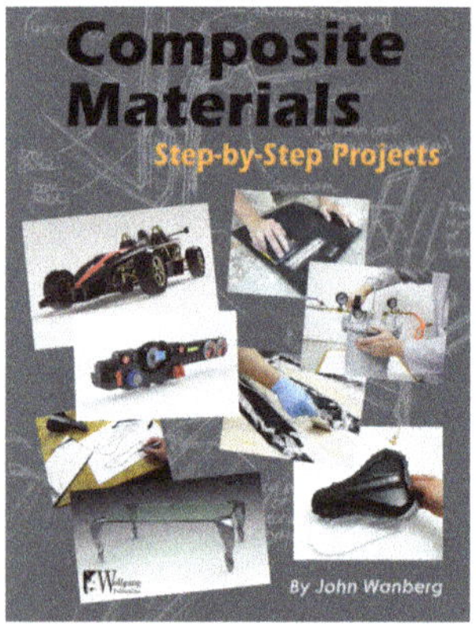

COMPOSITE MATERIALS - STEP BY STEP

In books one through three, Author and Professor John Wanberg, took pains to explain the why and how of building with Composite Materials. Each page was allocated nearly fifty-fifty between photos and text.

In Step-by-Step Projects, John takes a different approach. Instead of explaining the theory and what each component is made of, John cuts to the chase. Nearly every page is allocated to photos

The pictures lead the reader through a detailed how-to sequence. From making the mold, to cutting the fabric, and finishing the part, all the information is here. Projects include everything from fabricating speaker enclosures to hood scoops and cell-phone cases. Some require only simple molds, while others rely on more sophisticated vacuum bagging methods.

144 Pages $27.95   Over 400 photos - 100% color

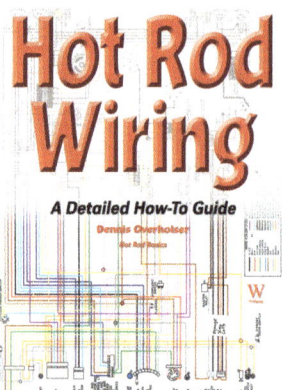

HOT ROD WIRING

There is one job that most mechanics farm out, and that that jog is wiring, but no more. Today you can pick the best components, the appropriate harness kit, and install everything yourself – with help from this new book from Wolfgang Publications. Whether it's an old skool '32 Ford with a flathead for power, or a modern kustom with fuel injected V-8 and a set of airbags, the information needed to wire that hot rod can be found

between the covers of Hot Rod Wiring from Wolfgang Publications. The electrical components used on modern hot rods have changed over the years. The stereo systems draw more power, and the number of accessories goes up and up. Hot Rod Wiring reflects these changes, and helps the reader determine how to pick the best components and design the best electrical system.

144 Pages $27.95   Over 400 photos - 100% color

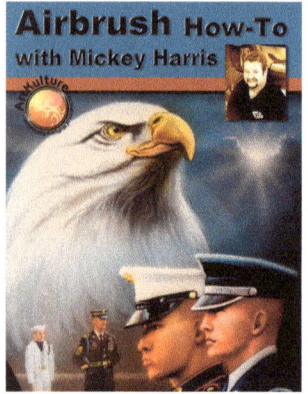

AIRBRUSH HOW-TO WITH MICKEY HARRIS

With over 35 years of experience under his belt, Mickey Harris is the ideal author to share with new and experienced airbrush artists what he's learned in a lifetime of airbrush work.

Mickey's new book starts with a little history - how he and a small group of his peers began to use the airbrush without any masks to paint T-shirts, motorcycles, hot rods and human bodies. Next comes Mickey's take on

what makes a good airbrush, followed by some of the strokes that make up the foundation of any good airbrush painting. How to Make a Living with an Airbrush is Mickey's version of Business 101 for airbrush artists.

The rest of the book is given over to twelve airbrushing sequences. Each one starts with a sketch and ends with a completed mural or graphic painted on a panel, a truck or maybe a hot rod.

144 Pages $27.95   Over 400 photos - 100% color

For a current list, visit our website
www.wolfpub.com

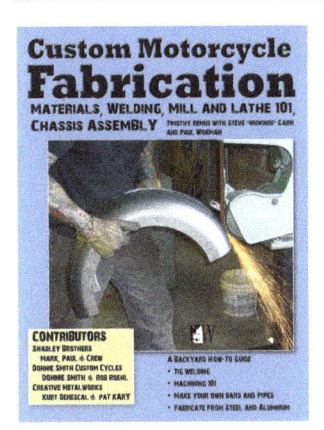

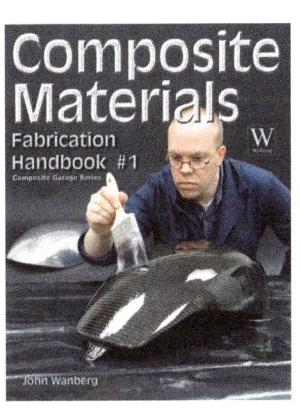

CUSTOM MOTORCYCLE FABRICATION

Owner of Bare Knuckle Choppers and long time motorcycle builder and fabricator, Paul Wideman is the perfect author for this book. With experience as both a hands-on builder and technical editor for Cycle Source Magazine, Paul has exactly the skill-set needed to write a book on fabrication.

Some commonly fabricated parts like handle bars and exhaust systems are covered as separate topics, along with sections on building simple brackets and mounts.

Learn how professionals like Paul bypass the catalog and build their parts from scratch instead. This is an essential building book, helping you build the necessary skills needed to assemble a truly unique kick-ass motorcycle.

144 Pages $27.95   Over 400 color images - 100% color

LEARNING THE ENGLISH WHEEL

Despite the fact that thousands of English wheel machines have been sold the past ten years there is currently no book dedicated to English wheeling. Owners of these machines are at a loss on how to really use them - because of the lack of DETAILED published material.

This book covers all aspects of English wheeling, from making your own wheel to learning the basics, from fabricating high-crown panels to reverse flares.

The photos used through the book serve to illustrate both what makes up a good English wheel, and how – exactly – to use an English wheel. Side bars and interviews done with famous wheelers and fabricators from around the world help to give personal insight from the best of the best.

144 Pages $27.95   Over 300 photos, 100% color

SHEET METAL BIBLE

Sheet Metal Bible is a compendium of sheet metal fabrication projects, everything from simple shaping operations to multi-piece creations like fenders and motorcycle gas tanks. Each of these operations is photographed in detail. Meaty captions help the reader to understand what's really happening as a flat sheet of steel slowly morphs into the convex side of a gas tank.

While some of the craftsmen work with hand tools, others prefer the English Wheel. The book is filled with work by legendary fabricators like Ron Covell, Craig Naff, Rob Roehl and Bruce Terry.

So whether your project needs parts made from aluminum or steel, is simple or complex, there is something in this new 176 page book to help you turn that dream into reality.

176 Pages $29.95   Over 400 photos, 100% color

COMPOSITE MATERIALS FABRICATION HANDBOOK #1

While most books on composites approach the subject from a very technical standpoint, Beginning Composites presents practical, hands-on information about these versatile materials. From explanations of what a composite is, to demonstrations on how to actually utilize them in various projects, this book provides a simple, concise perspective on molding and finishing techniques to empower even the most apprehensive beginner.

Topics include: What is a composite, why use composites, general composite types and where composites are typically used. Composite Materials Fabrication Handbook includes shop set up, design and a number of hands-on start-to-finish projects documented with abundant photographs.

144 Pages $27.95   Over 300 photos, 100% color

Wolfgang Publication Titles

For a current list visit our website at www.wolfpub.com

ILLUSTRATED HISTORY
Ultimate Triumph Collection	$49.95
American Police Motorcycles - Revised	$24.95

BIKER BASICS
Custom Motorcycle Fabrication	$27.95
Custom Bike Building Basics	$24.95
Custom Bike Building Advanced	$24.95
Sportster/Buell Engine Hop-Up Guide	$24.95
Sheet Metal Fabrication Basics	$24.95
How to Fix American T-Twin Motorcycles	$27.95

COMPOSITE GARAGE
Composite Materials Handbook #1	$27.95
Composite Materials Handbook #2	$27.95
Composite Materials Handbook #3	$27.95
Composite Materials - Step-by-Step Projects	$27.95

HOT ROD BASICS
How to A/C Your Hot Rod	$24.95
So-Cal Speed Shop's How to Build Hot Rod Chassis	$24.95
Hot Rod Wiring	$27.95
How to Chop Tops	$24.95

CUSTOM BUILDER SERIES
How to Build A Café Racer	$27.95
Advanced Custom Motorcycle Wiring - Revised	$27.95
How to Build an Old Skool Bobber Sec Ed	$27.95
How To Build The Ultimate V-Twin Motorcycle	$24.95
Advanced Custom Motorcycle Assembly & Fabrication	$27.95
How to Build a Cheap Chopper	$27.95

LIFESTYLE
Bean're — Motorcycle Nomad	$18.95
George The Painter	$18.95
The Colorful World of Tattoo Models	$34.95

MOTORCYCLE RESTORATION SERIES
Triumph Restoration - Unit 650cc	$29.95
Triumph MC Restoration Pre-Unit	$29.95

SHEET METAL
Sheet Metal Fab for Car Builders	$27.95
Advanced Sheet Metal Fabrication	$27.95
Ultimate Sheet Metal Fabrication	$24.95
Sheet Metal Bible	$29.95

AIR SKOOL SKILLS
How To Draw Monsters	$27.95
Airbrush Bible	$29.95
How Airbrushes Work	$24.95

PAINT EXPERT
How To Airbrush, Pinstripe & Goldleaf	$27.95
Kosmoski's New Kustom Painting Secrets	$27.95
Pro Pinstripe Techniques	$27.95
Advanced Pinstripe Art	$27.95

TATTOO U Series
Advanced Tattoo Art - Revised	$27.95
Cultura Tattoo Sketchbook	$32.95
Tattoo Sketchbook by Jim Watson	$32.95
Tattoo Sketchbook by Nate Powers	$27.95
Into The Skin The Ultimate Tattoo Sourcebook (Includes companion DVD)	$34.95
American Tattoos	$27.95
Tattoo Bible Book One	$27.95
Tattoo Bible Book Two	$27.95
Tattoo Bible Book Three	$27.95
Tattoo Lettering Bible	$27.95

TRADE SCHOOL SERIES
Learning The English Wheel	$27.95

GUIDE BOOKS
Honda Motorcycles - Enthusiast Guide	$27.95
Vintage Dirt Bikes - Enthusiasts Guide	$27.95

Lightning Source UK Ltd.
Milton Keynes UK
UKHW050703170822
407422UK00005B/146